AF849476

Psychology Revivals

Event Knowledge

Originally published in 1986, *Event Knowledge: Structure and Function in Development* was first undertaken because the authors were interested in certain phenomena of cognitive development in early childhood. In particular, they were struck by the discrepancy between young children's apparent competence in everyday activities and their apparent incompetence on certain cognitive tasks. The research was designed in an attempt to identify the basis for children's competence in everyday life. It evolved into an effort to find links between the everyday and the experimental realms, the hope that they could explain both the successes in one and failures in the other.

Based on initial concerns and assumptions, the program of research described here was designed to explore how young children's knowledge of their everyday world – its spatial-temporal structure, the people and objects that occupy it, and their activities – is organized and used, both in practical tasks and in abstract thinking. The approach was novel and it was hoped it would provide the foundation for a new approach to a theory of cognitive development. Today it can be read in its historical context.

Event Knowledge

Structure and Function in Development

Katherine Nelson

In collaboration with:
Janice Gruendel, Elizabeth A. Slackman, Judith A. Hudson, Robyn Fivush, Lucia A. French, Joan Lucariello, Amy Kyratzis, Susan Engel, Susan Seidman, Anthony Rifkin, Catherine Constable

Routledge
Taylor & Francis Group
LONDON AND NEW YORK

First published in 1986
by Lawrence Erlbaum Associates

This edition first published in 2026 by Routledge
4 Park Square, Milton Park, Abingdon, Oxon, OX14 4RN

and by Routledge
605 Third Avenue, New York, NY 10158

Routledge is an imprint of the Taylor & Francis Group, an informa business

© 1986 by Lawrence Erlbaum Associates, Inc.

All rights reserved. No part of this book may be reprinted or reproduced or utilised in any form or by any electronic, mechanical, or other means, now known or hereafter invented, including photocopying and recording, or in any information storage or retrieval system, without permission in writing from the publishers.

Publisher's Note

The publisher has gone to great lengths to ensure the quality of this reprint but points out that some imperfections in the original copies may be apparent.

Disclaimer

The publisher has made every effort to trace copyright holders and welcomes correspondence from those they have been unable to contact.

For Product Safety Concerns and Information please contact our EU representative GPSR@taylorandfrancis.com. Taylor & Francis Verlag GmbH, Kaufingerstraße 24, 80331 München, Germany

A Library of Congress record exists under ISBN: 9780898596571

ISBN: 978-1-041-27698-2 (hbk)
ISBN: 978-1-003-75571-5 (ebk)
ISBN: 978-1-041-27718-7 (pbk)

Book DOI 10.4324/9781003755715

EVENT KNOWLEDGE

Structure and Function in Development

Affiliations of Contributors

JANICE GRUENDEL, *Department of Mental Retardation, State of Connecticut*

ELIZABETH A. SLACKMAN, *Developmental Psychology Program, City University of New York*

JUDITH A. HUDSON, *Department of Psychology, S.U.N.Y., Albany*

ROBYN FIVUSH, *Department of Psychology, Emory University*

LUCIA A. FRENCH, *School of Education, University of Rochester*

JOAN LUCARIELLO, *Graduate Faculty, New School for Social Research*

AMY KYRATZIS, *Developmental Psychology Program, City University of New York*

SUSAN ENGEL, *Developmental Psychology Program, City University of New York*

SUSAN SEIDMAN, *Rockland Children's Psychiatric Center, Orangeburg, N.Y.*

ANTHONY RIFKIN, *Developmental Psychology Program, City University of New York*

CATHERINE CONSTABLE, *Bloomsburg University of Pennsylvania, Department of Speech and Hearing Sciences, City University of New York*

EVENT KNOWLEDGE

Structure and Function in Development

KATHERINE NELSON
Graduate School and University Center
City University of New York

In collaboration with:
Janice Gruendel, Elizabeth A. Slackman, Judith A. Hudson, Robyn Fivush, Lucia A. French, Joan Lucariello, Amy Kyratzis, Susan Engel, Susan Seidman, Anthony Rifkin, Catherine Constable

LEA LAWRENCE ERLBAUM ASSOCIATES, PUBLISHERS
1986 Hillsdale, New Jersey London

Copyright © 1986 by Lawrence Erlbaum Associates, Inc.
All rights reserved. No part of this book may be reproduced in any form, by photostat, microform, retrieval system, or any other means, without the prior written permission of the publisher.

Lawrence Erlbaum Associates, Inc., Publishers
365 Broadway
Hillsdale, New Jersey 07642

Library of Congress Cataloging in Publication Data

Nelson, Katherine.
Event knowledge.

Bibliography: p.
Includes index.
1. Cognition in children. I. Gruendel, Janice.
II. Title.
BF723.C5N44 1986 155.4′23 85–4516
ISBN 0–89859–657–2

Printed in the United States of America
10 9 8 7 6 5 4 3 2 1

Contents

Preface

> Um, we get a cart, uh, and we look for some onions and plums and cookies and tomato sauce, onions and all that kind of stuff, and when we're finished we go to the paying booth, and um, then we, um, then the lady puts all our food in a bag, then we put it in the cart, walk out to our car, put the bags in our trunk, then leave.

This report from a 5-year-old child about "what happens" when you go grocery shopping is illustrative of the data gathered in our investigation of young children's event knowledge. Although mundane in themselves, such reports provided us with unanticipated discoveries about children's knowledge of the real world, how that knowledge is structured, and how it functions in children's thinking. As a case in point, in the example above the information is presented in a general form, in a coherent temporal sequence, and contains "slots" ("all that kind of stuff"), roles ("the lady"), and possible "slot fillers" (different foods). The characteristics of generality, temporal sequence, and categorical (i.e., slot filler) structure were all unexpected on the basis of models of young children's thinking current at the time we began this research in the mid-1970s.

We first undertook this project because we were interested in certain phenomena of cognitive development in early childhood. In particular, like a number of other investigators a decade or so ago, we were struck by the discrepancy between young children's apparent competence in everyday activities and their apparent incompetence on certain cognitive tasks. In the former domain one could observe complex language use and impressive memory and reasoning skills, whereas in the latter one found that preschoolers performed poorly on experimental tasks assessing classification, memory, logical problem solving, and even language. Donaldson (1978) provides a good overview of observations of both types and a discussion of their implications.

We designed the research described here in an attempt to identify the basis for children's cognitive competence in everyday life. It has evolved into an effort to find links between the everyday and the experimental realms, in the hope that we can explain both the successes in one and the failures in the other. Further, we have sought to understand how cognitive competence in everyday activities may support eventual successes on abstract experimental tasks. This is an ambitious undertaking, and we do not claim to have a complete explanation of the processes involved, although we do believe that we have made headway toward it.

Because we believed that understanding children's competence (rather than their failures) was the key to explaining the discrepancies in their performance, we began by examining what they knew about their everyday world, in the expectation that this would give us a clue to the larger issues. We were fortunate in having at hand a tool for investigating this question, namely, the script model of event representations put forth by Schank and Abelson (1975, 1977) and described in Chapter 1. We quickly found that this tool was not only effective but also extraordinarily productive of hypotheses about the characteristics of the young child's mind, its capacities, and its limitations. We present here the fruits of our investigation as it has developed thus far.

Based on our initial concerns and assumptions, the program of research that we describe here was designed to explore how young children's knowledge of their everyday world—its spatial-temporal structure, the people and objects that occupy it, and their activities—is organized and used, both in practical tasks and in abstract thinking. This enterprise differs from the majority of studies of cognitive development in being centrally concerned with the content and function of mental representations, their role in guiding the child's activity and thought, and their place in the development of higher mental processes. Thus we are concerned with all the usual functions of cognition—memory, speech, conceptualization, fantasy, problem solving—as they develop in the young child. We view these functions in relation to children's representation of real world experience.

We believe that the representation of events constitutes a basic form of the child's real world knowledge. That is, we work from the premise that event schemas are the initial form by which children represent experience to themselves, and that more abstract structures may be derived from these schemas over time and with development. The assumption that studying how children organize their everyday experience in the real world can not only give us clues to competencies that might otherwise be overlooked, but also can uncover important factors in the development of abstract cognitive operations is somewhat novel. We hope that the case we present for it is a convincing one, because we believe that it provides the foundation for a promising new approach to a theory of cognitive development. In the chapters that follow, we build on the premises set forth here to uncover developmental phenomena and to construct an explanatory account of them.

The research reported here was first undertaken as a joint project with Janice Gruendel, who was then a graduate student when I was located at Yale University. Her initial contribution, both theoretical and practical, was immeasureable. The research had barely been launched, however, before I moved to the Graduate Center at the City University of New York, and Janice Gruendel moved on to a career in government concerned with children's development in its broadest sense. Fortunately, at CUNY I found a number of students who were excited by the research we had begun to carry out and its implications, and who joined me enthusiastically in further explorations. Most of them are represented as authors of chapters in this book. The studies reported here have been carried out over 8 years, 6 of them at CUNY, where the group concerned with these issues has met on a regular basis to discuss the progress of the research. The work has been supported almost from its inception by grants from the National Science Foundation (BNS 77–01179, 78–25810, 79–14006, 82–08904), which we gratefully acknowledge.

A number of people who have not shared in its authorship have also assisted on this work. Lindsay Evans was a research assistant during its early stages and made substantial substantive contributions. Kathleen McCartney contributed one of the early studies at Yale. Margo Morse, Jayne Berrier, and Peter Feigenbaum carried out various analyses and collected some of the data. Sahli Cavallero contributed helpful criticisms and suggestions. Caryn Greenstein assisted in assembling the bibliography. We are grateful to all of them for their help.

The collaborators on the book, authors of individual chapters, are listed on the title page in the order of chapters authored. The book is a collaborative effort rather than an edited volume. Each chapter (except Chapter 10, which was an independent contribution) was read and critiqued by the whole group prior to its final revision. The authorship of different chapters represents the primary contributors to the work in the various areas covered, but is not always inclusive of those who have made contributions in a particular area. With the exception of Chapter 10, all of the research was carried out as part of the NSF-supported "script project" and I therefore am ultimately responsible for any errors; by no means, however, can I claim credit for all the substantive contributions reported here.

Much (but by no means all) of the work reported here has appeared or will appear in a different form in journal articles or topical chapters. We acknowledge sources in the text where appropriate.

We are grateful for the comments and criticisms of numerous colleagues and anonymous reviewers who have read or listened to reports of this work in various forms. We are above all indebted to the many children, their parents, and teachers who have participated in our studies and generously allowed us to test our ideas with them.

Katherine Nelson

1 Event Knowledge and Cognitive Development

Katherine Nelson

Understanding the mind of the child has always been a major goal of developmental psychologists. What are the limitations and the potentialities of child thought? How do the child's thought structures and processes differ, if they do, from those of the adult? How do they develop, if they do? These are basic questions for developmental theory and they have been answered differently by different theorists.[1] Each theory approaches the mind of the child with different assumptions about the nature of the investigation.

The premise of the research reported in this book is that the key to understanding the child's mind, and thus cognitive development, is to be found by examining what children know. This may seem an obvious approach, but it can be contrasted with approaches that examine what children don't know or can't do and with approaches that examine how they perform in novel situations. Both of these are standard strategies in the study of cognitive development.

Having elected to study what children know, we proceeded to inquire about their knowledge of their familiar everyday world, in particular, their knowledge about familiar events. We have analyzed our findings to discover the structure as well as the content of that knowledge, how these change with age and experience; and we have provided opportunities for children to demonstrate how they use such knowledge in both familiar settings and on unfamiliar tasks. In the chapters that follow, we describe our research in these areas, research that has led us to propose some new conceptions regarding the nature of congitive devel-

[1]The major theories currently influential in the field are those of Piaget, Vygotsky and variations on the information processing theme. These will be considered in the light of the research reported here in the final chapter.

opment. We think that this perspective can illuminate a number of old theoretical issues and we discuss these in the concluding chapter.

In this chapter, I present some of the basic concepts of our approach. In particular, I discuss the assumptions involved in the study of generalized event representations (GERs), because, unless these assumptions are understood, both the aims and the results of our research may be misinterpreted. In the first half of the chapter questions relating to representation in general are discussed, beginning with the general question of the role of representation in cognitive development and proceeding to the rationale for studying specifically the representation of events by young children. The next sections consider representation in the cognitive system in terms of layers and levels. By layers we refer to the different types of representation that may evolve, such as event schemas and categories, which may be developmentally related and which also interact with one another. By levels we refer to those knowledge representations that are accessible to conscious thought and those that are not.

In the latter part of the chapter I discuss the particular assumptions of the script model of event representations that we have used as an analytic tool in our research, and the developmental implications and questions that we have addressed in our research.

EVENT REPRESENTATION

The Representation of Real World Events and Cognitive Development

Current models in cognitive science are explicitly representational models of mind. That is to say, they posit symbolic representations of states and relations in the world as the content on which cognitive processes operate. Mental representations are what knowing, believing, and thinking are about. What is represented and in what form determines to some extent the outcome of a cognitive operation (or thought process). However, mental representation has generally played a less central role in most discussions of cognitive development than it has in cognitive science generally. Although some theories have claimed an important role for changes in the form of representation with development (Bruner, Olver & Greenfield, 1966; Kosslyn, 1980), most studies of cognitive change have been concerned with basic operations such as seriation, classification, inference, or deductive reasoning rather than with representation per se. When the content or structure of knowledge representations have been considered, it generally has been in the framework of logical classes or taxonomic categories rather than other possible forms of representation such as schemata.[2] The hypothesis on

[2]But see Mandler (1980, 1983) for an alternative framework similar to the present one.

which the present work is based, that the content and structure of knowledge representation is an important source of observed changes in cognitive functioning, deserves more thorough exploration than it has received thus far.

The study of cognitive development, like most studies of cognition generally, has tended to focus on knowledge of objects and their relations or on other objectified entities such as categories and numbers. Thus the present research focus on event knowledge is also a departure from tradition. Events, as defined here, incorporate objects and relations in a larger whole. Events are dynamic, taking place through time. The research reported here indicates that even very young children represent events as complex and dynamic, that is, as holistic structures involving internal change over time. Both of these characteristics—holistic structure and internal variation in structural relations over time—are important in considering the implications of the content and structure of children's event representations for theories of general cognitive development. The representation of a holistic structure implies a strong proclivity for structural organization in the mind of the young child, an implication considered in detail in subsequent chapters. The representation of change over time within the event is even more provocative in that some models of cognitive development (e.g., Piaget & Inhelder, 1971) have claimed that young children are incapable of accurately representing changes of the state of objects. However, the results of our research indicate that representing changes through action within an event is no problem for the young child. This, in turn, implies that the representation of changes of state is not per se a problem in cognitive development.[3]

We go further to suggest that events, incorporating changes of state, are the initial content of mental representations, and that stable mental elements (e.g., concepts, categories) are derived from them. Because positing events as a basic form of mental representation is novel in studies of cognition in general and cognitive development in particular, we have devoted considerable effort here to describing the structure of young children's event knowledge and its function in thinking, talking, and acting.

For some years, it has been acknowledged that young children may exhibit greater cognitive competence in their everyday activities than they do in the cognitive tasks that experimenters set for them (e.g., DeLoache, 1981; Donaldson, 1978; Gelman, 1978; Nelson, 1977). The usual explanation for this observation has been that children have difficulty interpreting abstract tasks within the framework that the experimenter has devised, and thus are unable to

---

[3]In their study of imagery, Piaget & Inhelder (1971) proposed that children first rely on static images and come to represent changes of state only in late childhood. These studies, however, were based on children's ability to represent their knowledge externally through drawings, a form that bears an unknown relation to their internal representation. It should be noted that this paradigm requires translating a dynamic external event into a stable external form. The child's mental representation of the event is not observed, of course, but only the required translation.

bring to bear their full competence in experimental settings. We see this as only one part of the explanation. We believe that the young child's cognitive processing is contextualized in terms of everyday experience. What the child knows—what is available in terms of represented information—is based on everyday experience. Cognitive processes operate on representations; and, although the processes available may be very powerful, if young children are unable to represent and thus to operate on information that is not in some way part of their own prior experience, they will be limited in their performance on abstract tasks.

With time the child's cognitive system subjects the initial representations of everyday experience to further analysis, yielding more abstract cognitive structures. These abstractions make it possible for children to construct novel representations of events, ones not previously represented through experience; the children then become able to perform in novel abstract tasks at the same level that they do in the familiar everyday world.

Related to this hypothesis on the limitations of children's thought is the more complicating observation that the child's knowledge about everyday events inevitably includes information about the social and cultural world. We consider it a major advantage of the present approach that it integrates the social contribution to cognition in a natural way by making it part of the child's event representations. Because it takes into account both aspects of experientially derived representations, the approach we set forth here can also explain the successes of the child in the everyday world and the failures on abstract tasks. We spell out these implications in the chapters to follow.

In the remainder of this chapter we explain in greater detail the reasoning behind these views, describe the script model within which the research took place, and outline the research questions that we have been concerned with. In the next section the rationale for focusing on events and their representations, and the assumptions about the cognitive system that are entailed by this focus are discussed.

The Representation of Event Knowledge by Young Children

We focus on event knowledge because it appears to be central to young children's thinking—and to adults'—and because, as noted previously, its structure has important implications for understanding some basic characteristics of the child's cognitive system and its development. One of the intuitively appealing advantages of taking events, in all their complexity, as the basic unit of representation is that phenomenologically the world is experienced as a series of ongoing events.[4] However, in concentrating on event schemas we do not deny the exis-

---

[4]We make no claims about perceptual processes here, nor do we make any claims about the form of cognitive representation, whether propositional, imagic, or something more abstract than either, for example.

tence and importance of other representational structures such as taxonomic categories; indeed, we propose that these are related to event representations in interesting ways (Chapter 9).

A compelling reason for focusing on event representations in young children's thought is that real world knowledge comes to the child almost exclusively from direct experience. Older children and adults are taught about the world through books, oral instruction, television, and other media, but all of these require that the learners represent to themselves aspects of the world conveyed through language. These indirect knowledge sources are not available to the young child because children are unable to make use of language to construct world knowledge independently of their own prior experience for several years after first learning to talk.[5] Thus, what young children know comes primarily from the analysis of their own experience rather than from mediated sources.

That children gain knowledge from direct experiences by no means implies that the young child is a lone experiencer of the world (as sometimes does seem implied in the Piagetian model of development). On the contrary, the social and cultural world provides experiential context for the child. Experience does not come to the child as raw encounters with a neutral physical world. Rather, in some important sense, all knowledge of the world is social or cultural knowledge. At the other extreme, this latter statement may be misinterpreted as the claim that cultural agents are the only determinants of what the child experiences. However, that social and cultural agents (e.g., parents) set the context for the child's learning does not imply that they determine what the child experiences. The interactive model to which we subscribe emphasizes that the developmental state of the child's cognitive system and his or her current state of knowledge at least enter into what the child comes to know of an experience and how it is integrated into the knowledge system. These latter factors are the subject of the bulk of the investigations reported here. (See Nelson, 1973, for an illustration of this kind of model.)

A further point central to our conception of how event representations enter into cognitive development is that cognitive development is an "underground" process that takes place through operations on representations. The initial representation of an experience limits subsequent derivations and transformations from it, but that initial representation is only the beginning of the process. This assumption is compatible with general information processing models (e.g., Sternberg, 1984), although, unlike many such models, in the present conception change is an inevitable outcome of the organizing system. In information processing terms, the cognitive representation of an experience involves a process of organizing "data" from experience, a data structure, and a process of utilizing the data structure (see Palmer, 1978). Different data structures may be involved in different representations, and they may call on different processes to organize

[5]Research suggests that even television is highly dependent on the verbal message and that for this reason young children are likely not to understand many of the things that are presented on it.

the data initially. For example, a particular experience may be analyzed as a whole schema, whereas the language heard within it may be parsed to produce a set of propositions, its parts may be categorized for some purpose, or all of these may go on simultaneously to produce different types of representations of the same experience. At another level, processes such as pattern analysis and categorization may operate on the initial representations to produce derived structures (e.g., Bowerman, 1982; Maratsos, 1983), or the representation may be utilized in some other cognitive operation, such as problem solving. None of these processes is assumed to be at the level of conscious awareness; all are, in Campbell's (1979) term, "cryptic."

Although we claim that, for the young child, world knowledge is derived almost exclusively from the representation of experience, this claim does not imply that all knowledge is based in experience. Rather, cognitive operations of sufficient power (e.g., pattern analysis, categorization, inference, transformations of different kinds) can produce structures that do not exist in the real world and therefore can never have been experienced. It is our assumption that more abstract kinds of representational structures can be derived through cognitive operations on the initial representation of an experience. However, this assumption also implies that the initial representation provides a significant constraint on subsequent representations, inasmuch as derived representations cannot contain information about the world that was not present or implied in initial representations. That is, although the cognitive system may analyze, categorize, and make inferences about the information represented, it cannot supply missing information.[6] For example, if a child has been bitten by a dog, but in the excitement and fear of the experience did not note the shape or color of the dog and perhaps misrepresented its size, no amount of analysis of the representation of the experience will produce a reliable answer to the question, "what breed was the dog?" There is now a large body of experimental data on eyewitness accounts of accidents that make a similar point (e.g., Loftus, 1975).

The point to be emphasized here is that what children represent of an experience has important implications for their possible abstract cognitive organizations based on that experience. Thus it becomes important to ask: Are the representations that young children set up different in important ways from those of older children or adults? If so, we may be able to explain on this basis some of the commonly observed developmental differences in cognitive functioning. If not, we need to look elsewhere for such explanations. These are some of the questions that we address here. In the course of doing this, we explore the ways

[6]However, it can make guesses about it. Here we run into the distinction between knowledge and belief or between certainty and probability. Of course, no representation of experience can be accepted as indubitably true because of the fallibility of perception and conception. Nevertheless, experience has a greater probability of being faithfully represented than does unsubstantiated guesswork. It should be noted that young children may be insensitive to the distinction between knowing and believing.

in which children (and people in general) impose structure on their experience to produce flexible, functional representations.

Layers of Representation. In the previous discussion, an implicit distinction was made between the immediate experience of an event and its possible cognitive representations. This distinction rests on the ordinary distinction between perception and cognition, where cognition includes both representations and processes operating on those representations. The essential distinction between immediate perception and subsequent representation is important to understanding many aspects of the cognitive functioning of young children, as is noted in the following chapters. However, it is also useful to consider immediate perception as the first representational form of an experience. From this view, it follows that cognitive processes may operate either on perceptual representations or on cognitive representations, which may be more abstract representations of the same event. For young children these sometimes seem to be in conflict. A nice illustration of this was seen in Bruner's (1966) demonstration that young children more frequently responded correctly in Piaget's conservation of liquids task when the perception of a transformation was blocked than when they were able to observe the transformation.

An important point highlighted by the consideration of immediate perception as an initial representation is that cognitive processes such as categorization, pattern analysis, inference, and so on, operate not on real world phenomena but only on the mental representation of those phenomena. The further implication is that giving the child access to perception of an event is no guarantee that characteristics of the event considered relevant for some purpose by the adult will become accessible to cognitive operations, for the evident reason that those characteristics may not enter into the child's perceptual representation.

Caution along this line is necessitated by the research that has demonstrated that perception of an event is strongly determined by expectations, by prior schemas, and by other cognitive and affective states (Bransford & McCarrell, 1974; Neisser, 1967; Posner & Snyder, 1984). Different individuals may perceive the same objective event differently. An obvious implication of this fact is that children may be expected to perceive events differently than adults do, in view of the differences in their general knowledge base, goals, intentions, and belief states. Given our assumption that immediate perception is a first representation from which other representations are derived, the fact that immediate perception is biased in different ways has implications for possible subsequent representational structures that are constrained by the initial perception. The constraint works both ways: the initial perception of an event is constrained by prior knowledge, and the acquisition of new knowledge is constrained by the initial perceptual representation. The constraints are not complete, of course, or no change of any kind in the system could take place.

Although the perceptual representation is necessarily the most basic, or the first stage, other layers of representation need not be conceived of in terms of stages, but rather as a dynamic system in which different types of information are represented in different structures (see Schank, 1982, for a similar conception). The layer that is of most interest to the present investigation is that of schematized general representations, in particular of event schemas, that is, general event representations (GERs) (Nelson & Gruendel, 1981) or scripts (Schank & Abelson, 1977).

The term schema, as used in cognitive psychology, refers to structures that organize data configurationally. Schemas have been contrasted with categories (Mandler, 1979, 1981), and in many ways they seem to be the most natural form for representing experience, given its multidimensionality and multimodal characteristics. In discussing schemas and categories, Mandler (1979) described a schema as:

> an organized representation of a body of knowledge . . . a spatially and/or temporally organized cognitive structure in which the parts are connected on the basis of contiguities that have been experienced in time or space. A schema is formed on the basis of past experience with objects, scenes, or events and consists of (usually unconscious) expectations about what things look like and "what goes with what." The parts . . . of a schema consist of a set of variables, or slots, which can be filled, or instantiated, in any given instance by values that have greater or lesser degrees of probability of occurrence attached to them. (p. 263)

Mandler also noted that schemas are hierarchically organized, with information of a more specific nature embedded under nodes containing more general information. For example, a kitchen schema may embed a refrigerator schema, which has its own organizational properties. A restaurant-going schema may embed an ordering schema and a paying schema. A schema is neither an image, a proposition, nor a category. More abstract than the first, more complex than the second, different in structure from the last, it must be viewed as a unique type of representational structure.

In terms of layers of representation, general event representations (GERs) for familiar events stand midway between immediate perceptual representations and paradigmatic abstractions such as hierarchical categories (see Chapter 10). GERs appear to be very concrete in the sense of incorporating temporal and spatial specifications, even when contrasted with such other schematic structures as story schemas or games. Event schemas are derived from concrete experience of events and thus represent "how the world works." Nonetheless, they are very much abstractions from experienced reality, containing as they do generalizations about possible entries rather than specific values, as a memory for a specific episode does. Although schemas are abstractions from experience, they are not the only such abstractions. Elements that occur in events and scenes—i.e., objects, people, actions—become represented in their own right as concepts that may participate in other representational structures besides the schemas in which they are originally embedded (Nelson, 1982). At a still more abstract level, these concepts may be organized into hierarchical structures, such as taxonomic categories, or into logical or mathematical systems. The relation between these more abstract layers and the general experience-derived schema is of great developmental interest and is considered in Chapters 9 and 11.

It is probable that all types of representations—specific memories, general schemas, abstract concepts—may be used within the cognitive system in the manipulation and transformation of old knowledge to produce novel constructions, such as plans, predictions, and imaginative thought. A question addressed in our research is whether young children can generate novel constructions from their general schemas, or whether they are "schemabound," tied to their experientially-derived representations.

Levels of Representation. The human mind operates on at least two levels—the conscious and the nonconscious. It is necessary to posit the existence of representations at each level, although whether it is necessary to assume the same form at each level is an open issue (see Anderson, 1978; Palmer, 1978). It seems more informative to think of these distinctions in terms of explicit and implicit knowledge, or to use the terms introduced by Campbell (1979), phenic and cryptic knowledge. These latter terms imply accessibility and inaccessibility to conscious awareness, whereas consciousness itself is limited by the span of immediate apprehension. Phenic representations appear to be limited to images and symbols (language and other symbolic systems). Cryptic representations may be more abstract. Knowledge that is at first explicit may become implicit with time and thus may become less accessible; knowledge that is initially implicit may sometimes (but not always) be made explicit through reflection. Much of the young child's knowledge appears to be implicit, and one way of conceiving of cognitive development is as a process of making the implicit explicit.[7]

Interplay between explicit and implicit event knowledge in early childhood is apparent in an example reported by Schank (Nelson, 1977) from his young daughter, who directed: "Next time when you go to the market, I want you to buy straws, pay for it, and put it in the package and take it home OK?" (p. 227). This explicit "store script" becomes over time implicit, so that the child will state only the need for the shopper to buy straws. Yet the implicit that has begun as an explicit proposition seems to remain readily accessible to conscious reflection, and when asked the child will report what happens when you go to the store. On the other hand, knowledge that was not explicitly stated initially, that was derived cryptically from an initial representation, seems to remain inaccessi-

[7]A good deal of recent experimentation and theorizing can be explained in this way, including the positing of various "meta" systems, such as metacognition, metamemory, metalinguistics. See also Gelman & Gallistel (1980); Piaget (1978); Rozin (1976).

ble to explicit formulation, except through effortful conscious reflection and reconstruction (e.g., Reber & Allen, 1978; Reber & Lewis, 1977). As is apparent in the report to follow, we cannot be sure that all of the child's knowledge of an event is explicitly statable; and, while the relation between the explicit and the implicit in event representations is an important aspect of their development, it is one that is difficult to untangle.[8]

As the foregoing remarks imply, there is another level of representation that must be taken into account in order that its relation to the cognitive levels can be made explicit. This is the external representation of knowledge (see Mandler, 1983). Our research has relied primarily on children's verbal reports of their experiential knowledge. This reliance assumes a correspondence between the verbal report and the internal—both explicit and implicit— representation, although we are only too aware that in any given case the verbal report may incompletely and inaccurately represent the child's actual knowledge state. Nonetheless, children's verbal reports have shed important light on the structure and content of their knowledge, as the following chapters show and as our subsequent observations using other techniques of inquiry have confirmed.

Operations. The basic premise underlying the developmental model set forth here is that the initial representation of experience forms the basis for more abstract mental representations, derived through operations of various kinds. The research program we have undertaken does not involve an investigation of these processes, although we have provided evidence for their products. Insofar as these are cryptic processes, uncovering evidence for their operation is a challenge to research ingenuity. Our reading of the field is that in most cases implicit assumptions about the operation of cryptic cognitive processes substitute for explicit statements, thereby obscuring both differences and similarities in assumed theoretical mechanisms.

On the basis of what is known about young children's thinking (e.g., Siegler, 1978), we assume that at least the following processes operate at the nonconscious, cryptic level on all types of representations: pattern analysis, categorization of similar elements (with similarity defined along several different dimensions), correlation of co-occurring elements, linear ordering (i.e., sequencing), organization into higher-level units (i.e., categorizing), and inferencing (i.e., filling in informational gaps on the basis of prior knowledge).

Young children also appear to form implicit rules of behavior for themselves and others. These presumably derive from their analysis of "the way things are"

[8]Recent research on automatic and nonautomatic processing and on the difference between procedural and declarative knowledge (Mandler, 1983) suggests that these may be related to the distinctions made here, but they are not quite the same. These issues, although important, are only indirectly related to the research reported here.

and are not subjected to testing against alternative rules. It is of interest that their event schemas seem to support these kinds of inductions and that in early childhood they equate "the way it is" with "the way it should be." Such equations are readily observable, for example in young children's insistence on maintaining a given bedtime routine.[9]

In summary, we have outlined here a general view of mental representation and organization subject to developmental systemic change. This view assumes a continuum from immediate preception to abstract representational structures of varying types, subject to cognitive analysis and transformation through a set of operations that take place at a cryptic level of cognition. Development of the system is conceived to be the result of changes produced by these operations, driven by but not fully determined by new input. To the extent that these ideas are correct, they suggest that different representational structures should emerge at different points in development, as the initial representations are operated on to provide the derived more abstract structures.[10] The event representation is seen as a beginning step toward abstract representational structure, and the focus of this research program is directed toward the analysis of its structure and function.[11]

EVENT STRUCTURE AND EVENT REPRESENTATIONS

Thus far we have discussed events and event knowledge without defining these terms explicitly, although the term *event* has had a number of interpretations within psychology. Events are sometimes defined as simply change, for example, the movement of a bouncing call. The events we are concerned with here are of a more macro order; they involve people in purposeful activities, and acting on objects and interacting with each other to achieve some result. Because these events are organized around goals, they usually have been given conventional labels and are conceived of within boundaries. For example, for a particular

[9]The maintenance of routines may serve emotional needs, but these needs may in turn reflect the kind of cognitive structures and behavioral rules that we are concerned with here. The relation between affect and cognition in early childhood is at present poorly understood.

[10]Whereas developmental processes of this kind can be expected to take place within knowledge domains throughout development, the developmental state of the cognitive system as a whole also influences what is possible. See Nelson and Nelson, 1978 for a discussion of this and related issues.

[11]Accepting the validity and importance of the event representation in the thinking of young children does not necessarily involve accepting all these developmental assumptions. Indeed, there are disagreements among some of the investigators working in this research program on some aspects of the system sketched here. Nonetheless, it is important to lay out these assumptions and their rationale in order that the research reported here can be interpreted within its theoretical framework, and to avoid possible misinterpretation of its claims.

individual, "grocery shopping" may begin with making a shopping list or with getting into the car, and may end with bringing the groceries home and unpacking them. The shopping event, however, does not include planning menus or eating dinner; it is bounded by its goal-defined activities, in this case obtaining food and other sundries. This discussion immediately raises the question whether children are aware of goals and are thus sensitive to boundaries in the same way.

Events themselves have structure: they proceed according to a temporal-causal sequence, and they can be seen to be hierarchically organized, in that embedded within the whole event are smaller segments of activities, each of which may be analysed as an event in its own right. For example, the shopping event includes the car driving event, which has its own procedural structure. We can, therefore, speak about the *event structure* (ES) of shopping, for example. The *general event representation* (GER) for shopping is also structured in the same way that the event itself is; or rather, it can be said to represent that structure. However, there is no guarantee that important characteristics of the ES will be represented in any given GER; in particular, children's GERs may be quite incomplete in this respect. Further, a person's verbal description of the event may incompletely reflect the actual structure that is represented in the GER. Thus the three—the event itself, its mental representation, and its public verbal representation—need to be kept separate in our discussions.

The script model discussed in the next section does not adhere to these distinctions between external event, internal representation, and external description. These distinctions are not important to the computer model of understanding discourse for which scripts were originally proposed, because the internal representation in the computer is a faithful rendition of its input, and its output is in turn a faithful rendition of the internal model. However, as argued previously, we cannot make similar assumptions about the internal and external representations of children (or, for that matter, of adults). One of the reasons for adopting the GER terminology is that it makes fewer assumptions with respect to structural characteristics than does the script, which implies a particular structural model. Thus the script, as an event schema, is a type of GER. Our investigation was aimed in part at determining whether children's GERs fit the script model. We use GER as a general term; ER when we want to cover both specific and general representations, as in discussions of memory; and script when we have evidence or firm belief that the GERs we are discussing fit the script model. We also use the term script-like GER to indicate that the representations in question may not meet all of the criteria of a script.

At this point also a distinction can be introduced between the episode and the event. These terms stand in relation to each other as token to type. The child experiences an episode of an event and may have a memory for an episode and a schema for the event. The term "event" is used generically throughout this book.

SCRIPT THEORY

The research that we report in this book was originally conceived within the general model of scripts as set forth by Schank & Abelson (1977). This is one possible model of event representations, which may turn out to be a good description of the kind of structured information children and adults have about events they take part in. The script model as originally proposed may, however, turn out to be inadequate to such descriptions, and it should be noted that Schank, one of its original proposers, has since turned away from it toward a more complex, dynamic account of the human memory system (Schank, 1982). In any case, our research relies on this model primarily as an analytic tool rather than as a rigid theoretical claim about the true structure of event knowledge, and we have felt free to depart from its claims when the research seemed to warrant it. In this section we present the essential characteristics of the script model of general event representations as a background to our own research.

What is a Script?

According to Schank & Abelson (1977) a script is an ordered sequence of actions appropriate to a particular spatial-temporal context and organized around a goal. Scripts specify the *actors, actions* and *props* used to carry out those goals within specified circumstances. The script is made up of *slots* and requirements on what can fill those slots. That is, the script specifies roles and props and defines obligatory and optional actions. For each of these slots there are *default values* that are assumed if the person, object, or action is not specified when the script is instantiated in a particular context. For example, in a restaurant script a waiter or waitress is assumed, as are a menu, food, a bill, and a tip. Persons hearing a story about a restaurant can easily fill in these items from their general script knowledge.

There are certain basic characteristics that differentiate scripts from other kinds of schematic organizations, as well as characteristics that are shared with schematic structures in general. The most important of the general characteristics is that the script, like other schemas, is an organized body of knowledge such that a part implies the whole and the whole is more than the sum of the parts. This characteristic endows the script with its inferential power. When a situation is understood sufficiently well that an adequate script has been developed for it, the script user can predict all of the necessary components and has expectations about optional components even when they are not explicitly stated.

Another important characteristic shared with other schemas is that scripts are general structures. Whether the script knowledge is based on only one episode or a repeated series of the same event, the resulting structure is expected to apply to all episodes of that event. It is not specific to a single experience. This characteristic is highly relevant to the way in which scripts affect memory development and the organization of world knowledge.

The script structure is differentiated from other schematic structures by its basic elements—actions—and by the temporal and causal connections between acts. Scripts represent events that occur over time, and thus the links between their component acts are temporal links, one act following another; in the most tightly woven structures the links are causal as well as temporal (see Chapter 3). Since scripts are specified in space as well as time, changes within scripts are often associated with changes in the location of the action. Thus temporal links may have both causal and spatial components.

Like the events that they model, scripts exhibit hierarchical structure in that they are composed of subscripts or scenes (Abelson, 1981). For example, the restaurant script includes entering, ordering, eating, and paying scenes, each of which has a script structure of its own. The child's school day script embeds subscripts of work, play, and eating lunch (see Chapter 4). Within a script there may be alternative paths that are taken under different circumstances. For example, the path taken for paying in an expensive French restaurant is different from that in an inexpensive coffee shop. In addition, the overall script category may contain different tracks. The fast food (e.g., McDonald's) restaurant track includes subscripts and sequences different from the standard restaurant track or the cafeteria track. This distinction has an important bearing on the complexity of the scripts that children of different ages build up.

Abelson (1981) distinguished between weak and strong scripts, a weak script being one that specifies the components but does not specify the order in which they are to occur, whereas a strong script specifies order as well. We have made a similar distinction between scripts that are temporally invariant and those that are not. In addition, the temporal invariance can derive from causal connections or from simple convention (see Chapter 3). However, seldom does a script reveal one of these structures in its entirety; rather some of its substructures may have one basis or another, making it more or less strong or weak. For example, the child's birthday party script is relatively weak, many of the event components occurring in any order (e.g., opening the presents can come at the beginning, middle, or end). However, some components are strictly ordered by convention (e.g., singing Happy Birthday before blowing out the candles), and others exhibit logical or pragmatic necessity (e.g., blowing out the candles before cutting the cake and eating it).

Sometimes we refer to an event as "scripted," and differentiate between event types in terms of the degree to which they are scripted. Here we refer to the ES and make a distinction similar to Abelson's (1981) between weak and strong scripts. A scripted event is one that lends itself to easy formulation of a GER because it has strong temporally invariant structure, recurs frequently, and has goals, roles and props well understood by the participants. Getting dressed and eating lunch are examples of typical well-scripted events.

An important characteristic of scripts is that their format includes, and is in fact organized around, information about social goals and activities. Thus scripts integrate into one structure knowledge about objects and their relations and knowledge about the world of people and their interactions. These are not two separate domains in this model but parts of the whole representation of events. For this reason scripts are especially apt as initial representations for children, insofar as children depend on direction and guidance from adults in carrying through daily activities; thus the events they participate in inevitably include both types of information.

In summary, the important structural characteristics of scripts include their wholeness, their boundedness, their sequentiality, their causal structure, and their capacity for hierarchical embedding. In addition, the openness of the general structure allows optional and conditional paths and alternative slot fillers, which substitute for one another in different instantiations. The substitutability principle is shown in Chapter 9 to be important in considering how more abstract cognitive structures may be derived from the basic script.

Origin and Functions of Scripts

Scripts primarily represent culturally defined events as a consequence of the fact that virtually all the events we take part in are culturally defined. Scripts, therefore, are necessarily learned, the product of experience. Adults inevitably guide and direct such learning, implicitly or explicitly teaching children how to take their part. Children in turn, through the process of participatory interaction, learn the script even as they act within the scripted event. Partial knowledge of the script, supported by the knowledge of others, is sufficient to guide action and interaction and to lead to more complete acquisition.[12] The degree to which script structures result from inherent principles of cognitive organization and the degree to which they are dependent on structural guidance from adults are open questions. We address some of the knotty issues of acquisition and development in Chapters 4 and 7.

The question of the origin of scripts inevitably raises the issue of the relation between the general representation and memory for a specific episode. To an important degree, the GER must derive from a specific experience or set of experiences. Yet, as is shown in Chapter 5, memory for an episode and a general schema for the event are interacting but distinct types of representations. We propose that the GER and the specific memory are two different representational processes, both derived from the initial experiential representation.

With respect to the function of scripts, research with adults has demonstrated that the event schemas individuals bring to a situation influence their interpretation of new experiences, their understanding of stories and ability to carry on

[12]In this way script theory is related to Soviet activity—see Wertsch, 1984.

discourse, and enable them to form plans and make inferences and predictions. Some of the research on these issues is discussed in Chapter 3. The extent to which these functions of scripts apply to young children as well as adults is explored in Chapters 6 through 10.

A point that is emphasized throughout this report is that the GER provides the individual with the capability of establishing *cognitive context* within a familiar situation. By this is meant that, when a child (or adult) has an established GER for a situation, the GER provides interpretive context for the persons, actions, objects, and relations to be found in that situation. The context is cognitive in that it exists in the representation itself. A specific episode may fit well with this cognitive context or conflict with it in certain ways. Thus reliance on the cognitive context provided by the script may either facilitate or hinder comprehension of the episode.

The importance of the cognitive context proposal can be seen in the fact that children's performance on cognitive tasks often appears to be context bound. That is, the young child's competence (as measured by performance on a task) is apparently dependent on and varies with different situations. For example, although experimental research has established that young children typically fail to conserve in a standard Piagetian type task, different task contexts can affect the presumed age of attainment of conservation and the quality of the child's response (e.g., Beilin, 1977; Gelman, 1978). The child's response often seems to depend on the naturalness of the task context (Donaldson, 1978). The notion of cognitive context can help to illuminate these observations.

We believe that the observed difference between situations where children perform well or poorly is that between those for which children have established a relevant GER and those for which they have not. When a GER is available, the child can supply a context for what is going on and thus interpret the situation appropriately; but, when it is not available, the child has no framework for interpretation or may call on the wrong framework. As noted earlier, it is not only a matter of interpretation of the task demands but rather a limitation of the young child's representational system. When the child has an already established representation on which problem-solving processes can operate, success at the task is possible. But, when no relevant representation is available, it is necessary to construct one from scratch, using whatever features the situation offers. This demand competes with task performance and may lead to inappropriate task interpretation. Thus the GER actually supports or fails to support task performance itself (see Chapter 6 for examples of these effects).

The notion of cognitive context can also aid in understanding how children are freed of their dependence on others for guiding behavior in a situation and from the immediate perceptual array for interpreting speech and action. That is to say, cognitive context can replace supportive perceptual context and thereby enable the child to engage in independent thought and action that is not tied to the immediate present. These consequences of the GER proposal form the basis for the research in Chapters 6 and 8 and are considered at greater length in Chapter 11.

A summary of the functions of scripts for the individual, then, includes predicting action and interaction, supporting the interpretation of discourse, action, and task demands, organizing memory, making plans, and serving as a base for the derivation of abstract knowledge structures. These functions are considered in detail in the light of the research reported in this book.

DEVELOPMENTAL IMPLICATIONS AND RESEARCH QUESTIONS

A number of developmental issues have been raised that are relevant to the research reported here. Some are conjectures about the nature of development that we believe to be true but that are not tested in the research reported here, nor are they critical assumptions behind it. For example, it was suggested that children may not distinguish between belief and knowledge or between what is and what should be. And it was conjectured that implicit knowledge becomes explicit through reflection, whereas explicit knowledge becomes implicit through use. Neither of these conjectures is crucial to the present research endeavor. Other developmental proposals are more in the nature of assumptions about the representational system that fit the kind of developmental model we propose, but that have not been tested in this research. We therefore include them in our explanations of developmental phenomena as untested assumptions. Among these are the following:

- Differences in initial perceptual representations imply differences in derived structures as well as in cognitive performance.
- Because schemas in part guide perception, perceptual representations of the same event may differ for children to the extent that their schemas for that event differ.
- Cognitive analysis of initial representations leads to more abstract, integrated and differentiated representations.

Finally, there are developmental issues that we have investigated as part of this research program, the results of which we report in subsequent chapters. The central issues are the following:

- Do the event representations of young children differ from those of older children and adults? If so, are the differences to be found in the structural characteristics of event representations, in their content, or in both? Are children's ERs, like adults', organized around goals?

• How are scripts for familiar events acquired? How do they develop? What are the respective contributions of participation, observation, social direction, and cognitive analysis? Are GERs formed on the basis of one experience, or are many needed? How different does a novel event need to be in order to lead to the formation of a new ER different from one already available? Are ERs set up piecemeal, bit by bit, or do they develop from a more global structure to a more detailed, internally elaborated one?

• Are episodic memory and scripts related as competing or as complementary event representations? Does this relation change with development?

• Are scripts effective in providing cognitive context in familiar situations? How does such context affect understanding and use of language?

• Do children generate novel constructions from general schemas?

• What is the developmental relation between event schemas and more abstract categories?

There are, of course, other questions that might be raised. For example, the place of affect in the acquisition, structure or function of GERs has not been considered here, nor have individual differences in their characteristics. In the final chapter we point out some of the unexplored territory that the present research has opened up.

PLAN OF THE BOOK

Each of the chapters to follow focuses on one set of issues among those raised above and reports studies that have been undertaken to address these issues. In the course of the book, we discuss first the structure of children's event representations using the script model as a guide, and point out the ways in which structure changes and does not change with development. The examination of structure in Chapters 2 and 3 brings out the complexity of children's knowledge representations and the inclusion of logical relations and concepts within them. These chapters demonstrate that young children's thought is not limited in many of the ways previously claimed, and they also suggest some dimensions along which development takes place. Chapter 2 foreshadows the more systematic discussion of these issues in Chapters 3 and 4 by reporting the results of the first studies of children's scripts, most of which have not previously been published.

Chapters 5 through 8 report studies that demonstrate how event representations function in children's memory and language development. In these chapters, the supportive effects provided by cognitive context are brought out in terms of use of relational language, acquisition of new language terms, engagement in mother-child discourse, play, and story production. The facilitative effects of GERs on children's episodic memories is examined in Chapter 5. The new theoretical perspective that is brought to bear on issues in these areas has in many cases suggested new solutions for old problems, which are discussed as well.

In Chapter 9 relations of GERs within the representational system itself are considered in the light of experimental evidence showing a developmental relation between scripts and taxonomic categories. This discussion brings out the function of scripts in cognitive development in its most basic sense. The claim here is that not only do event representations function to support performance, but they lead themselves to developmental change in the system.

Chapter 10 reports a clinical application of the script claims, demonstrating that a language intervention program designed on the basis of the script model supports the needs of language disordered children and leads to improved performance (and presumably improved language competence) in that setting. Although this work was carried out independently of the other research reported here, we believe its practical as well as theoretical implications are important enough to warrant inclusion here.

In the final chapter, the general developmental implications of the work carried out thus far are discussed in terms of general developmental theory, and directions for future research are indicated.

2 Children's Scripts

Katherine Nelson
Janice Gruendel

The first question to be addressed in our research was whether children have script-like event representations, and, if so, whether their content and structure change over time with experience and general cognitive development. Experimental evidence on these questions is presented in this chapter and will be elaborated in the chapters to follow. The experiments were based on informal observations suggesting that young children do seem to rely to a large extent on script-like representations in organizing their knowledge of the world. The following letter from an 8-year-old girl exemplifies these observations. This child, whose usual home was in Iowa, composed this letter to her grandmother describing her experience in Japan, where she had just spent the first few weeks of a year-long visit.

> Dear Grandma,
>
> I miss you VERY much. I wish you could come and see us. Me and Annie know the way to school most of the way, after the bus ride. You see, it's rather hard to remember the way to the bus stop. We're having pretty much fun in school, even though Annie says that it's not so great. I think it's pretty nice there. When I came in to school today, first you have to wait around for the mothers and fathers to talk to the teachers. I usually go in to the playground at the back of the school to wait. Well, when you get into school, then today I saw this list of things on the board. Miss Stewart, my teacher, said that this list was the things I was supposed to do today (and the other kids too). You don't have to do them in order. In fact, I got them all mixed up when I did them. The math was stuff like 8 + 7 = (now a box for you to write the answer in). There's also stuff like 60 + 7 = (box) and "Which is two behind four on the number line?" Then in SRA (Select, Read, and Answer), you select a card from the card box, Read the story on it, in a notebook answer the

questions at the end, and then check it with another card. The next thing I did was (I think) do spelling. Spelling is a lesson in which you have a book and you answer the questions in it about spelling. Then there was a recess. After recess, there was something called handwriting. Handwriting is when you have another book in which you copy sentences and then the teacher looks over them and checks them. That's to see how good your handwriting is and to improve it. Oh, no, I forgot reading! I don't know where that comes in. Oh, well, reading is when you come up to the teacher and read part of a book. Then you go to your desk and, in your reading workbook, answer the questions about that story you were reading. Then comes lunch, I think. (Maybe I've gotten all mixed up.) After lunch, there's lunch recess. And after lunch recess—oh, no, I have gotten mixed up!—there's handwriting. Then you do the stuff you haven't finished up. And then there's when Miss Stewart reads to you. Oh, no, there's Japanese. I have to fit that in. In Japanese class you learn Japanese words. On Wednesdays, I'm going to go swimming; and today I had P.E. That may sound like a lot of things to do in school, but somehow the teachers have fitted it all in all right. And then I guess you don't want to know very much about going home. In school, I've made friends with Tina, John (I guess), and a girl who I don't know her name. I also like Miss Stewart because she always helps you when you're having problems (especially in math).

We live in a small apartment that isn't so interesting because it isn't very big. It has our bedroom, (me and Annie's), the living room (which is Mommy and Daddy's bedroom), the kitchen, which is where we're typing right now, and the bathroom. It may sound a little bit confusing about the living room because of the beds; but in Japan people put down mattress beds at nighttime, and take them up in the morning, because that gives you a lot of extra space, so that you don't have a whole room just sitting there with nobody in it all day. When you come in to Japanese houses you have to take your shoes off to keep the tatami clean (A tatami is a straw mat on the floor.) Goodby I have to eat dinner.

Lots of love,
Elizabeth

This letter illustrates at once several points about children's scripts that were gradually revealed in the research reported here, but that can be clearly seen in this one example. One first notes its everydayness—nothing about it is particularly notable, given its topic and its writer. It succeeds in conveying in an organized form the experience of school from Elizabeth's perspective. But consider this point a bit more closely. There is nothing in the letter to indicate that this school is in Japan except for the mention of Japanese lessons. That is, what Elizabeth has chosen to write about is precisely the sort of experience that she has been used to having at home in Iowa. Even accepting that most school experiences are the same no matter where (with minor variations), and that the most salient experience in the life of an 8-year-old is school, it is striking that virtually the entire letter is taken up with a description of the school day. This letter was written early in September and probably reflects Elizabeth's efforts to formulate to herself an account of the school routine that was still new. Although she had a familiar school schema on which to build from prior experience, she needed to put the parts together in a new way and to note departures from the previous script.

When talking about home, she does not report a routine but notes the things that are different from her previous experience: the mattress beds and taking off shoes before coming in the house. These segments illustrate two essential aspects of organizing knowledge of new experience: organization and integration of a new routine from old and new parts; and acquisition of novel parts.

But this letter illustrates more about children's formulation of experiential knowledge. Note how Elizabeth moves back and forth in the school segment between the specific, first person-past tense account (''When I came in to school today'') and the general, second person-timeless present tense account (''first you have to wait around for the mothers and fathers to talk to the teachers''). The relation between these two forms in both narration and in the knowledge representation is apparent in even the youngest children's reports, and for that reason is a matter of some interest in our research.

Note also both the effort to report things in order and the awareness that she has made errors. We suggest later that the errors emanate from the list-like nature of the parts (indeed, the parts were listed on the board) in contrast to a causal or hierarchical structure among them. Nonetheless, like most children, Elizabeth, with more experience with the routine, will soon be able to report the sequence flawlessly (Fivush, 1984).

There is also a type of hierarchical structure to the account. Under math, examples of problems are embedded; under SRA is the select and read routine; and so on. Each subpart has its subroutines and slots, to use the computer analogy.

This example gives a feeling for how a child may organize event-based knowledge and use it in description. Elizabeth, of course, is a very articulate 8-year-old. We began our investigation of event knowledge by interviewing children much younger than Elizabeth, as young as 35 months. In contrast to her very coherent account, many of the responses of these children to the interview questions were very brief and sometimes fragmentary, and we were faced at the outset with the problem of determining whether or not they provided evidence of script-like knowledge.

Toward this determination we considered what the alternatives to GERs might be. One alternative that has been commonly accepted in developmental psychology is that the young child's knowledge is completely unorganized and consists of randomly assembled elements that might be associated with particular cues. If this were the case, we would expect the child's verbalization to consist of specific salient props, without any evidence of sequential organization. Related to this conception is the notion that the child's knowledge store is instance oriented, that is, that the child remembers bits and pieces of particular experience but does not have general knowledge or organization. In this case, we would expect idiosyncratic episodic output. On the other hand, if the child's event knowledge were organized, but not in a script-like form, it might consist of categories associated with the event (for example, "Lunch has sandwiches, milk and cookies"). If types of schemas other than scripts, such as scenes, organized the knowledge, we might find such things as descriptions of the room where events took place. Or, if knowledge were organized around affective cues, we would expect the child to include mention of likes and dislikes.

In contrast, we expected children's scripts to exhibit certain specific structural characteristics, based on Schank and Abelson's (1977) account described in Chapter 1, as follows:

1. Because scripts are organized sequentially through time, with a temporal, spatial, and causal structure that determines which elements are required, which are optional, and when alternative paths may be entered, children's scripts should exhibit an invariant sequential structure. That is, acts and scenes should be reported in sequential order, or the order should be indicated through other devices such as appropriate answers to questions.

2. Because scripts are organized around goals, the accounts that children give should reflect this goal orientation, either explicitly or through such devices as emphasis on the Central Act, which specifies achievement of the goal (e.g., "eating" in a lunch script).

3. Because scripts are general rather than specific structures, they describe and predict what generally happens, not what happened in a particular episode. Therefore, children's verbal output should exhibit a general, even skeletal, form and should include slots for variables, indicated by the use of general terms for elements that may vary from one occasion to another, for example, particular foods or games that can fill the slot for "what you play" or "what you eat."

4. Because scripts (at least those we are concerned with here) are derived from shared social experiences and are presumed to rely on common organizing principles, they should exhibit a high degree of commonality across those who share the same experience. Although each individual script is organized from the point of view of the person involved, the degree of idiosyncracy should be relatively low.

5. If scripts reflect the underlying cognitive structure, they should be consistent from one time to the next for a given child. That is, the same sequence of events should be expected to be reported on each occasion, unless the script has undergone developmental change. Moreover, it should indicate implicit underlying structure through such devices as definite reference to elements that are not explicitly identified (for example "the teacher").

Of course we could not expect each child's response to contain evidence for all of these characteristics, because we did not expect a one-to-one correspondence between the underlying event representation and its explicit verbalization. However, evidence that these characteristics were present in some degree in most children's narratives and that the aforementioned alternative types of knowledge organization (or disorganization) were not characteristic to any large degree would be persuasive in favor of a script model of children's event representations. In the remainder of this chapter the initial studies that provided evidence of this sort are summarized, and the further questions that these studies led to are set forth.

EVIDENCE FOR CHILDREN'S SCRIPTS—THE FIRST STUDIES

Preschool children were subjects in most of the studies reported in this chapter. We were interested primarily in studying very young children because we hypothesized that some of the pervasive findings of preschoolers' failing on cognitive tasks such as classification might be explained by the way they typically organize their knowledge about the world. That is, if we could show that young children rely on script-like representations, but do not have readily available hierarchical classification systems, we could expect to find systematic performance effects on tasks such as classification. Such effects would not indicate lack of organization but rather a specific type of organization of knowledge that leads the child to interpret information in a particular way, namely, in terms of relations among the elements included in the event schema. It is important to note that the script model was designed to apply to adult memory and has been shown to affect adult information processing on certain tasks. Our hypothesis, then, did not suggest a more primitive type of representational system for the young child, but one that might be primary in the sense of developing earlier than other, more abstract systems and that might be the only system available in early childhood. We also aimed to establish a baseline with preschool children to compare with event reports of older children and adults. We expected to be able to discover in that way dimensions along which the representations of younger children differed from those of older children and thus to propose a sequence of developmental change.

We thus sought to determine whether preschoolers had organized knowledge about their own everyday experiences, and, if so, whether the organization could be characterized in terms of the script model that we had adapted from Schank & Abelson's (1977) work. We focused initially on intensive study of a relatively few children attending a day care center affiliated with Yale University. The children in the center ranged from 2½ to 6 years and came from families in which the parents were students, faculty, or staff members at Yale. The socio-economic, racial, and national backgrounds of the children were quite diverse.

General Method

These first studies designed to explore evidence for children's script-like knowledge used primarily a verbal interview format that was employed as well in many of our later studies. In this paradigm, the child is taken to a quiet corner of the day care center or school and, after being given time to become comfortable with the interviewer, who has had prior acquaintance with him or her in play situations, is introduced to the tape recorder and asked a sequence of questions. The question sequence begins with the introductory statement, "I know you know a lot about . . . : Can you tell me what happens when you . . . ? If the child responds and then pauses the interviewer says (when appropriate) "You certainly know a lot about . . . Can you tell me anything else about . . . ?" When the child indicates no, or if he or she needs further prompting, the interviewer uses selective sequential prompts, such as "What's the first thing that happens?" and "What happens next?" or "What happens after . . . ?"

From the total response protocol (tape recorded and later transcribed for analysis), a script may be constructed that shows the child's indication of what follows what, whether or not it was reported in an unbroken sequence. Elements that follow specific probes are identified. The entire protocol is then analyzed for number of acts reported, specificity of the acts, terminology, inclusion of specific slot fillers, links between acts and other matters of interest. For example, in analyzing the structure of a script, use of causal and temporal terms to connect acts that are variable or invariant in sequence are of interest (see below and Chapter 3). Examples of children's scripts for making cookies and having a birthday party are shown in Table 2.1.

Study 1. Common Scripts

In the first study, eight children (48 to 61 months) from the day care center were interviewed, first in the verbal format as previously described and then with commercially available props (a school, a house, and a model of McDonald's plus Fisher-Price "people") to encourage the acting out of scripts. Three eating situations were probed: eating lunch at the day care center, where all of the children had a common experience and therefore should report a common script; eating dinner at home, which might vary from child to child; and eating at McDonald's, where the set sequence should also lead to common reports. In this first study we were most interested in whether children would report common, required acts in correct sequence.

The protocols derived from the transcripts of the tape recorded sessions, supplemented by the observer's notes, were first analyzed in terms of the acts reported by each child. An act was defined as any action or change in state, regardless of size or generality. "We eat" and "after the main course we have dessert, usually ice cream" would each be counted as one act. The mean number

TABLE 2.1
Examples of Cookie and Birthday-Party Scripts
from 3–8 Years

Making Cookies

Well, you bake them and eat them. (3;1)

My mommy puts chocolate chips inside the cookies. Then ya put 'em in the oven . . . Then we take them out, put them on the table and eat them. (4;5)

Add three cups of butter . . . add three lumps of butter . . . two cups of sugar, one cup of flour. Mix it up . . . knead it. Get it in a pan, put it in the oven. Bake it . . . set it up to 30. Take it out and it'll be cookies. (6;9)

First, you need a bowl, a bowl, and you need about two eggs and chocolate chips and an egg-beater! And then you gotta crack the egg open and put it in a bowl and ya gotta get the chips and mix it together. And put it in a stove for about 5 or 10 minutes, and then you have cookies. Then ya eat them! (8;8)

Birthday Party

You cook a cake and eat it. (3;1)

Well, you get a cake and some ice cream and then some birthday (?) and then you get some clowns and then you get some paper hats, the animal hats and then and then you sing "Happy Birthday to you," and then then then they give you some presents and then you play with them and then that's the end and they go home and they do what they wanta. (4;9)

First, uhm . . . your're getting ready for the kids to come, like puttin' balloons up and putting out party plates and making cake. And then all the people come you've asked. Give you presents and then you have lunch or whatever you have. Then . . . uhm . . . then you open your presents. Or you can open your presents anytime. Uhm . . . you could . . . after you open the presents, then it's probably time to go home. If you're like at Foote Park or something, then it's time to go home and you have to drive all the people home. Then you go home too. (6;7)

Well, first you open your mail box and you get some mail. And then you see that there's an invitation for you. Read the invitation. Then you ask your parents if you can go. Then you . . . uhm . . . go to the birthday party and you get a ride there, and after you get there you usually wait for everyone else to come. Then usually they always want to open one of the presents. Sometimes then they have three games, then they have the birthday cake, then sometimes they open up the other presents or they could open them up all at once. After that they like to play some more games and then maybe your parents come to pick you up. And then you go home. (8;10)

From Gruendel (1980); reprinted from Nelson & Gruendel, 1981.

of acts for each event ranged from 5.67 for eating lunch to 8.00 for dinner and 9.14 for McDonald's. These numbers were based on the combined verbal and enactive conditions and may reflect the attractiveness of the McDonald's props as much as they do actual knowledge about the situations. As might be expected, children reported more acts in the condition with props than in the verbal condition alone.

One way of looking at the commonality of reporting across children is to compare the number of children who mentioned each act in each event. For the lunch situation, nine acts were commonly mentioned, and the average number of children (out of six, since two children did not respond to this question) who mentioned each act was 3.78 or 63%. For dinner, eight acts were mentioned, with an average of 4.5 (of six) per act, or 75%. For McDonald's, 11 acts were mentioned, with an average of 5.72 (of 7) or 82%. In addition to these common acts, some acts that were idiosyncratic to each child were mentioned. Nonetheless, these figures appear to indicate a very high level of consistency across children in the representations that they had built up of these events.

The high degree of agreement on common acts suggests the possibility that there is a basic level of event conceptualization similar to the basic level of object categorization posited by Rosch, who also suggested such a possibility (Rosch, 1978; see also discussion in Chapter 9). We found in this study and confirmed in subsequent studies that children broke up the larger event into units of a common size (eat, play, clean up, etc.) rather than reporting subsidiary or irrelevant actions. Details of basic acts were seldom mentioned except when specifically probed. For example, although playing before lunch could mean riding bikes, playing games, playing with dolls, and so on, these were seldom mentioned. Similarly, how and what was eaten was seldom specified, with the exception of dessert and hamburgers at McDonald's. This general level of reporting appeared to be related to the fact that a variety of specific activities, people, and objects could be included in each act. Only by ignoring specifics—that is, by defining the open slots—could the child report a general sequence that would apply to any day.

In addition, children appeared to be sensitive to the central act of each event, as indicated by the fact that "eat" was mentioned by all children in all three events. Nonetheless, although in general children focused on the event specified in the interview, there was some indication that those events were less bounded than they would be for adults: the children often went on to report after-lunch events at the day care center, even going home after nap, and included going to bed in their dinner at home scripts.

An important finding in this study was that the children reported acts in the correct sequence for each event virtually flawlessly, with only the order of paying at McDonald's commonly out of sequence (reported at the end rather than after receiving food).

There were several indications that an implicit structure was being tapped through these interviews. Children's use of certain linguistic forms, for example, definite articles, pronouns (e.g., she, they), and deictic terms (e.g., this, there) without prior identifying reference indicated that, from the child's point of view, the referents were implied by the situation and did not need to be specifically introduced. Such reference is often taken as an indication of egocentrism on the part of the young child, but such egocentrism also implies that the child is drawing on cognitive representations that are independent of immediate perception.

Contrary to what might have been expected from the literature, personal and idiosyncratic elements did not dominate the reports and were not especially frequent, although disruptions of the routine were often mentioned, as in the report "someone spilled the milk." The enactive condition brought out more personal and fantasy material than did the verbal condition, not surprising considering that the children were engaged in a playful activity rather than a truthful report (see Chapter 8 for some comparisons of these activities).

In summary, this study provided initial strong evidence that children as young as three years had built up general, sequentially correct script-like representations of familiar routine meal situations.

Study 2. Script Development

In the second exploratory study, we attempted to investigate the way in which children's representations of a situation might develop as they gained more experience with that situation. Development of the script might occur in two different ways. It might begin as a very general structure that was gradually filled in with greater detail; there was some suggestion of this in the fact that even the youngest children gave very general, skeletal accounts in Study 1. Or, alternatively, the script might begin with the assembling of details, perhaps largely idiosyncratic, and over time become more general and abstract as experiences accumulated. To investigate these possibilities, we studied the "eating lunch at the day care center" script as it developed over the first 3 months of the child's experience in the center.

Fourteen children were interviewed within the first week of the opening of the center in the fall and again 3 months later. Seven of the children were new to the center, and seven were returning from the previous year. Both verbal reports and acting out with props were used, as in the first study.

A number of different quantitative measures of the completeness of the script reports by new and returning children at Time 1 and Time 2 were computed and are displayed in Table 2.2. It can be seen that children with prior experience, either from the previous year or over several months, give longer accounts, and this difference does not disappear as the new children gain more experience.

TABLE 2.2
Summary Statistics Comparing Old and New Students at Time 1 and Time 2 on Length of Event Sequences (Study 2)

	Script Length (Acts)	*Act-Probe Ratio*	*No. of Acts Recalled to 1st Question*	*Total Number of Acts Recalled in Sequence*
Time 1				
New	5.4	1.24	1.86	5.86
Old	9.1	1.94	3.83	8.57
Time 2				
New	8.6[b]	1.32	4.6	8.43[b]
Old	11.3[b]	2.34[a]	5.5	11.43[c]

[a]Differs from New at $0.10 > p > 0.05$
[b]Differs from T_1 at $p < 0.025$.
[c]Differs from T_1 at $0.10 > p > 0.05$.
Based on Table 10.2, Nelson, 1978.

Analysis of the length of spontaneous sequences in terms of the number of probes needed to elicit a given number of script elements—the act/probe ratio—also showed that both prior experience and subsequent experience made a difference. As shown in Table 2.2 this ratio increased from Time 1 to Time 2 and for old versus new children. Similar results are found when the number of acts in response to the first question and the number of acts sequentially ordered are examined.

Although there were differences in the quantity of responses given by new and returning children, there were no apparent qualitative differences. New children mentioned the same types of acts at the same level of generality as did the returning children. For example, children in both groups mentioned that you drink milk, eat lunch, and get dessert.

Although the results of this study are highly suggestive, there were inevitable confounds that suggested the need for control in further research. The old and new children were not well matched for age; returning children tended to be older than first timers. Moreover, some of the differences found on the initial interview may be attributable to the new children's uneasiness in the situation. Nonetheless, the difference seen at Time 2, indicated that the effects might be real and enduring and suggested the importance of further studies of script development (see Chapter 4).

An interesting side outcome of this study was the finding that the new children mentioned other people in their scripts far more often than did the returning children. These other people were almost always family members, suggesting that these children were still having difficulty in differentiating their day care scripts from their ''lunch at home'' scripts. This tendency was seen as well in the answers to questions such as, "how do you know when it's lunch time?" The new children responded with "Daddy says I have to eat," "Mommy told me," or the like. None of the returning children gave such responses.

As for the developmental alternatives previously outlined, this study suggested that scripts might develop, not from specific detail to general account, but rather from a skeletal structure first differentiated from an older script and gradually becoming more elaborated.

In summary, these first studies demonstrated that young children know about and appear to rely on the sequential structure of familiar events. They establish structures organized around the main or goal acts of an event. The building up of such structures appears to proceed from a simple skeletal frame with slots for alternative fillers. The process is thus neither random nor unorganized.

Study 3. The Effect of Context

Having determined that even the youngest preschool children produced script-like accounts of their day care experience after very minimal experience there, we investigated whether these accounts were affected by the context in which the questions were asked. That is, were children relying on the cues they obtained from the Center in formulating their accounts? We therefore designed a study that posed questions about lunch and dinner through interviews in both the preschool and at home.

Twelve girls and 8 boys between the ages of 3 and 5 years attending the Gesell Nursery School in New Haven participated in this study. There were ten 3-year-olds and ten 4-year-olds. For the most part, children came from middle- to upper middle-class families.

Each child participated in two sessions, one at school before lunch and one at home before dinner, with a week's time between interviews. On each occasion the child was asked two questions: "What happens when you have lunch at school?" and "What happens when you have dinner at home?" The setting for the initial session and the order of questions were counterbalanced across subjects. There were no order effects of either type in the analysis.

The analysis was carried out in terms of numbers and types of acts. An analysis of variance on number of acts reported with age, event, and setting as factors revealed that, as shown in Table 2.3, number of acts did not vary according to the context of questioning, whether in school before lunch or at home before dinner. The values were in fact virtually identical. Although lunch tended to elicit longer responses than dinner, this difference was not significant. The apparent age difference in number of acts did not reach a significant level ($p = .06$). In this situation, then the specific event and the context of questioning did not affect amount of output, which ranged between three and five-plus acts reported.

Again, reports concentrated on central and common acts. "Eat" and "play"

TABLE 2.3
Mean Number of Acts by Age and Context in Study 3

	Lunch	*Dinner*	$\bar{X}$
School context	4.65	4.00	4.32
Home context	4.70	3.90	4.30
Age 3 (N = 10)	3.90	3.35	3.62
Age 4 (N = 10)	5.45	4.50	4.97

were the most common acts mentioned in the lunch scripts, and "eat" and "go to bed" were the most common for the dinner scripts. For both events, 36 out of 40 scripts contained "eat," which is, of course, the central or goal act in each event.

As in the previous studies, children gave general accounts. To examine this effect more closely, we analyzed the language terms used in describing activities. We had observed in the first studies that children tended to use the timeless present form of the verb rather than the past tense and also used the general "you" form, as in "you eat." Although these forms are appropriate to general timeless accounts, their use by preschoolers had not been previously reported; and there were some claims in the literature that children of 4 or younger were not capable of taking the perspective required by the timeless verb form (Cromer 1968; McNeil 1970). It appeared that, if children did use these forms appropriately in giving script reports, this was an indication that they understood the difference between a general, impersonal, timeless account and a narrative that was told from a specific personal point of view about a specific happening. Children in this study almost always (94% of the time) used the timeless verb rather than the past tense in reporting events, as shown in Table 2.4. Children used the general "you" or "we" more than half the time, and more frequently in the lunch situation than in the dinner. It may be that dinner was conceived to be more personal, less socially shared than lunch. It is notewor-

TABLE 2.4
Per cent Use of Tense and Pronoun Forms in Study 3

	Tense			*Pronoun*			
	Timeless Present	*Past*	*Future*	*I*	*We*	*You*	*They*
3 years	95.4	3.3	1.2	43.8	37.1	16.3	2.8
4 years	93.3	6.4	0.3	36.0	43.1	12.4	8.4

thy that "I" was used less than 50% of the time and that the general timeless verb was the dominant form used by even the youngest children.

General terms for acts, such as "we play" and "we eat," were also frequent in these reports, as in the previous studies. It is not possible to specify a priori whether a particular act description is general or specific, or whether terms for different acts represent the same level of generality. For terms like "play," "eat," and so on, there is no standard of generality or abstraction to refer to as there is for general category terms such as "food" and "furniture." Therefore, in order to verify that the accounts were at a consistent level of generality, we compared each child's description of a given act in a given script at Time 1 and at Time 2. We coded each act in terms of whether it was repeated at the same level of generality in the second session or was described in more general or more specific terms. For example, a child who reported "we play" in the first session and "we play dolls" in the second would be scored as moving from more general to more specific. At both ages, 75% or more of the repeated acts were reported at the same level, whereas 10% were more specific and 10% to 15% were more general. Overall, then, acts were reported at a consistent level of generality, and there were no age or event differences. This finding supports the suggestion that there may be a basic act level of description that applies to scripts and that children respect this level of description from an early age.

Because of the possibility that children's script reports were dependent on the context of reporting, the consistency of a child's script across contexts was of interest. We devised a measure to indicate how predictable a script given on one occasion is from knowledge of the same child's script on a previous occasion. This measure is determined by dividing the number of acts mentioned on both occasions (number of repetitions) by the mean number of acts mentioned on each occasion. If scripts were totally predictable (i.e., script output is automatic and not subject to error or decision processes) the index would be 1.00. If scripts were totally unrelated (as might be expected if the child is responding on the basis of idiosyncratic salient recent experience) it would be 0.00. Each child's script was also analyzed for sequence consistency by taking the number of repeated acts produced in the same sequence on each occasion and dividing by the total number of repetitions.

In this study within-child consistency ranged from .41 to .60 for different ages and events. There were no significant differences between ages or events. It appeared that even the youngest children were moderately consistent, an indication that they were drawing on a stable event representation. Sequence consistency was virtually perfect (.94 to 1.00) for both ages and both events. That is, if two acts were mentioned by a child in sequence at Time 1, they were given in the same sequence at Time 2.

It might be argued that act consistency reflects the simple probability of an act's being mentioned. That is, if certain acts are very salient, then they will be mentioned by most children on both occasions. This explanation might apply to the lunch event, which was an experience common to all the children. A Spearman rank correlation of the probability of mentioning an act across children and contexts with the consistency index for that act was performed and proved to be significant for the lunch event (rho = .92 $p < .001$). However, for dinner the correlation was not significant (rho = .56, $p > .05$). Thus, high group agreement on lunch acts was reflected also in within-child consistency, but within-child consistency did not appear to be a simple function of overall probability for the dinner script. That is, although a child might have an uncommon dinner script, he or she was likely to report the same script on both occasions.

In summary, this study replicated the findings of the first two studies with regard to the generality and sequentiality of script reports and showed in addition that children were consistent in their reports regardless of context. Their scripts were not dependent on cues from the immediate environment. They reported no more when they were in the location or at the usual time when the event took place than when they were in a different spatio-temporal context. We may conclude that their script reports are based on the cognitive context provided by the GER, brought forth by the interviewer's questions, and not on the immediate perceptual context.

Study 4: Script Variation as a Function of Event

The foregoing studies were all concerned with eating events. To answer obvious question as to how general these findings are for different types of events, the next study included events with which children might have varying amounts of experience and that varied in type and degree of invariant structure. Of course, in relying on naturalistic experiences, these variables could not be controlled to the extent that might be possible in a laboratory setting. On the other hand the lab has its own drawbacks for this type of work as further research has shown.

The events were chosen to reflect differences in familiarity, social character, centrality of the child's role, affectivity, and the basis for and variability in the temporal structure. The six events were: *getting dressed in the morning, making cookies, going to the grocery store, going to a restaurant, going to a birthday party, and having a fire drill.* On the basis of our intuitions about how these variables might affect the script, we made some predictions about the characteristics of the children's reports. These variables and their characteristics are shown in Table 2.5.

Variation in the number of acts reported could be expected on the basis of the number of distinct acts an event affords. In addition, familiarity with the event, affective attitude toward it, and personal involvement might all be expected to influence how much is recalled. In general, we expected both theoretically and on the basis of previous research, that older children would report more acts than would younger children. We also predicted that grocery store, fire drill and making cookies would produce relatively low amounts of recall because of either

TABLE 2.5
Theoretical Ordering of Events in Study 4

	Frequency of Experience	*Centrality of Child*	*Affect*	*Temporal-Causal Structure*
Getting dressed	Very high	High	Low	Segments consistent, sequence variable
Birthday party	Low	High	High	Segments consistent, sequence variable
Restaurant	Medium	Low	Medium-high	Sequence consistent
Fire drill	Very low	Medium	High?	Sequence consistent
Making cookies	Medium-low	Medium-low	Medium-high	Sequence consistent
Grocery shopping	High	Low	Low	Endpoints consistent, segments variable

lack of personal involvement (grocery store) or unfamiliarity (fire drill, making cookies).

The consistency measure described earlier may reflect how well established the script is for a child. Thus intrachild consistency is presumably some function of experience with the event, and we expected that the highly familiar getting dressed routine would be high on consistency; restaurant and fire drill might also be high because of their high salience and affect. On the other hand, if the experience of making cookies was relatively unfamiliar as we expected, that should have led to low consistency. Grocery store and birthday party might also have been expected to be low on consistency, not simply because of lack of familiarity and/or involvement, but because each has a less highly structured and invariant temporal sequence.

The structure of the event may also be reflected in how the child links its component acts. The use of temporal terms such as "then," "when," "before," and "after" indicates sensitivity to the temporal structure of the event. Such use increases with age, of course, but it may also vary with type of event. The structure of the event itself may influence the extent to which these terms are used. Some events, such as going to a restaurant or making cookies are very tightly woven in terms of their causal and temporal relations. Others, such as grocery shopping and getting dressed, are composed of similar acts more loosely strung together. Birthday party, on the other hand, is composed of a number of essential elements, but these elements can be put together in varying ways. Thus, the temporal structure in the child's report, and therefore the temporal terms used, could be expected to vary.

In brief, a frequent, highly affective, central, consistent event should lead to better organization and higher commonality and consistency of script output than an infrequent, peripheral, low affect, inconsistent event. These hypothetical orderings admittedly represented guesses about the frequency and salience of events in children's lives and, especially in the mid-range could be expected to vary considerably from child to child. For example, for a particular child making cookies may be a common experience in which the child plays a central role and finds the activity very exciting, whereas for other children it may be an infrequent or absent experience.

Twenty children between the ages of 2,11 and 4,5 years (younger group) and twenty between 4,6 and 5,6 (older group) from the Gesell preschool in New Haven participated in this study. Each child was interviewed twice at 3 to 4 week intervals. The interviewer presented the child with six cards on which topics were named and asked the child to choose one in turn to talk about. In this way the child was given an opportunity to participate in the procedure, even though the children could not actually read what was on the cards. All children talked about all six topics.

Overall, 5-year-olds reported more acts than 4-year-olds ($p < .001$), as shown in Table 2.6. Events varied significantly ($p < .001$) in number of acts reported. For the older children, the top four events (getting dressed, birthday party, restaurant, and fire drill) all differed significantly (.05 or less) from making cookies and grocery shopping; they did not differ among themselves; and cookies was significantly greater than shopping. For the younger children, a less differentiated pattern emerged, with fewer significant differences between events, although the order was the same as for the older children (see Table 2.5). The results are generally in line with expectations: birthday party was expected to be high; grocery store and making cookies were expected to be low.

There were no overall age differences in within-child consistency, but there was a difference among events ($p < .02$). No single factor appears to explain the orderings of events on consistency. Getting dressed and restaurant were high, as expected; but fire drill was low on consistency, perhaps because the children had had too few experiences with it. Although there were no overall age differences on consistency, there were age differences for individual events. Getting dressed was relatively low for the younger children and high for the older. It may be that, although both groups of children had had considerable experience with this routine, the 4-year-olds were only beginning to take responsibility for it themselves and thus to have to predict its details. To the extent that a person must plan ahead, the script must become much more reliably established and automatic. The younger children presumably had not yet reached this point.

For restaurant the situation was almost reversed: the younger children showed higher consistency than did the older children. Clearly, this cannot reflect the

TABLE 2.6
Means for Number of Acts and Consistency by Event and Age Study 4

	Number of[1] Common Acts	Mean Number Acts		Act Consistency		Sequence Consistency		# Temporal Terms Used[3]	
		Y[2]	*O*	*Y*	*O*	*Y*	*O*	*Young*	*Old*
Getting dressed	18	2.36[d]	3.62[b]	.41	.62	.89	.84	19	62
Birthday party	16	2.08[cd]	3.59[b]	.35	.53	.90	1.00	15	62
Restaurant	11	1.92[cd]	3.38[b]	.70	.49	.94	.94	27	49
Fire drill	12	1.67[c]	3.31[b]	.35	.53	.90	.94	16	49
Making cookies	9	1.53[c]	2.75[a]	.36	.43	1.00	.95	20	46
Grocery shopping	8	1.28	2.03	.71	.67	1.00	1.00	14	40
Means		2.12	3.42	.48	.55	.94	.95	18.5	51.3

[1]Number of acts mentioned by 2 or more children.
[2]Y = Younger children, 3–4 1/2 years; O = Older children, 4 1/2–5 1/2 years.
[3]Total number of temporal terms such as then, when, before, after, first used by all children in the age group.
[abcd]Means sharing superscripts do not differ among each other but differ from means without shared superscripts at the .05 level or better.

effect of responsibility, as suggested for getting dressed. Rather it may reflect the greater likelihood that older children had had experience with a wider variety of restaurants; thus their restaurant scripts may have been more complex, consisting of different paths that may be taken. Complexity of the event must then be taken into account as well. Contrary to prediction, grocery store was high on consistency; it may be a more highly structured, or perhaps more familiar, event than we expected. Consistency of sequencing was very high in this study for all events, as it was in the previous studies.

The use of temporal terms was aggregated across children and terms at each age, as is also shown in Table 2.5. Here our initial expectations were not borne out, and different patterns appeared at the different ages; although because of the nature of the data, these could not be compared statistically. The expectation that highly structured events would be associated with the use of temporal terms was at least partially supported for the younger children, with restaurant and making cookies high on this measure. This was not the case for the older children, whose use of temporal linking terms was correlated with amount of output (r. = .64; younger: r = .24). This finding supports the supposition that when the child is just learning to use temporal terms productively, they will be used first and most frequently in those contexts where the temporal structure is most compelling. Thus, at the younger age, event structure determines use, as predicted; whereas at the older ages, children use temporal terms to indicate temporal sequence as needed, regardless of how tight that structure is felt to be. In addition, their relatively longer accounts require greater use of temporal terms than do short accounts. These speculations are borne out by the detailed analysis of the use of relational terms in this study and by an experiment on the use of "before" and "after" (both reported in Chapter 7).

In summary, this study demonstrated that different real world events affect the length and consistency of children's scripts. These effects are not a simple and direct reflection of experience, affect, or event structure, although there are indications that each of these may be important. Experience (getting dressed) and salience (restaurant, birthday party) appear to lead to longer accounts, whereas familiarity with the event appears to have the greatest influence on consistency, as reflected both in ranking at different ages and changes with age.

Study 5. The Language of Scripts and Episodic Narratives.

The findings that even 3-year-olds could respond appropriately with general script accounts, and could formulate those accounts in the general terms that were appropriate to them, contrasted with the commonly accepted position that young children focus on specific instances. One possible explanation for our results is that the young children in our studies did not differentiate between the specific and the general, and their use of the general language in their script reports simply mimicked the question form (e.g., "What happens when you . . . ?"). If this were the case, we should find similar responses to both general and specific questions, but formulated linguistically in terms appropriate to the respective questions. On this basis, we undertook to determine whether the script accounts contrasted with accounts of a specific episode and, if so, in what ways. For this purpose, children were asked on one occasion to tell "What happens?" and on another occasion to tell "What happened?" A more detailed analysis of this study is reported in Chapter 5; for the present purpose only the language analyses are reported.

Nineteen 3-year-olds and 19 5-year-olds attending two temple-affiliated summer day camps in New York City were interviewed in the second month of the two-month programs. Sixteen children at age 3 and 15 children at age 5 completed both interviews. Each child was interviewed twice at approximately a one-week interval. In each interview, children were asked about having both a snack at camp and dinner at home. The general interview format was, "What happens when you have snack at camp?" or "What happened when you had snack at camp yesterday?" followed by general probes (e.g., "Anything else?"), then specific probes (e.g., "What happens next?"). Half the children in each age group were asked the general question in the first interview and the specific question in the second interview; the order was reversed for the other half. Children's responses were tape recorded and transcribed for analysis.

Analysis of the use of the past tense revealed that children at both ages distinguished between the general and specific questions in their reports ($p < .001$). When asked "What happened?" they answered with at least the form of a specific past tense recounting. When asked "What happens?" they gave a general timeless account 80 to 98% of the time (see Table 2.7). There was also an Age × Event interaction resulting from the 3-year-olds's giving more general accounts of dinner in the specific condition than they did for snacks—almost half their verbs were present tense in this condition. Three-year-olds apparently had

TABLE 2.7
Results of Study 5

	Question			
	General		*Specific*	
	Age 3	*Age 5*	*Age 3*	*Age 5*
Mean number				
Propositions reported	5.48	11.25	4.26	8.78
Percentage of tense use:				
Past	18	7	74	73
Present	82	88	25	26

not discriminated the specific demand of the "What happened?" question as well as the older children had, and they reverted to the more general account form for the highly familiar dinner event. Overall, children reported more acts in the general than in the specific condition and more specific acts and fewer general acts in the specific condition. The drop in standard script acts in the specific condition may reflect the fact that these become backgrounded, taken as implicit in the context of the more explicit recounting of a specific event.

This study demonstrated that even 3-year-olds respond differentially to questions about specific past events and general event structures. The fact that they appear to respond more readily to general than the specific questions, as indicated by their longer reports, suggests that their memory for specific episodes may be dependent upon the prior development of general event representations. This question is taken up in Chapter 5. Other aspects of the language used in script reports are discussed in Chapter 7.

Study 6. Scripts and Stories: Evidence for Underlying Structure[1]

A crucial question raised by the results of the aforementioned studies is whether the children's verbalization of general event sequences reflects an underlying script-like knowledge structure or whether there is some "output generator" that organizes the report regardless of the form of the underlying knowledge base. For the purpose of untangling this question, an analysis of the relationship between children's scripts and their stories about the same event was undertaken. Two aspects of the data were considered important. First, if scripts depend on an underlying structure, they should be consistent from one report to another, as we already found in the first studies; moreover, they should be more consistent over time than stories, which by definition are episodic variations. Second, if scripts are based on an underlying structure, they should provide a basis for story construction; the script structure in children's stories should then be evident.

More precisely, the rationale for the analyses in this study is the following: If the child has an underlying GER, when the child is asked to generate a description of an event, the GER may be instantiated and copied in part or as a whole to produce the script. When the child is later asked to reproduce the same script, either the GER may be again instantiated and copied or the memory of the first script output, if it exists, may be copied. Copying a memory does not rule out the production of the original script from a set of specific episodes or from some other form of knowledge store. However, consistent production of the same script, independent of memory for the previously produced specific script, would implicate an underlying script-like representation of the sort hypothesized.

[1]For more details on this study see Gruendel, 1980.

For this purpose, one group of children were asked to produce stories about the same events used by children in a script condition, and the act and sequence consistency scores for story generation were used as a comparison to the script scores. It was assumed that children would create stories about events "on the spot," that is, the stories would be novel constructions rather than copies from already existing story representations. Recall of the story would then have to rely on an episodic store of the initial production. However, if memory for a story produced 3 weeks earlier was poor, consistency of content and form would be low in this condition. Thus, lower consistency for stories than for scripts would provide support for the hypothesis of an underlying GER, rather than an all-purpose store plus output mechanisms for different types of narratives.

Forty children at each of three ages, 4, 6, and 8 years from pre-schools and schools in suburban New Haven County participated in this study. Half the children at each age were assigned randomly to the script condition and the other half to the story condition. Children were seen in two sessions at 3-week intervals.

In the first session, children in the script condition were asked to tell, "What actually happens when you are . . . ?" where the blank specified one of four events: having a birthday, planting a garden, making cookies, or building a campfire. Only neutral probes were given (e.g., "Anything else?"). For children in the story condition, the instructions asked the child to "Tell a make-believe story about . . ." where the blank again was to be filled in with one of the four topics. In both conditions, the order of events was counter-balanced, and each child responded to all four topics. Three weeks later, the experimenter returned and explained to the children individually that "the taperecorder had not caught" their words clearly. The children were then asked to "Tell me again what you told me last time, just the same as last time." The instructions were identical for the children in both groups.

Act consistency was central to the data analysis. As in the other studies, sequence consistency was very high at all ages and for all topics and tasks, with an overall mean of .90. Act consistency scores were influenced by both task and age. These scores are shown in Table 2.8, where it is seen that act consistency scores were significantly higher in the script task condition than in the story condition (overall means of .63 and .53 respectively, $p < .025$). A significant task by age interaction resulted from an increase with age in the script task and a decline with age in the story task. A significant topic effect reflected the lower consistency score for birthday party than for the other topics. As we have noted in Study 4, birthday parties have a variable structure, and therefore may be expected to show less consistency.

The significant difference in act consistency between the two tasks was predicted on the grounds that the script would be a direct output of the GER, whereas the story would be a novel construction, dependent on episodic memory for its retention over the 3-week interval. Yet the absolute difference between the

TABLE 2.8
Act Consistency by Task; Age, and Event Topic Study 6

Act Consistencey	*Garden*	*Cookies*	*Campfire*	*Birthday*	*Mean*
Script task					
4-year-olds	.62	.57	.56	.41	.55
6-year-olds	.69	.63	.69	.61	.65
8-year-olds	.70	.67	.76	.68	.70
Story task					
4-year-olds	.55	.59	.53	.43	.53
6-year-olds	.57	.60	.62	.54	.58
8-year-olds	.46	.50	.51	.50	.49
Means	.59	.59	.61	.52	.58

two conditions is not large and does not provide a strong argument for a stable underlying representation.

However, children did not produce exclusively, or even mostly, stories in the story condition. Preschool children's productions in particular were scripts rather than stories. To the extent that the children's stories were actually scripts, we could expect the act consistency scores to be as high in the story condition as in the script condition. In order to examine act consistency for stories alone, the data were analyzed in terms of narrative types produced.

Three types of event narratives were identified: episodes, scripts, and stories (other possible types such as lists or unordered acts did not occur). A production was classified as episodic when it referred to a particular occurrence of an event. Markers for episodes included the use of "I" as subject, action specified in the past tense, and the use of specific personal, temporal, or spatial qualifiers such as "On my 8th birthday" and "When I was three." Reports might be complete or partial episodes, that is, episodes embedded in a general script. Scripts were identified as general event descriptions consisting of a sequence of acts, marked by the neutral "you" as actor and timeless verb. All productions by children in the script condition were actual event descriptions, that is, scripts, scripts with partial episodes, or total episodes.

Very few of the children's productions in the story condition met all the criteria for classification as a story (see Chapter 8). Rather, children in this condition produced descriptions of actual events in the form of scripts and episodes and three types of story-like constructions. Story variants included *elaborations* in which the narrative included a story beginning, end, and/or protagonist, but with an internal script act sequence rather than a story episode, or in which the protocol was based on a script embedded in a larger event description. *Transformations* included productions in which the child varied or violated one component of a script sequence. A *problem-resolution structure* most resembled a proper story, for it included at least one problem-resolution sequence and often included several other formal story characteristics as well.

In the story condition, only 8% of the 4 year-olds' productions were story variants, the remaining 92% being actual event descriptions. Story variants accounted for 38% of the productions of the 6 year-olds and 50% of those of the 8-year-olds; all nonstory productions were actual event descriptions. The distribution of productions by category, task and age is shown in Table 2.9. As can be seen in this table, scripts accounted for the majority of productions in both tasks, an average of 87% in the script condition and 55% in the story condition. In the script condition, the number of scripts produced increased with age from 73% for the 4-year-olds to 94% for the 6- and 8-year-olds. It is also evident that complete or partial episodes declined with age for both task conditions.

For the purpose of comparing act consistency for stories and scripts, each child's two productions were identified as (a) both event descriptions (scripts or episodes), (b) both stories (or story variants), or (c) an ED in one session and a story in the other. The distribution of the reports by age in these groups is shown in Table 2.10 where it can be seen that, for 4-year-olds, 89% of the responses were EDs in both sessions with stories accounting for only 4%. By 8 years, story matches account for 35% of the total. This regrouping permitted the comparison of act consistency scores within the story task for those responses that matched in type, that is, the comparison of consistency for stories from one session to the next, and of scripts from the two sessions. These scores are also shown in Table 2.10.

Across ages, mean act consistency was highest for the actual event description group and at .63 is equal to that for the event descriptions in the script task condition. For the story match group, the mean score was .40, lower than that found for the story task as a whole. The mixed output group achieved a score at the same level as the story group (.41). These findings confirm that the presence

TABLE 2.9
Percent of Protocol Types by Task Conditions, Test Time and Age Study 6

	Time 1			*Time 2*		
	Age			*Age*		
Script Condition	*4*	*6*	*8*	*4*	*6*	*8*
Scripts	73	94	94	80	88	91
Partial episodes	20	4	1	14	11	5
Episodes	7	2	5	6	1	4
Story condition						
Scripts	66	58	41	60	63	54
Partial episodes	15	4	6	25	9	4
Episodes	9	0	3	9	0	2
Elaborations	6	26	19	4	20	9
Transformations	4	10	17	2	8	19
Problem-resolutions	0	2	14	0	0	12

TABLE 2.10
Act Consistency Scores by Type of Match and Age in the Story Condition Study 6

Match type	*Age*[1]			*Mean*
	4	*6*	*8*	
Actual match	.54(89)	.70(56)	.62(46)	.63
Story match	.35 (4)	.50(23)	.30(35)	.40
Mixed responses	.42 (7)	.42(21)	.38(19)	.41

[1]Number of responses in each category in parentheses.

of the actual event descriptions in the story condition increased overall story task consistency and minimized the real difference between the production and recall of actual event descriptions and stories.

This finding of high act consistency for the script task and low consistency for the stories provides strong evidence that scripts reflect the organization of the underlying event representation. The argument here is that asking a child to tell a story involves constructing a novel production from information that may be organized in memory in different ways. Asking the child to give a script, however, requires only that the child construct an account that reflects the organization of information available in the GER. The difference in the two processes becomes evident when the child is asked to reproduce the same narrative 3 weeks later. In the case of the novel construction, the child is dependent on memory to reproduce the previous story and the fallibility of memory results in low consistency. In the case of the script, the child does not need to rely on memory but can again draw directly upon the GER, with resulting high consistency of content across the two tasks.

This study also suggested that children's story productions were derived from their scripts, at least when stories about familiar events were requested. This was particularly striking in the youngest children's productions, which were primarily script accounts rather than stories or story variants. This finding will be considered in more detail in Chapter 8.

SUMMARY AND CONCLUSIONS

The studies reported in this chapter provide ample evidence that very young children possess well-organized knowledge about the familiar events of their everyday life; that this knowledge is readily accessible to verbal recounting; and that it reflects certain basic characteristics of the situational script model.

The fact that children's sequencing of acts is both veridical and consistent over time is one of the most important outcomes of this research in the light of claims by Piaget (1969) and Fraisse (1963) that children's memories are disordered because children are unable to impose a temporal sequence on events. When reporting on real life experiences, children order their invariant temporal sequences correctly. However, when the acts in an event do not occur in an invariant sequence (as in the case of birthday parties) children are less consistent in their reports.

In general, children's reports of a given sequence show a striking degree of interchild commonality and intrachild consistency. Although each narrative contains a relatively small number of acts, they are not a random selection, nor are they based on idiosyncratic notions of salience. Rather, the selection reflects the most central and important acts, linked together into a causally related sequence.

The analysis of common acts suggested that children might be recalling events in terms of a general basic level of events, as suggested by Rosch (1978). Evidence for such a basic level is found in the fact that there are few shifts to either a more general or a more specific level from one time to another, as well as in the consistency of reports within and between children. How this basic level of analysis is derived is an open question, but one that may well provide a key to further understanding of the relation of this type of representation to more complex cognitive operations.

The generality of children's scripts has been highlighted, not only in the common basic level of acts reported, but in the language forms used for these reports, including the use of the timeless verb and the general you form, as well as the use of general verbs that cover a variety of possible specific activities, such as play or eat. This level of generality contrasts with the more specific forms used in the accounts of particular episodes.

Few age differences in the structure of children's scripts were found in these first studies. Even the 3-year-olds produced sequentially ordered accounts, using the same general terms and focusing on central and anchor acts. Older children produced longer scripts, but differences appeared to be in the elaborations on the basic skeletal script of the younger child. The youngest children appeared to utilize similar form and content and were as consistent from one session to the next as older children. Thus, questions relating to the development of scripts have not been definitively addressed in these studies. Subsequent studies provided further information with respect to what develops and what does not in children's scripts. These are considered in Chapter 4.

Additionally, these experiments left open certain structural questions, such as the place of goals in children's scripts and the role of causal relationships between acts in the formation of the script. Moreover, it is not clear whether the resulting structure is dependent on adult definition or whether it is a natural outcome of the child's experience. Most activities that young children take part in are directed by adults, who verbalize the intended sequence. Whether children who were not exposed to such verbalization would produce that structure anyway is a question for further research.

Overall, these studies demonstrated that children as young as 3 have well-developed event representations for familiar routine events and exhibit many of the characteristics of scripts, including generality, sequentiality, and agreement on main and central acts. That their scripts are unaffected by the context of the task supports the notion that scripts themselves provide cognitive context; they vary, however, between events, being affected by such factors as familiarity, participation, goal orientation, and the invariant sequence of the event structure.

Our investigation up to this point, had raised many more questions than it had answered, and the chapters to follow report further research into these problem areas. In particular, the structure of scripts needs further elucidation. It is not enough to say that very young children have scripts, unless the structure of their scripts can be shown to be similar to that of older children. Thus far we have shown that the primary developmental differences found are in the length of scripts, but not in their sequencing or in their consistency across children and across time. In the next chapter, we examine in more detail the causal and temporal structure of scripts and their heirarchical arrangement in order to shed light on the development of these characteristics, which will be taken up as well in Chapter 4. Also in that chapter an examination of microdevelopment over weeks of experience with an event is presented, and the question of influences from both internal and external sources on that development is considered.

We have raised here many issues relating to the use of language, to memory for specific episodes, and to story generation for consideration in later chapters. In addition, the specific cognitive processes that make possible script formation, or that are supported by GERs need to be considered. The understanding of causal relationships, of the reversibility of sequences, the ability to make inferences are all at issue here, as well as the connection between GERs and other conceptualizations. Finally there is the question of the relation between ERs and action—are ERs simply cognitive structures without implications for performance, or do they guide action in real life situations? These are the issues that we discuss and attempt to resolve to some degree in the succeeding chapters.

ACKNOWLEDGMENT

The studies reported in this chapter were carried out in collaboration. Janice Gruendel helped in their design and served as experimenter in Studies 1 and 2. Study 5 was carried out as part of Gruendel's dissertation at Yale (1980). Lindsay Evans served as experimenter and aided in data analysis for Studies 3 and 4. The first two studies were reported in Nelson, 1978.

3 Actions, Actors, Links, and Goals: The Structure of Children's Event Representations

Elizabeth A. Slackman
Judith A. Hudson
Robyn Fivush

As the research reported in Chapter 2 has shown, children make sense of mundane events in their lives in certain characteristic ways. For example, when asked about what happens at a birthday party, a young child will talk about such events as opening presents and eating cake but will not mention cutting the cake or picking up the fork to eat it. If asked about the same event a month later when the child is not likely to remember what was first reported, the child will reproduce much the same account and in the same order. If the child does report the sequence differently the second time, the order of eating cake and playing games is more likely to be changed than the order of blowing out candles and eating cake.

This example illustrates some of the structural characteristics of children's event representations that have emerged in our research on children's scripts. Specifically, children report events in a way that suggests that important or typical actions for an event are represented at a higher level than variable or optional information, and that children are highly sensitive to event sequence, especially when the actions consistently occur in the same order in the real world. As noted previously, that young children possess such structured event knowledge is at first surprising in light of other research findings demonstrating that young children perform poorly on a variety of conceptual and logical reasoning tasks. It might be expected that a well-structured event knowledge system would be a late development rather than being evident by 3 years of age (see Nelson & Gruendel, 1981).

In this chapter we spell out the structure of children's event knowledge as it has become apparent in our research on children's scripts. In addition, we explore here some issues that have arisen in the course of that research: How does the nature of the child's experience with the event affect the learning process? Are some events easier to learn than others? Does the structure of the event representation change with age or experience?

In considering these questions, it is important to distinguish among the three levels of the representation system that are involved in the representation of real world events. To recapitulate these distinctions, outlined in Chapter 1, the first is EVENT STRUCTURE (ES), or how events are organized in the real world. Some events are more tightly connected than others in terms of the causal or enabling relations between component acts. For example, the birthday party event has fewer constraints on the sequence of play games and eat cake than the restaurant event has on the sequence of enter, order, eat, and pay. The representation of events is not simply a matter of mapping onto these structural characteristics, however. Thus, the second level of the representational system is EVENT REPRESENTATION (ER), or how events are represented in memory. Event structure in the real world is translated into the structure of an event schema primarily through participatory experience with the event. The nature of that experience significantly influences both the form and the content of the event representation. Finally, the verbal description (or other externalization of event knowledge) is termed the SCRIPT and is presumed to reflect the form of the underlying representation. The externalized script may not necessarily capture all that is actually represented. A variety of measures may be instructive in revealing different aspects of the underlying schema.

The context in which we explored the structure of children's event knowledge is clarified by a review of the assumptions of the Schank and Abelson (1977) script model on which we originally based our investigations. Then, a discussion of the major findings of script research conducted with adults reveals how well the assumptions of the model have predicted the organization of adults' event schemas and serves as a basis of comparison in discussing structural aspects of children's event representations.

THE SCRIPT MODEL OF EVENT REPRESENTATIONS

Schank and Abelson's (1977) model was originally designed as a computer model to simulate inferential processes required in understanding textual material. Later, a more dynamic formulation that more adequately captures event representation in people, was proposed (Schank, 1982). Because our research on event representations was based on the 1977 model, we focus here on the specifics of that earlier formulation as a point of departure.

A script is a temporally and causally organized event representation constructed from experience in the real world that specifies appropriate action sequences in particular contexts. The representation is a generalized structure made up of slots or categories of event information such as actors, actions, and props that are filled according to the requirements of a particular event. For example, in the restaurant event, the actors are waiters and customers, actions include entering the restaurant and ordering, and props include menus and food. Associated with these open slots are a range of more or less probable alternatives, called slot fillers. For example, what is ordered in a restaurant may range from a hamburger to a filet mignon, and the likelihood of each being ordered depends on the type of restaurant. Because an event schema is an organized whole, the content for any one slot constrains what can fill the remaining slots.

Each event schema has a central or goal act and also specifies which acts and information categories are required and which are optional across contexts. Although required items must occur in the standard script for a particular type of event, the probability of optional items occurring is less than one. For example, the restaurant script predicts certain required actions, such as entering the restaurant, ordering something to eat, and eating, which is the central or goal act. Waiting for someone to show you to your table is included as an optional act because in some restaurants you seat yourself. The number of options an event has depends on the level of inclusiveness at which the event is described. The restaurant event includes more options than the particular types of eating places that it subsumes; that is, there is a different track for eating at a gourmet restaurant than for eating at a fast food place, with accompanying differences in actors (waiters or self-service), actions (standing in line to get food or having it brought to your table), and props (hamburgers or Coquilles St. Jacques). Finally, the event schema contains information about order of occurrence. In a restaurant, for example, you expect to get dessert after rather than before the meal.

Thus, event schemas represent the structure and variability of our experiences with real world events, and this knowledge is used to guide and interpret behavior in familiar situations. In addition, event schemas can be used to monitor comprehension of oral and written discourse. Event schemas are automatically activated whenever a familiar event is encountered or referred to; they guide encoding or retrieval of the actions in the event while also indicating start and stop rules for memory search. In this manner, event schemas provide an implicit, automatic mechanism for comprehension and recall.

Finally, event schemas provide the basis for inferential or constructive processing. Expectations for what should occur are specified by default values for various slot fillers. That is, appropriate slot fillers are inferred from the event schema even when this information is not explicitly mentioned, for example in a story. Inferential processes can also produce distortions in memory, as information not explicitly given may be falsely recalled and more typical slot fillers may be remembered in place of less probable ones.

TABLE 3.1
Schank & Abelson's Prototypical Restaurant Script

Script:	Restaurant (the script header)
Roles:	Customer, waitress, chef, cashier
Goal:	To obtain food to eat
Subscript 1:	Entering
	move self into restaurant
	look for empty tables
	decide where to sit
	move to table
	sit down
Subscript 2:	Ordering
	receive menu
	read menu
	decide what you want
	give order to waitress
Subscript 3:	Eating
	receive food
	ingest food
Subscript 4:	Exiting
	ask for check
	receive check
	give tip to waitress
	move self to cashier
	move self out of restaurant

Hierarchical Organization

Event representations may be organized in two major ways: hierarchically and temporally/causally. Event representations are composed of major scenes[1] that consist of subsequences of actions. For example, the restaurant event includes such scenes as entering, and ordering. (See Table 3.1, adapted from Schank & Abelson, 1977.) The ordering scene subsumes other sequentially ordered actions, or subscripts, such as asking for a menu, deciding what to order, and telling the waitress what you want. Within scenes, some acts are more important or central to a particular scene than others. These are referred to as *main cons,* or *main conceptualizations* (Schank & Abelson, 1977). According to the model, there is at least one maincon or main act in every scene. In the ordering scene, for example, the main act is the customer's giving the order to the waitress.

[1]The scene, as used by Schank and Abelson, extends the dramatic metaphor implied by the script and refers to a subsequnce of actions. Scenes have also been referred to as subscripts. The use of scene in this sense differs from the static notion employed in Mandler and Parker's (1976) work on picture scenes, also referred to as scene schemas (Mandler, 1983).

The main act expressing the event goal (to eat) is the most important of the main acts because it is around this goal that the entire event is organized. The main acts in each scene for an event constitute subgoals that are necessary for realizing the overall goal. Thus, the goal in the restaurant, to eat, is achieved by realizing the sequentially ordered subgoals of entering the restaurant, finding a table, and ordering the meal. Schank and Abelson's model assumes that event representations are originally derived from plans that are carried out in order to achieve a goal. An event representation is formed when a particular plan has been carried out enough times for it to become routine. Plans are at a more abstract level of schematic representation than event schemas. As we discuss later in the section on children's scripts, there is reason to believe that, for children, event schemas precede plans rather than the reverse and goals may not motivate schema development for children in the same manner as for adults.

Temporal/Causal Structure

All event representations are temporally ordered. Schank and Abelson (1977) argue that they are causally connected as well. They conceptualize event representations as ''giant causal chains'' and specify five different types of causal and enabling connections in which component actions are related. The two most basic types are: ''action results in a new state,'' and ''states can enable actions.'' For example, in the restaurant event, the action of entering the restaurant results in the new state of being inside. Being inside, in turn, enables you to go to your table. The succession of causal and enabling connections is what moves you through the actions of the event—whether in the course of enacting the event or in discourse comprehension. Each action either directly causes or enables the next in the order in which the actions typically occur in the real world. Three other types of causal links that are derived from the basic two are: ''states disable actions,'' ''states or acts initiate mental states,'' and ''mental states lead to actions.'' For example, not having a menu prevents you from ordering, having to wait a long time for your food may make you angry at the waitress, and being angry may lead you to leave a small tip or no tip at all.

However, not all event schemas are organized in terms of causal or enabling relations between component actions. Some events consist of loosely associated collections of actions that do not have specifications on sequence. In this connection, Abelson (1981) contrasts ''strong'' and ''weak'' scripts. Strong scripts are based on events that include constraints on order as well as on the occurrence of particular actions. A restaurant script is a strong script in this sense. Weak scripts, on the other hand, are based on stereotyped sets of events that lack consistent sequencing properties. For example, the particular set of actions that occurs at a circus is predictable, but the sequence is not.

We have seen that the script model assumes a number of structural features of event representations. At one level, the representation is a temporally organized whole consisting of necessary or main acts and organized around the major goal of the event. At another level, it is a hierarchical structure in which main acts subordinate variable or optional acts. We now discuss some of the research that has been conducted to assess how well the model matches the actual organization and processing characteristics of event knowledge in adults.

Script Research with Adults

Three basic methods have been used in the investigation of event knowledge in adults: script generation, recall of script-based stories, and script judgment or verification tasks. In script generation, similar to the method used with children described in Chapter 2, people are asked to describe the actions of routine events such as going to a restaurant, or visiting the doctor. These accounts are then scored for the type and organization of actions reported. In addition, people's scripts are compared to determine the extent of agreement on the structure of the event. In recall of script-based texts, people are asked to read a text that is based on a familiar event and then are asked to remember the material in recognition or recall tasks. The assumption in this paradigm is that the pre-existing script guides text comprehension, and thus the narrative is stored in terms of the script representation, including invited inferences, default values, goals, and the possible distortions in the original narrative that these may lead to. When incomplete or misordered texts are presented, measures of false recognition or intrusion errors provide evidence for the existence and structural characteristics of the underlying representation. Finally, in script judgment or verification tasks, people are given script texts in whole or part and are asked to perform tasks that similarly reveal how they organize the event in memory.

In a landmark study, Bower, Black and Turner (1979) provided evidence that adults represent routine events in accordance with the script model. When asked to generate event descriptions of a number of different events, people agreed substantially on the component acts and their sequence. In addition, subjects agreed on how to segment the script actions into chunks or scenes. After reading script-based texts, people tended to confuse in a recognition task items that were consistent with the script but that had not been mentioned in the stories. Additionally, the importance of the event goal was shown by the finding that obstacles in the story that were related to the overall goal were better remembered than obstacles that were irrelevant to the goal. In general, then, the findings constitute evidence for the psychological reality of the model. Specifically, they are in accordance with assumptions of a hierarchical structure in which component actions are organized by scenes and subordinated to an event goal.

Other research using a script judgment paradigm has found that people agree on which actions are central to an event (Galambos & Rips, 1982). In memory tasks using script-based stories, Abbott and Black (1980) found that people falsely recognize scene headers (superordinate, or main acts) more often than scene actions (subordinate, or variable acts). Walker and Yekovich (1984) similarly found that for peripheral (i.e., variable) script actions, the number of false recognition errors is influenced by the number of times the action is implied in the text; whereas, for central script actions, the number of textual implications has no effect. Thus, central script concepts have a higher initial probability of being falsely recognized because of their structural importance, but peripheral actions have a lower baseline level of activation that can be enhanced by the number of other references to them within the text. Finally, Graesser, Gordon, and Sawyer (1979) found more false recognition alarms for typical than for atypical script actions. Although one script judgment study failed to find consistent scene boundaries (Mandler & Murphy, 1979), these results may reflect a mismatch between personal versions of the script and the one presented in the study (Barsalou & Sewell, 1984). Taken together, these findings provide converging evidence for the assumption of hierarchical organization of event representation in adults. At the same time, the Mandler and Murphy (1979) results show that there may be considerable variability among individuals in the specifics of that organization.

Researchers have also tested the assumption of the temporal organization of scripts. Using the script generation paradigm, they have shown that people agree substantially on the sequence in which actions should occur (Barsalou & Sewell, 1984; Bower et al., 1979). Stronger evidence comes from research showing that, when people are given scrambled versions of script-based stories to recall, they spontaneously rearrange the actions to their canonical serial position during recall, even when instructed to remember the sequence in the presented order (e.g., Bower et al., 1979). Further, actions in ordered (strong) scripts are more difficult to recall out of order than those of unordered (weak) scripts.

Other research on the "gap size effect," however, has failed to find evidence for temporal organization in scripts (Bower et al., 1979; Galambos & Rips, 1982; Nottenburg & Shoben, 1980). In this research, it is assumed that, if event schemas are stored temporally, then actions should be retrievable from the representation in the order in which they occur in the event. For example, given the priming statement, "receives a menu," a person should be able to recognize "places an order" faster than "left a tip" because the first action is closer to the serial position of the priming statement than is the second. The failure to find gap size effects has been taken to mean that events are not temporally stored. However, if events are organized hierarchically, as the centrality findings seem to indicate, the failure to find evidence for temporal organization in this paradigm may indicate that the event knowledge is accessed in terms of hierarchical structure; the existence of temporal organization in memory is not necessarily negated. People may be more likely to retrieve event knowledge in terms of its temporal sequence when they are required to reconstruct that sequence, as in a production task (Barsalou & Sewell, 1984). The findings of temporal organization in research employing the script generation paradigm support this interpretation.

In summary, the evidence suggests that adults do organize event knowledge in accordance with the basic assumptions of the Schank & Abelson model. At the same time, and not surprisingly, it shows that people are more flexible and variable in their use of such event knowledge than was specified by the original model.

EVENTS AS EXPERIENCED BY CHILDREN

Thus far, we have discussed structural characteristics of event representations in adults. People learn about the structural characteristics of events through experience with real world events. Whether or not structural characteristics are represented in a GER depends on the type of experiences we have had. For example, for the difference between main and variable acts to be represented, we must either directly experience variations in an event or have them pointed out to us by others. By the time we become adults, we have already constructed event representations for many of the routine activities in our lives, such as going to a restaurant, visiting the doctor, or taking a trip.

For an extended part of their childhood, however, children are engaged in learning about a variety of real world routines as basic as the steps involved in getting dressed. In addition, as children gain more knowledge and experience, their event representations presumably change as well. Before discussing the research on the structure of children's event representations, we need to consider some of the experiential factors that may mediate children's experience with events and thus with the resulting event representation, in the context of their changing perceptions of real world events. Amount of experience with an event, the age of the participant, the goal of the event, the type of participation (e.g., active or passive), and labelling or verbal rehearsal of the event may all contribute to the learning process. Some speculations on their influence follow in the discussion below. (See also the discussion in connection with Study 4 in Chapter 2.)

Event Familiarity

Different stages of schema organization characterize different degrees of experience with an event. Taylor and Winkler (1980) described four stages of development in adults: a rudimentary (or episodic) phase, a stereotypic phase, a relative expert phase, and an automatic phase. In the rudimentary stage, knowledge of a particular example is used to make inferences about other apparently similar instances. An example of this would be a child's making assumptions about what happens when you go to a restaurant based on a single experience of eating at McDonald's. In the stereotypic phase, only the most representative attributes are featured. In the restaurant example, these might include prototypical actions that occur in any restaurant, that is, ordering, eating, and paying. In the stage of the relative expert, there is greater attention paid to inconsistencies; for example, in some restaurants (e.g., fast food type) you pay before you eat. Finally, in the fourth stage, the schema seems to become automatic or "mindless." Thus, when you go to a restaurant, you automatically know what to do without necessarily being aware of the steps in the process.

Although these stages were derived from adult research, they may apply to children's script development as well. For example, with regard to the first stage, Nelson (1980, Chapter 2) found that children formed a general schema for what happens in a fire drill after only one experience. Similarly, Fivush (1984; Chapter 4) found that kindergarteners used the term "sometimes" to describe an event that had occurred only once. In addition, with more experience, the school scripts became more complex, as in Taylor and Winkler's third stage.

Age of the Participant

In developmental research in general, there is a danger of confounding age and experience. Nowhere has this been so elegantly demonstrated as in Chi's study (1978) showing the recall of chess positions by child chess experts to be superior to the recall of adult novices. Script research is particularly susceptible in this regard, given that scripts are descriptions of familiar events and older children necessarily have more experience with many events than younger children. Research on story schemas shows that children are less able than adults to maintain input order of stories that are presented in a noncanonical form (Mandler, 1978), and younger children are less able than older children to recover story structure from distorted versions (McClure, Mason, & Lucas, 1979). There is some evidence that such flexibility with age is true of event knowledge as well. Given the attendant increase in flexibility of scripts with experience, however, it is important not to conflate the two when drawing inferences about the causal or contributing factors in event representation. Children of different ages participating in the same event may have different perspectives on that event because of different degrees of experience with it. These issues are discussed more fully in Chapter 4.

Event Goal

As discussed previously, for Schank and Abelson (1977), event representations are derived from plans for achieving goals. Given that plans and goals are more abstract than scripts, this proposal poses some problems for a developmental theory. What motivates children to form an event schema? One possibility is that children do not initially build up event representations on the basis of their own plans, but rather through observation or participation in adults' plans (Nelson & Gruendel, 1981). For example, the child may learn the grocery store routine simply by accompanying the parent on shopping trips. Another possibility is that, although children may not have the same goals as adults, they may nonetheless have goals appropriate to their own perspective. For example, whereas the adult's goal in grocery shopping is to buy food, the child's goal may be to ride in the cart.

Salience/Affectivity

The salience or affectivity associated with an event may highlight aspects of the event and make it more memorable. Birthday parties or trips to the circus may be well remembered because of their entertainment value. Other events may receive greater attention because of the centrality of the child's role or degree of participation. Events that are somehow significant for the child may require less repetition of occurrence or experience with the event to produce a well-organized event representation.

Participation in the Event

The degree of involvement in an event may range from vicarious to direct participatory experience. Vicarious exposure may include the relating of an event by someone else, stories, television, movies, and so on. Event representations may be constructed by any of these means—separately or in various combinations.

What is not known is the relative importance of these avenues of learning and how this may change with development. There is some evidence in the literature on schematic representation that the degree of active involvement facilitates the ability to draw logical inferences. For example, a greater degree of involvement may enhance constructive processing and make logical relations more salient; the effect may also diminish with age (Paris & Lindauer, 1976). Research has also shown the importance of physical activity on memory for spatial layouts (e.g., Feldman & Acredolo, 1979). Greater involvement appears to enhance representation, and the effect is particularly pronounced the younger the child. Whether this is because of physical activity, the inducement of planning, or more purposeful, goal-directed behavior, is not clear.

The degree of participation may serve to emphasize relations between acts; the impossibility of reversing a logical sequence, for example, may be much more apparent when the sequence has been directly experienced.

Verbal Descriptions

Verbal description of events may influence children's event representations both when it is used by others to direct the child and when it is used by children to monitor or rehearse their own activities. In both cases, language is used as a means of defining the event and thus of enhancing representation.

Others may prime the child for the event through verbal descriptions and set up expectations before it is experienced. Such preparation provides clues to the child about what is considered important about the event; it provides, in effect, a relief map for the event in which main acts are stressed. Further, the description segments the event and specifies beginning and ending points that indicate event boundaries. Labelling of activities identifies what goes with what and indicates hierarchical relationships, such as the reference to subscripts by the heading label of the larger script. Finally, logical and temporal terms may mark different types of relations between acts.

In rehearsing or retelling an event, children not only reinforce what has been learned, but may prompt feedback from others in the form of corrections or embellishments. In this manner, children extend and refine what they know and adjust their knowledge of the event to conform to more socially shared versions.

We have just considered some of the important influences on children's event schemas; the next section discusses research evidence on children's scripts showing how such influences operate together in the construction of organized event knowledge.

STRUCTURAL CHARACTERISTICS OF CHILDREN'S EVENT REPRESENTATIONS

The form and content of event representations are inferred from performance on a variety of measures. The most common and most direct measure is the script interview, or script generation paradigm (e.g., Nelson & Gruendel, 1981; Chapter 2). Other measures include memory for script-based stories (e.g., Hudson & Nelson, 1983, McCartney & Nelson, 1981), picture sequencing tasks (e.g., Fivush, 1981), and enactment with props (Nelson, 1978).

As described in Chapter 2, in the script interview, children are asked "What happens when . . . ?" with reference to a particular familiar event. This question is then typically followed by general probes (e.g., "Anything else?"), and more particular probes designed to uncover the child's knowledge of temporal sequence (e.g., "What happens first?" "What happens next?").

As summarized at the conclusion of Chapter 2, the generation research has shown that even very young children organize their event knowledge in accordance with the script model. Specifically, when interviewed about familiar events, they report a common set and sequence of acts and organize their scripts according to a temporal sequence. The event is reported in a generalized form by the use of the second person pronoun and the tenseless present form of the verb ("you do x"), indicating that the representation is a generalized structure referring to the usual instantiation of the event rather than to a specific incident. Finally, script accounts are consistent on these measures across time and children. We provide in the following section a more detailed review of the structural characteristics and types of acts included in children's scripts.

Hierarchical Organization

Chapter 2 discussed the findings from early script research designed to explore whether children would produce event descriptions sharing a common structure. In Study 1, 3- and 4-year-old children were asked about what happens at mealtime in three different settings: at a day care center, dinner at home, and dinner at McDonald's. The structure of the event was then empirically derived from children's protocols. An analysis of the scripts revealed consistent structural features that were common to each mealtime setting and mode of reporting (verbal or prop assisted).

The acts that were most commonly mentioned by children were identified as main acts. Of the main acts, the central (goal) act and the (final) anchor act were mentioned most frequently. For example, main acts mentioned were: you play . . . get ready . . . get food . . . eat (the central, goal act); . . . throw away plates . . . take nap'' (anchor act). Although they tended not to report them spontaneously, when probed children also demonstrated knowledge of variable acts and items. For example, for the main act, ''play,'' optional acts (ride tricycles, swing on swings), and actors (play with [John] or [Mary]) were mentioned. Children reported variable acts in two ways. As in the play example above, the acts consisted of lists of possible actions. In other cases, the variable acts formed an action sequence. For example, the actions of the main act, ''get ready,'' subsumed the sequence ''go inside . . . wash hands,'' which constitutes a subscript.

In this connection, another type of hierarchy has been shown in children's scripts in which acts subsume optional objects rather than other acts. For example, in the grocery store event (Study 4), the set of particular grocery items selected constituted a variable list, such as, ''You buy X (milk, eggs, bread).'' These findings suggest, then, a common underlying structure in children's event representations in which there is a basic level of temporally organized main acts that may stand in a hierarchical relation to other acts or objects.

McCartney and Nelson (1981) confirmed the relative importance of main and variable acts in an experimental study investigating children's memory for script-based stories. This and other research using script-based stories with children is based on the same assumptions as the adult research, namely, that the pre-existing GER guides story comprehension; thus, recall of the story will be affected by the characteristics of the script, producing superior recall of some components and distortions or omissions of others. Based on information from children's scripts, McCartney & Nelson specified a priori what the main and variable acts were in stories constructed about a typical evening in the life of a young child. Two stories were constructed, each containing activities of a dinner script, a television script, and a bed script. Both stories contained the same main acts but varied in emphasis. In one story, the bed script was emphasized by adding filler (variable) acts, and, in the other, the dinner script was emphasized in a similar way. Five- and 7-year-olds recalled anchor (first and final) acts and main acts in general better than filler acts. There were no age differences in number of main acts recalled, although older children recalled more filler acts than younger children did. This suggests that a basic level of event representation develops first, and then filler acts are added to it.

In summary, we know that children agree on the set and sequence of acts for a scripted event, describe it at the same level of generality, and consistently parse it at the same points. In addition, they are able to use script knowledge to guide their recall of script-based stories.

If children as young as 3 have event schemas, what is it about the representation of events that develops? McCartney and Nelson's study suggests that one development is the addition of lower-level filler acts to the main acts at the basic level. In the research discussed later, we see that scripts also become more complex with age and experience in both the number of main acts reported and in the elaboration of different types of variable acts.

Specifically, three types of variable acts have been identified in the course of our research on children's scripts: *optional, alternative,* and *conditional.* An optional act is one that may or may not be performed; that is, you may or may not order dessert after dinner. An alternative act is one that vies with another for the same slot in the event sequence. For example, at a restaurant you may either check your coat or keep it with you. Finally, conditional acts are those that require that certain preconditions be met for an event to take place. These are often optional, but need not be. In a restaurant, for example, retrieving your coat when leaving the restaurant requires that you first check it.

Gruendel's dissertation (1980; see Study 6 in Chapter 2; also Chapter 8) showed that, with age, not only did children report more acts, but their scripts became more complex. In that study, children ages 4, 6, and 8 were asked to generate event descriptions of four events: birthday party, making cookies, planting a garden, and building a campfire. After a 3-week interval, they were again asked for their scripts. Analysis of the protocols revealed that all children from 4 to 8 produced scripts with a high degree of act and sequence commonality—both among children and between script interview sessions. For each event, there were several acts that were mentioned by 70% or more of the children. Although the number of main acts increased with age and also varied by event, this again confirms that main acts constitute a reliable structural characteristic of children's event representations.

Gruendel found evidence of change in the elaboration of event knowledge between the ages of 4 and 8. She categorized children's protocols in terms of single acts, simple sequences, and qualified sequences. The latter category included: (a) "if then," or "when" clauses specifying preconditions for occurrence of acts ("If you're like at Foote Park or something, then it's time to go home and you have to drive all the people home"); (b) optional acts ("Sometimes then they have three games"); and (c) optional orders of acts ("Then . . . uhm . . . then you open your presents . . . or you can open your presents any time.") Most acts fell into the category of simple act sequences. By ages 6 and 8, no single acts were reported at all. Approximately two thirds of the protocols were of the simple sequence type, and one third were of the conditional type. (See Table 3.2.) That is, the major structural development occurred between the ages of 4 and 6, through an increase in the use of more complex hierarchical structures.

In the research described so far, the development of structure of children's event knowledge has been assessed by comparing scripts of older and younger children. As discussed in the previous section, however, older children differ from younger children not only in age but also in amount of experience in the world. Therefore, in the aforementioned research, age and experience have been unavoidably confounded. This was noted as a problem in Study 2 of Chapter 2. In a study designed to explore the effect of experience alone, Fivush (1984) investigated the development of school scripts in children of the same age. (This study is discussed in detail in Chapter 4). Children were interviewed about the school day routine on the second day, and during the second, fourth, and eighth week of school. An analysis of the scripts they gave revealed that, as of the second day, children produced generalized, well-sequenced reports. The main acts of the event were organized in a horizontal, temporal sequence. For example, many children produced the following sequence: "turn names over . . . have meeting . . . go to a minigym."

On later interviews, a hierarchical organization was evident in that certain "header acts" subsumed lists of possible actions that could be performed in any order. For example, children mentioned that at meeting you might do math, or reading, or some other form of academic activity. Over time, not only were more acts reported, but there was an increase in the number of conditional acts, such

TABLE 3.2
Percent of Scripts at Each Age by Act-Sequence Category

	Age		
	4	*6*	*8*
Single act	4	0	0
Simple sequence	85	62	61
Qualified sequence	11	38	39

Based on Table 10 in Gruendel, 1980.

as, "Then I do art project if I have time" (preconditions of time); or, "At snack, the teacher reads us a story" (specification of time or duration). Optional and alternative acts increased only in the context of the main act minigym, such as, "And then you go to the playground or minigym."

How do children become aware of event structure? One way discussed earlier is through the regularity and consistency of the event itself. The school routine, for example, is a highly defined one in which action boundaries and sequence are clearly demarcated from nursery school age on. Labelling of activities may also be expected to highlight what is important. Fivush (1984) found that the header act, meeting, was labelled by the teacher to announce that group discussions would take place at a particular location in the room. Finally, change of physical location may operate as a tag for particular activities. Fivush found that transitions between actions involved a change of location twice as often as not.

In summary, although the basic organization of event knowledge does not appear to undergo significant change with age or experience, the inclusion of conditional, optional, and alternative acts with increased age or experience shows that, at a more advanced level, event representations become more flexible and probabilistic. Such factors as the sequence's regularity of occurrence in the real world, labelling of event components, and change of physical location may all provide important clues to the structuring of the event for children.

Event Goal

Research on children's awareness of event goals shows that the central or goal act for an event may change with development. This was the finding in a study by Fivush (1981) assessing 4-, 5-, and 7-year-olds' knowledge of two familiar events: having a birthday party and going to a restaurant. In a picture selection task, children were shown ten pictures for each event, eight pictures that were relevant to each event and two that were irrelevant. For example, one of the relevant pictures for the restaurant event showed someone ordering from a menu, and one of the irrelevant pictures showed a child brushing her teeth.

The children were told about an imaginary child who had never participated in the event and were asked to choose the three most important pictures for the child "to know what happens." It was anticipated that this instruction would focus children's attention on those acts they considered essential to the event. Although some children selected irrelevant pictures as well as relevant ones, children at all three ages chose "bring presents" and "blow out candles" as central acts for the birthday party event. On the other hand, for the restaurant event, there was little consistency across age. Only for the 7-year-olds was "eat" the most frequently chosen act (which, as we saw above, matches the adults' choice), in addition to "order" and "pay." Four-year-olds' choices did not consistently match on any particular act as central, and for 5-year-olds, the acts "order" and "pay" were most commonly agreed upon. It may be recalled that in the studies (1, 2 and 3) in

Chapter 2 involving events organized around eating, the goal act of eating was usually included in the child's script. In these studies, however, the event was personally significant to the child and was told from his or her own point of view.

Thus, it appears that the central act for an event may be different for adults and for children and that this discrepancy may vary with the event itself. The degree of match may depend partially on the relevance of the event to children and adults. Whereas birthday parties are presumably entertaining for children, going to a restaurant may be less interesting from the child's point of view and may be an instance in which the child participates in the adult's script. Interestingly, though, with increasing age the child apparently comes to take the perspective of the adult.

In the research described earlier, Gruendel (1980) similarly found convergence with age on the perceived event goal. She designated a priori what the probable central act would be for each of the four events that children were interviewed about (birthday party, planting a garden, making cookies, and building a campfire), and then determined their importance to each age group by means of a frequency of mention measure. For example, for the campfire event, she assumed the central act would be lighting the fire, and the percentage of children at each age group mentioning this as central act was calculated. She then derived *high mention acts* for each event as well; that is, those acts mentioned by 90% or more of the children of each group.

A comparison of the two measures showed that degree of common agreement on the central act increased with age. For the 4-year-olds, high mention acts occurred only for two of the four events, and there was no match between the designated central act and high mention acts for any of the four events. For 6-year-olds, in contrast, high mention acts were found for three events, two of which matched designated central acts; for 8-year-olds, high mention acts were found for all events and all matched the designated central act. These findings strongly indicate that agreement on the central act for an event increases with age. Gruendel also found, however, that, in addition to the central act, 8-year-olds mentioned other acts at 90% frequency as well, suggesting that there may be several acts that are of equal importance to the event.

These results suggest that young children either may not initially perceive the goal or outcome of an event as being important to the event or do not organize the event around the same goal as do older children and adults. There is some support for the latter possibility. Other findings by Gruendel suggested that the meaning an event has for the child changes with age. For example, for the birthday party event, younger children tended to organize their scripts around more object-centered actions (e.g., blowing out the candles), whereas older children included more socially centered actions (e.g., inviting the guests).

In summary, the evidence suggests that the goal for an event changes with age in accordance with the meaning an event has at a particular age. There may not be a single act around which the event is organized; rather, several obligatory acts may be equally important. Finally, the possibility remains that some event representations may be constructed not on the basis of the child's own goal, but rather in the context of an adult's plan.

Whether the goal of an event is their own or adult-based, there is evidence that very young children are implicitly aware of it. In a story recall study (Hudson & Nelson, 1983), stories based on the making cookies and birthday party events were presented to 4- and 6-year-olds. Two story versions of each event were heard: one in which the goal was mentioned in the beginning statement, and one in which a neutral statement replaced the goal statement. For example, for the birthday party event, the goal statement was "One day it was Sally's birthday and Sally had a birthday party." In the goalless story, this statement was replaced by "One day Sally was waiting by the window and looking for her friends."

The children were read stories about the events and were asked to retell them immediately afterwards and again one day later. At the end of the second recall session, the children were asked to give a title to the story as a way of determining whether they perceived the goal. Although the amount recalled was the same for the goal and goalless stories, which seems to indicate that the children were unaffected by the goal or that it did not direct their recall of the event, almost all the children could state what the goal was. Moreover, half the preschoolers spontaneously included a goal statement in their recall of the goalless stories, indicating that they inferred the goal even when it had not been explicitly stated. This suggests that, whether or not an event is initially organized around their own goals, young children are implicitly aware of what the objective goal is.

It seems, then, that children perceive an event structure that is the same across different occurrences of an event; that is, events are organized in terms of main and variable acts. However, events may also differ in their structure in the extent to which main and variable acts are temporally or causally related. Relations between acts are always temporally defined, although, as in a weak script, they may occur in variable orders, and they may be causally or spatially defined as well. Our investigations of children's scripts indicated that, in addition to these types of relations, children's reports also reflect awareness of the temporal invariance of the relations. A temporally invariant sequence is an action sequence that invariably occurs in the same order for reasons other than causality. For example, at the typical day care center, the scenes, such as snacks and story, could theoretically occur in any order, but they tend to be invariant by design. Social or cultural conventions often dictate invariant sequences, as for example, in singing "Happy Birthday" before rather than after blowing out candles on the birthday cake. We consider now the degree to which children's event representations reflect this differential aspect of event structure and how it interacts with age and experiential factors.

Birthday Party

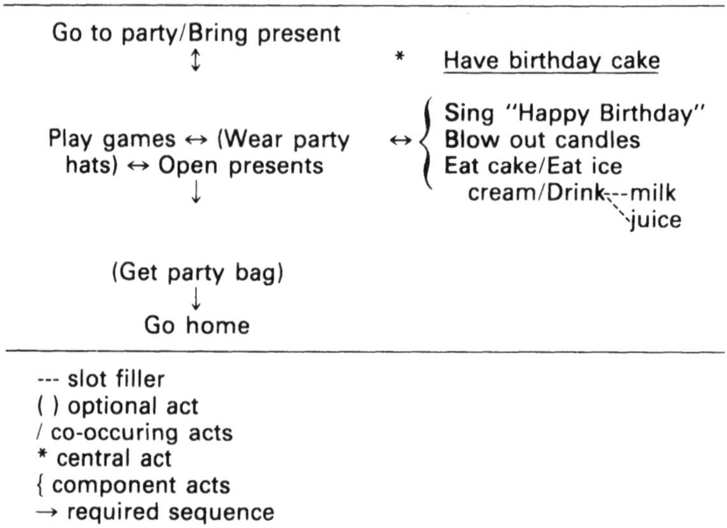

FIG. 3.1a Schematic Representation of the Birthday Party and Making Cookies Scripts

Temporal and Causal Structure

Nelson (1979b) investigated the influence of temporal and causal structure by coding the types of event relations between acts in children's scripts. An analysis of the lunch and dinner scripts of 3- and 4-year-olds from Study 3 in Chapter 2 showed that spatial-temporal relations, that is, those in which there was a change in the location of the action, were the most common type of link between acts in the children's reports. Causal links were also important and were of relatively greater importance for the younger children. Finally, among acts that were only temporally related, invariant relations were much more frequently represented than variable ones. It was concluded that children's first event representations are organized around spatial and causal sequences and that temporal relations are based on either or both of these. That is, location changes, causal structure, and invariant sequence appear to be basic relations in young children's event representations.

Hudson & Nelson (1983) also found causal structure to be important in guiding children's memory for script-based stories. In the study of children's recall of goal and goalless stories, logical organization of the events was also manipulated. Preschoolers' and first graders' recall of the causally constrained making cookies event was compared to their recall of the conventionally organized birthday party event. As Fig. 3.1 shows, the structure of the birthday party event is similar to the "weak scripts" defined by Abelson (1981), in that the

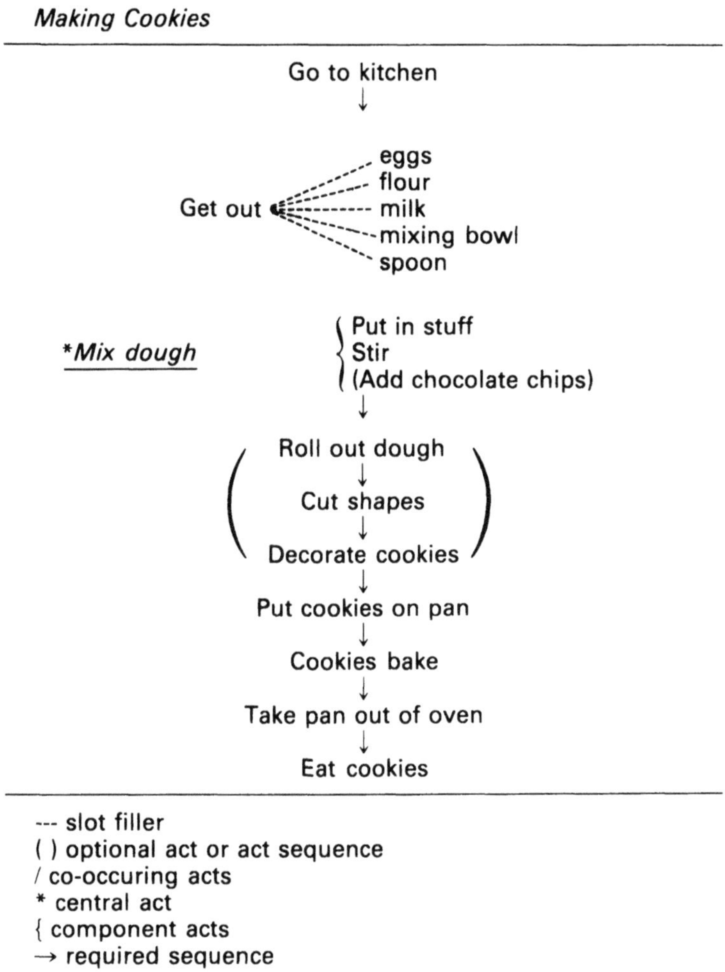

FIG. 3.1b

sequence of acts is more variable than for events such as making cookies (shown in Fig. 3.1), which is an example of a strong script in which most actions are causally related in an invariant sequence. Children of both ages sequenced the making cookies story better than they did the birthday party story, indicating that causal structure is reflected in better organized event representations in children as young as 4.

Children were also asked to recall misordered versions of the two events in which the canonical event sequence was disrupted. For example, in the birthday party story, the statement about bringing presents was given at the end rather than at the beginning of the story. In a manner similar to that found for adults, children made corrections in memory that preserved the canonical script sequence. They omitted one or both of the acts that were misordered, or they transformed statements to make them accord with the logical sequence of the event. For example, the statement about bringing presents was sometimes recalled as party favors being given to the children to take home. Preschoolers' performance was more affected by the misordered versions than was the older children's. That is, preschoolers were more likely than first graders to omit the misordered acts than to recall them in the illogical sequence presented, as the older children were able to do. These results suggest that young children are more constrained in general by the organization of their event knowledge than are older children. The greater difficulty of preschoolers in recalling logically inconsistent sequences intact suggests that they may be more dependent than older children on causal structure.

On the other hand, in the picture sequencing task described earlier, Fivush (1981) found that older children (7-year-olds) showed a high degree of consensus on the sequence of the birthday party event. This indicates that consistent act representations can be constructed for events that do not have inherent causal relationships between acts. It is possible that the older children abstracted a prototypical or most usual sequence for the birthday party as a result of their greater experience with the event. It might also be that the birthday parties 7-year-olds attended had a more invariant structure than those the 4-year-olds were familiar with.

Similarly, as reported in Chapter 2, when Nelson (1979a) interviewed young children about events varying along dimensions such as causal structure, frequency of experience, amount of child's participation, and affectivity (or interest of the event to the child), causal structure was not found to be more important than the other factors. Rather, each factor seemed to contribute to the organization of event knowledge. There was some suggestion that specific effects were associated with particular factors. For example, affectivity seemed to result in longer scripts, so that the children tended to report more about the birthday party event and less about the grocery store event. On the other hand, in addition to causal necessity, event familiarity also led to greater script consistency so that getting dressed was more consistent than making cookies. There were age differences, however, on individual events that suggested the interaction of several factors. Getting dressed, for example, was low on consistency for younger children and high for older children. For the restaurant event, on the other hand, the pattern reversed: Younger children showed higher consistency than older.

As discussed in Chapter 2, it was speculated that the reasons for these results were as follows. Although all children have had a great deal of experience with getting dressed, older children have been taking responsibility for it longer and are thus more practiced at predicting its sequence; thus, they are more consistent. The reversal in consistency for the restaurant event results from older children's greater experience with a wider variety of restaurants. This experience in turn leads to the availability of a number of optional pathways, resulting in lower consistency. Thus, experience, event complexity, and degree of participation all appear to contribute to the organization of an event schema.

In summary, causal structure does seem to be important in the organization of event knowledge and is especially important for younger children. However, these studies point up the difficulty of determining its relative importance by analyzing children's verbal scripts, in which age and the nature of the child's experience with the event also exert a significant influence.

The effect of such confounding variables has been minimized in two studies that have investigated children's acquisition of relatively unfamiliar events in laboratory settings. In one study (Slackman & Nelson, 1984) the event was presented in the form of a story. The narration was about "what happens when you visit a friend," and, although it contained activities familiar to children, the sequence of the event did not form a routine that children would be expected to have in common for the event. Preschoolers and first- and third-graders were asked to recall one of three versions of the event narrative over a consecutive 3-day period (one version on each day). The story versions were meant to simulate the structure of real world event schemas and thus contained obligatory as well as variable acts and details. Half of the story was tightly organized according to a logical sequence and was structured sequentially in the same way across the three versions with only minor slot filler variations. In the other half of the story, the acts themselves varied.

The acts in the causally connected portion of the story were better recalled and sequenced as of the first day, which indicates the importance of overall causal structure. Further, as of the first day, preschoolers' performance was more adversely affected in the arbitrarily organized portion of the story than was older children's. Thus, as found by Hudson & Nelson (1983), younger children seem to rely on logical structure in performing memory tasks more than older children do. The findings are also consistent with Brown's (1976) research showing the superiority of performance on logical compared to arbitrary sequences among preschoolers.

Finally, a study by Slackman (1985), has shown differential effects of event structure and degree of participation in the event. The unfamiliar event in the study ("What happens in the typical day of a toymaker") was modelled with toys and props for 4- and 6-year-old children over a 3-day period. For some children, the event was causally organized, whereas for others it was arbitrarily sequenced. Within each event version, some children acted out the event while telling about it (active condition); others simply related it verbally (passive condition). In the free recall phase that followed training, it was found that, as expected, active participation had resulted in better recall, whereas causal structure resulted in better sequencing of the event. Thus, in this controlled investigation, we confirmed that event structure constitutes an important influence on event organization in children, but other factors contribute to memory for the event as well.

In summary, children's event representations reflect not only the basic structure of real world events, but the extent to which the structure is qualified by the relations between acts as well. Children as well as adults represent and rely on the structure of events, particularly those in the class of "strong scripts." Finally, age and a variety of experiential factors have been found to mediate in the construction of event representation.

SUMMARY AND IMPLICATIONS

The findings that have emerged from our research have yielded important information about the organization and dynamics involved in the formation of event schemas in children. In general, the findings provide converging evidence for a remarkable level of cognitive organization in children as young as 3 years of age. The changes that occur are not in the basic organization, but in the degree to which it is qualified or elaborated upon, and appear to result as much from amount and type of experience with the event as from age-related changes in development.

The findings highlight some of the ways in which children's experience with an event relates to their representation of event characteristics. For example, we have found that events that hold more interest for the child contain more main acts; familiarity with an event results in greater consistency. We still do not know how all the relevant factors interact in the construction of children's event knowledge. For example, what is it about participation that facilitates learning? How often do children form event representations on the basis of their own goals or as participants in events whose structure is made explicit for them by others? To what degree does the more probabilistic and flexible nature of scripts reflect age or event familiarity? Additional controlled research is needed to illuminate the existing evidence and explore possible answers to these questions.

Another major finding of this research is that even very young children's event schemas represent causal and temporal invariances in real world events. However, because causal sequences are also temporally invariant sequences, the advantage of causality per se over invariance remains an open question. In addition, even if younger children perceive causality in events, this does not mean that they necessarily perceive causal relations based on a full understanding of causality. In fact, our evidence suggests otherwise: Younger children are more constrained by the organization of event knowledge and are apparently less flexible than older children in performing tasks that depart too much from that structure. This suggests that event structure may initially function as an implicit scaffold. Once event relations are fully understood, the child is freed to transform and manipulate event sequences by accessing knowledge about cause and effect contingencies.

On the other hand, that children implicitly perceive differences between invariant and variable events raises some provocative questions about the possible influence of causal event structure: Is causality learned from the structure of events? If so, how is it differentiated from invariant sequences? Is knowledge of causal relations somehow decontextualized from familiar event sequences?

In general, these results suggest that organized event knowledge, particularly when logically organized, may constitute the basis for much of the later abstraction and decontextualization of knowledge. The move from simple to more complex scripts may reflect a growing awareness of event categories and provide the basis for the representation of both syntagmatic and paradigmatic relations at a more abstract level (see Chapter 10). The theoretical significance of these findings is their suggestion that structured event knowledge may constitute the source of such higher-level cognitive operations as taxonomic organization and causal inference. The identification of the organizational characteristics of children's event representations can shed light on children's performance in a variety of cognitive tasks and suggest ways to structure learning situations to capitalize on how children naturally organize what they know about the world of events.

4 The Acquisition and Development of Scripts

Robyn Fivush
Elizabeth Slackman

One of the more intriguing findings to emerge from the research on young children's event knowledge is the qualitative similarity in how children of different ages report about events with which they are familiar. Children ranging in age from 3 to 8 years report familiar events in a general, spatially-temporally-causally organized framework. Yet there are also important differences associated with age. Older children almost always report more actions than younger children, regardless of which particular event is being reported. Moreover, older children's event reports tend to be more probabilistic; these children report both more conditional actions and more optional actions. As discussed in the previous chapter on the organization of event representations, conditionals specify prerequisite states that must be met in order for an action to occur, and optionals specify actions that may or may not occur during the event.

In this chapter, we deal with the developmental process in more detail. We explore not only how children's scripts change as a function of increasing age, but also as a function of increasing experience with particular events. First, however, it is important to emphasize again that we are focusing primarily on children's verbal reports. We assume (with good reason, as discussed in Chapters 2 and 3) that verbal reports reflect the organization of the underlying event representations. Because we focus on children's verbal reports, however, we are restricting ourselves to relatively linguistically sophisticated children; that is, preschool and school age children. This does not mean that we do not think children younger than 3 years of age represent events in a general, spatially-temporally organized framework. On the contrary, we believe that schematically organized event representations are a developmentally early and natural way of representing environmental events. Further, we can examine the consequences of this kind of representational ability in younger children's behavior, including language, symbolic play, and action routines. Each of these areas is discussed in subsequent chapters.

In this chapter, we examine how children's verbal reports about familiar events develop. In the first section, we outline our theoretical assumptions and speculate on how various social, cultural, and cognitive factors influence the acquisition and development of event representations. In the second section, we present empirical findings on script acquisition and development, and in the last section we draw some general conclusions and suggest some possible avenues for future research.

THEORETICAL ASSUMPTIONS

Scripts as Cognitive and Social-Cultural Knowledge

Basically, scripts are defined in terms of spatially-temporally organized event representations, but they are not assumed to be simple reflections of action routines experienced in the world. Both the organization and the content of the representation are influenced by a myriad of cognitive and social-cultural factors, and these influences are manifested in several ways. Scripts provide the background of shared social and cultural information necessary for social interaction to proceed smoothly. This information, in turn, implies that scripts develop in interaction with the social world. Moreover, the social context in which script-type knowledge is called on influences how that knowledge is used. That is, the social setting and the goals of the situation affect how script knowledge is brought to bear on the task at hand. Each of these issues is discussed in turn.

Scripts as Shared Cultural Knowledge. Our claim that scripts reflect cultural knowledge is based on the assumption that all events are culturally defined. Following from the work of cultural and cognitive anthropologists such as Geertz (1973) and D'Andrade (1981), we believe that even the simplest action routine is imbued with social meaning. The social meaning defines not only what this particular event is about, but also how it fits into the larger cultural context. For example, schooling is highly valued in western culture, and consequently school is defined as an important and necessary event in children's lives. We believe that this kind of cultural definition of what school is about influences how children come to understand and represent school as an event.

The larger cultural context influences event representations also by the kinds of cultural conventions that are assumed to be known by the members of the culture. That is, many of the default values, or variables that are expected to occur within an event representation, exist at a global cultural level and are imported into the particular event representation. Sex role stereotypes are a good example. Although these kinds of stereotypes are culturally defined, we also use them in assigning default values for particular events. Thus, when we think about "going to the doctor," we often assume that the nurse will be female and the doctor will be male. As the role of women in our society changes, these kinds of assumptions also change.

Scripts as Socially Constructed. Of course, the transmission of cultural knowledge is actually accomplished at a more local level. Scripts are learned and develop in the context of social interactions, and this has several implications for the process of script acquisition and development. We can speculate that the way in which events are talked about will influence how they are represented. More specifically, we think that these effects will be most evident at three points in the construction of an event representation: before, during, and after the occurrence of the event.

First, talking about an event before it is actually experienced sets up expectations about the event, and these expectations affect how the event is perceived and understood when it occurs. Expectations may highlight certain aspects of the event such that the highlighted aspects are more likely to be incorporated into the representation. Highlighting may also occur during the ongoing activity. Labelling different activities may call attention to those activities, and this may have the same effect as prior expectations.

Labelling may also influence the level at which the event is represented. For example, when a mother and child engage in the "getting dressed" script, the mother may first tell the child that they are going to get dressed and then label each article of clothing as it is put on. Later, when asked about getting dressed, the child may respond by naming each article of clothing in the order in which it was put on. On the other hand, the mother may simply tell the child that they are going to get dressed and provide no further verbal structure. In that case when asked, "What happens when you get dressed?", the child may simply respond, "You put your clothes on and then you have breakfast." These are both scripts, in that they are temporally organized sequences of activities; but the component activities of each script are reported at a different level of generality, perhaps due partly to the way in which the event was labelled.

These kinds of influences have been explored systematically in a study by Kyratzis, Lucariello, and Nelson (1984). In that study, they recorded four mother-child dyads in the process of establishing a new routine, "playing circus." The details of this study are reported in Chapter 7, but it may be noted here that the way mothers talked about the developing routine was reflected in the way that the children came to take part in it and to talk about it themselves.

Finally, the way the event is talked about after it is experienced may influence the representation. Again, mentioning particular actions may highlight those actions as an important part of the representation, or may help to define certain categories of actions. Subsuming a collection of different activities under the same verbal label may define a hierarchic organization of activities. For example, when the activities of going to various kinds of stores—such as grocery stores, clothing stores, and toy stores—are all labelled "shopping," they may come to be related to each other as subsets of the "shopping script."

All these factors operate at all stages of script development. That is, expectations about events may not only be formed before an event is ever experienced, but can also be generated about an already experienced event and change certain expectations about the next occurrence. Similarly, once an action category is defined, it will influence how future occurrences of those actions are understood and represented.

Another issue to be considered is the possibility that scripts can be learned vicariously. Not only do we assume that an event representation is not a simple reflection of the event as experienced, but we think it likely that the event does not even have to be experienced for a representation to be constructed. In a very real sense, scripts are cultural knowledge: they can be learned through the cultural media, which ranges from others' talking about the event, to stories about events, television, movies, and so on. There most likely is a difference in the event representation, depending on whether or not the event has been actively experienced. For example, we can all design a "walking on the moon" script from watching the astronauts on television and reading about their experiences; but this script is much different from, for example, a "hiking" script, for which we have personally experienced the event. Although this may not be a critical issue for adults, it may be quite important developmentally. Because children, and especially very young ones, have experienced fewer events than adults, they may depend to a larger extent on more vicarious avenues of event learning. It may be also that they do not distinguish between knowledge gained directly and that gained indirectly. There is some evidence, for example, that preschool children do not differentiate between stories and real life (see Chapter 8).

Scripts as Cognitively Constructed. Although scripts emerge in a social-cultural context, they are at the same time cognitively constructed by the child. Children's representations of a given event depends on their ability to comprehend and construct particular types of relationships between actions, such as causal connections, on their ability to relate event actions to a goal, and to understand and construct plans leading to a goal. Further, different types of events have different underlying structures. For example, as noted in the previous chapters, some events, like going to a restaurant, have an underlying logical structure. Nearly every action is a prerequisite for the action that follows; you must read the menu before you can order, you must order before you can eat, and so on. Other events, such as going to a birthday party, have only loose connections between the actions. Although you have to cut the cake before you can eat it, you can play any time during the party, you can open your presents at the beginning or at the end, and so on. Children must differentiate these structural differences in events in order to represent them accurately. Thus, the way in which events come to be represented by the child is a joint function of how the event is defined and organized by the culture, the underlying structure of the event itself, and the child's ability to comprehend and construct the social and structural organization of the event.

The Problem of Novelty

The term *script acquisition* implies that a new schema is constructed, such that the representation of this event is different and distinct from representations of other events. We should acquire a new script whenever we encounter a new or novel event. Upon reflection, however, it becomes clear that there is probably no such thing as a ''novel'' event, but rather that novelty is a dimension along which events can vary. A novel event can range from a small change in one of the variables of an otherwise familiar event to a truly unique experience. Further, we seldom find ourselves in a completely novel situation where we are unable to make reasonably intelligent predictions about what is likely to happen. This is because event representations are not isolated knowledge. They are related to the larger social and cultural context, as discussed previously, and event representations are also related to each other in several overlapping ways.

First, we have general knowledge about events. All events share certain categories of information, such as actors, actions, and props, and certain structural similarities, such as temporal sequence, and conditional and optional pathways; and we are able to use this kind of abstract knowledge about events in understanding a new event. The fact that even 3-year-old children organize their event reports in the same way as do older children and adults indicates that this kind of event information is available from a very early age.

Second, we always interpret new events in terms of what is already known about events. When we encounter a new event, we try to make sense of it in terms of familiar events; we search for an already established event representation that shares important aspects of the new event. For example, at one end of the novelty dimension, we can understand a dining experience that includes a novel food as just like all other dinners except that one of the props (what you eat) is different. This is the simplest kind of novelty to understand and may be expected to lead only to a new slot filler, or an optional path.

At the other extreme, the very first restaurant experience can be understood as just like eating dinner at home in that certain actions are the same (sitting down at the table, getting food, eating food) and the goal is the same (eating dinner), but other aspects are different from the home routine (reading a menu, selecting and ordering food, being served by a waiter, and paying). These exceptions are so extensive that a new event representation can be expected to be constructed for eating at a restaurant that is related to but different in important ways from, an eating at home script.

In the middle of the two extremes is the first fast food restaurant experience (assuming that a "standard" restaurant script has already been developed). Here, almost all the actions and props are similar to a traditional restaurant, but the sequence of activities (when you sit down, when you pay) and the procedures (how you order, how you find a seat) are different. It is unclear whether a new event representation will be constructed for this kind of a novel experience, or if it will be incorporated as an alternative path in the more general restaurant script. There may be some critical level of discrepancy that will lead to one outcome over the other.[1]

Our use of already established event representations in understanding new situations also suggests that events may be categorically organized. In the previous examples, it seems likely that there are "eating" scripts; and, when we encounter a new event in which the goal or one of the important actions is "eating," we use our knowledge about "eating" scripts to understand the new event. Thus, we can use information from more than one particular event representation to understand a new event and construct a new representation. Once a new representation is constructed, it too will be expected to fall in the category of those scripts that were useful for understanding this new event. Other examples of this kind of categorization are "entertainment" scripts, which include going to the movies, going to museums, the theatre, concerts, etc.; and "health care" scripts, which include going to various health care professionals, going to the hospital, and so on. (The notion of organized event hierarchies is discussed in detail in chapter 10).

Further, at least two of the social factors discussed in the previous sections have implications for defining novel events: how events are talked about and the belief that scripts can be acquired vicariously. Both factors operate in similar ways: They allow us to form a set of expectations about an event before we ever experience it.

Again, the example of walking on the moon is illustrative. Although this is an event that few of us have experienced and would certainly be considered novel, we can still generate a set of expectations for it. Clearly, these expectations would be greatly modified by the actual experience, but nonetheless they would allow us to understand the novel event by limiting our confusion and disorientation.

This example also emphasizes the interactions between knowledge about events and social-cultural knowledge. Our knowledge about events comes not only from our personal experience with events but also through indirect social

---

[1]Schank's (1982) model avoids these problems by proposing different dynamic levels of event representations. Which particular model is most enlightening with respect to these issues is not crucial to the present discussion.

and cultural channels. When we encounter a new event, both sources of information are brought to bear on understanding the new event and constructing a representation. The same relationships hold for the construction of event hierarchies. Both how the event is labelled by others and which similar events from our own experience we draw on in understanding new events influence which events come to be related to each other in a hierarchic fashion. These interactions will become clearer when we present some of the empirical work in the following sections.

Summary

This section has highlighted two of our major theoretical assumptions—scripts are social cultural knowledge; and, in some sense, there is no such thing as a novel event. In our discussion of these points, several important implications of our approach have emerged. First, scripts do not exist as an isolated representational system. They are not only organized in relation to each other, but are a part of a much larger knowledge base that includes our shared cultural and social beliefs and values. Second, even when we examine the development of one particular event representation, we must take into account various social factors that influence the developmental process. These include how the event is talked about before, during, and after its occurrence and whether the event has been actively or passively experienced. Finally, although young children seem to represent events in ways qualitatively similar to those of older children and adults, we cannot ignore the fact that young children have less related knowledge, both social knowledge and knowledge about other events, to draw on in order to understand and represent a particular event. Keeping these ideas in mind as theoretical background, we now turn to a discussion of the empirical findings.

SCRIPT ACQUISITION

Although there may be no such thing as a completely novel event, we do encounter events that are relatively unfamiliar, and we must address the problem of how an event is represented after the first experience.

The first possibility is that a general event representation is abstracted across a series of discrete event memories. According to this explanation, the first few experiences with the event are encoded as distinct, episodic memories. After several similar experiences, one matches across these episodic memories and abstracts out those features of the event that remain invariant across episodes. This process is analogous to the abstraction theory of concept formation. If this is the case, then, after the first experience with an event, the event will be reported as a set of details of that particular occurrence. We can expect it to be reported in the first person singular and the past tense, (e.g., "I did X,"), indicating a specific, personally experienced episode.

On the other hand, the event representation may be general from the outset. According to this account, after only one experience with the event, the representation is organized as a general set of expectations such that future occurrences of the event can be expected to contain the same basic elements and conform to the same organization. Evidence that the ER is a general representation could be found in a well-organized, temporally sequenced report, structured in the second person plural and the timeless present tense, (e.g., "You do X,") and containing little personally referenced or idiosyncratic information (see Nelson, 1978; Chapter 2).

Although this second possibility may seem counterintuitive, the empirical evidence from several studies favors this alternative. In one study (Study 4, Chapter 2), preschool children were asked about fire drills in school after only one experience with a fire drill, and they reported the fire drill event in the general, timeless form and included little or no idiosyncratic information. Thus, children appeared to have a general fire drill script after only one experience.

In another series of studies, Hudson (Hudson & Nelson 1984) asked children ranging in age from 3 to 7 to report about various events after the first experience. Events asked about included going to Disneyland, on an airplane trip, and a special class at school. Hudson found that, again, children were able to give general, well-organized accounts of events after the first experience (see Chapter 5 for the details of these studies).

The final piece of evidence comes from a larger study of kindergarten children's developing representations of the school day routine (Fivush, 1984). This research will be discussed in detail in the next section, but some aspects of the data may be noted here. First, children interviewed on the second day of school gave well-organized, temporally sequenced reports and structured their reports in the timeless present tense. Examples of kindergarten scripts after the first day of school are shown in Table 4.1.

TABLE 1
Kindergarteners' Scripts on the Second Day of School

"Play. Say hello to the teacher and then you do reading or something. You can do anything you want to . . . Clean up and then you play some more and then clean up and then play some more and then clean up. And then you go to the gym or playground. And then you go home. Have your lunch and go home. You go out the school and you ride on the bus or train and go home."
"I just go to school. Then we do stuff. And then we have lunch or snack and then we go home . . . We play a little and then we go to the gym sometimes, or else we can go to the playground. And then we have snack and then, in an hour, we have lunch. And then we can draw a picture or read and then we go home."

These reports, though not elaborate, are general: They appear to incorporate a set of expectations such that future occurrences of the event can be assumed to contain the same basic elements in the same organizational framework. We use the term *general* in a slightly different way than it is sometimes used. The term *general* here contrasts with *specific*, whereas *abstract* contrasts with *concrete*. Thus, the event representation is general in the sense that it is organized as a set of expectations, in contrast with episodic, autobiographical memory, which encodes specific details about one's personal past. However, the event representation can still be concrete in that it is based on actions experienced in the world. In later sections, we present some evidence that the representation, although general from the outset, does become more abstract over time.

This is an especially important distinction because it contrasts with the traditional distinction in the memory literature between episodic and semantic memory. According to Tulving (1972), semantic memory is a general knowledge base. It is essentially a storehouse of factual information, such as word meanings and category membership, and is organized in terms of semantic relationships. Episodic memory, on the other hand, is essentially personally referenced, autobiographical memory. It includes such information as what I did last summer and my third grade teacher's name. Episodic memory is organized in terms of spatial and temporal "memory tags," i.e., when and where the experience occurred. Although all information must have started out as autobiographical in the sense that we had to have learned the information at a particular time and in a particular place, information in semantic memory no longer retains its spatial and temporal "memory tags."

Using Tulving's definitions, scripts are both episodic and semantic. They are episodic in that they have a definite spatial and temporal framework. However, their spatial-temporal organization is a *general* organization. It is not tied to a specific occurrence of the event, but rather defines the organization of any and all occurrences of that event. Thus, scripts are general knowledge. They define a category of occurrences. When kindergarten children report the school day routine on the second day of school, they are assuming that the next occurrence of the kindergarten routine will be similar to the first occurrence in the same sense that we expect the next occurrence of a dog to be similar to previous occurrences of "dog." It is in this sense that we mean that a general representation is constructed on the basis of the first experience with a novel routine.

One further aspect of these data from the kindergarten study deserves special consideration. All of the children interviewed had nursery school experience, which certainly influenced their conceptions and understanding of the kindergarten routine. Children had expectations about kindergarten derived not only from their own previous nursery school experience, but also from what they were told about kindergarten by their parents and nursery school teachers as well as from more indirect means such as stories and television programs about school.

As our earlier theoretical discussion indicates, we believe that all these sources of information contribute to children's understanding of an event upon the first occurrence.

However, kindergarten differs from nursery school in several important respects. The teachers are different, the classmates are different, the physical location is different, and, most important, the activities and the schedule of activities are different. Children's reports on the second day of school reflected these differences. There were no intrusions of any nursery school activities in children's kindergarten scripts. For example, many of these children had attended the same nursery school, where one of the daily activities was "show and tell." Yet none of these children mentioned "show and tell" when reporting the kindergarten routine on the second day of school. The other side of this argument is that some activities were new to the kindergarten routine, such as putting your belongings in a locker and many children mentioned this activity. Even more impressive, their kindergarten scripts were temporally organized according to the kindergarten routine, which was quite different from the nursery school routine. Thus children had differentiated between these two similar routines after only one experience with the new routine.

In summary, the evidence indicates that a general script may be acquired after just one experience with a new event. The newly constructed event representation will be based on the actual experience with the event, on knowledge about all events and experience with similar events, and on expectations about the event derived from social interactions. Nonetheless, after one experience, a general framework is constructed such that future occurrences of the event will be assumed to be similar to the first occurrence. The initial script, however, continues to change and develop over time. This is the issue to which we now turn.

SCRIPT DEVELOPMENT

One of the problems in assessing how scripts develop is the confound between age and experience discussed in Chapter 3. We assume that scripts are based on experience with events in the world. Inasmuch as older children generally have more experience than younger children, it is difficult to determine whether the differences in their event representations are due to increasing experience with an event or to more general changes related to age and cognitive development.

A preliminary study addressing this problem was reported in Chapter 2 (see also Nelson, 1978). In that study, 3- and 4-year-old children were asked about lunch at their day care center during the first week of attendance. Those children who had been at the center the previous year reported more about it. Further, 3 months later, all the children reported more than they had earlier. Although these data suggest that experience with an event may lead to more elaborate representation, it is difficult to draw any firm conclusions because those children who had been at the center for a longer period of time were also older.

In this section, we try to determine how age and experience differentially affect the process of script development. In the first part of the section, we discuss the effects of experience, and in the second part we discuss the effects of age. In the last part of this section, we try to provide some perspective on how each of these factors may influence the process of script development.

Changes with Experience

One way to look at the representational effects of increasing experience with an event is to follow the same set of children over time as they build up more and more experience with a particular event. This is the approach we took in the study of kindergarten children's developing school scripts (Fivush, 1984). Kindergarten children were interviewed four times during the first 3 months of school—on the 2nd day and again during the 2nd week, the 4th week, and the 10th week. At each of these four interview times, children were asked an open-ended, "What happens when you go to school?" question and were encouraged to continue responding with general, "Anything else?" and "And then what happens?" probes.

Kindergarten was chosen as the event to be studied for several reasons. First, it is a highly routine event. Second, children amass a great deal of experience with the routine over a relatively short period of time. Thus, any changes in children's scripts can safely be attributed to increasing experience rather than to age changes. Finally, the school day is an event of relatively long duration and can be conceptualized either as one continuous event or as several discrete events, such as lunch, recess, reading, and so forth. By asking children about the school day as a whole, as well as about daily activities within the school day routine, we can gather information on the developing differentiation and hierarchization of the event representation. For this reason, in addition to being asked about the school day at all four interviews, children were also asked about two daily activities—a daily work activity, reading, and a daily play activity, minigym—at the second interview and at the last interview.

One of the problems encountered in asking children to report the same event again and again is that they may be learning how to report the event, or, just as problematical, they may simply be recalling their previous report. To explore this problem, we interviewed an additional group of children only during the 10th week of school. These children were asked both the general school-day question and the questions about the two daily activities, and their script narratives were compared to the narratives from the repeated interview group.

Overall, then, we were interested in how the organization and content of children's scripts changed as a function of increasing experience with a particular event.

TABLE 2
Kindergartener's Scripts During the Second Week of School

"We do art things. You go back in the class. Then we play. Then when the bell, we have a little bell in there, and when the bell rings, we go in the meeting. Like you sit in the square. Then we have snack. Then we go out to the minigym and then we come back. And we do some math. And then we have lunch. Then we play a little bit. We have nap. No, we don't, we don't play a little. After lunch, we have nap. And then we get our stuff. Then we go on the bus or someone picks us up. But I always go on the bus."
"Well, we have to turn our name over. And then all you could do your handwriting, or something like that, or you could play games. But the really first thing, you have to turn your name over. I mean, the really first thing, you have to put your stuff in the locker. And then you have to turn your name over. That's the first thing. And then we could start playing, or doing our handwriting. And then after we do our handwriting we could play again. And then she tells us to clean up. And then we have to sit on the blue line [for meeting]. And then we have snack. And then we, after that, we can play again. And then after we play, you have to clean up and go to lunch. Then we could write stuff after that. And then we go to nap time. I mean, after that, we go to nap time. And then after we wake up, then we could play for a few minutes or play outside or something like that. And then our mothers take us home."

Elaboration. Not surprisingly, children's narratives bccame more elaborate with increasing experience with the event. That is, over time they mentioned more component activities of the school day routine. On the 2nd day of school, the children mentioned a mean of 7.00 acts; by the 10th week, they mentioned a mean of 12.00 acts. Children interviewed only during the 10th week of school reported a mean of 12.46 acts, indicating that their reports were quantitatively similar to the reports of children repeatedly interviewed. To give the reader a sense of how children's scripts changed over time, Tables 4.2, 4.3 and 4.4 present children's reports during the 2nd week, the 4th week and the 10th week, respectively, to compare to children's reports on the second day of school, which

TABLE 3
Kindergartener's Scripts During the Fourth Week of School

"You have to put our stuff in thc lockcr. And then we have to turn over our name. And then sometimes we can play. And then we have to sit on the blue line. And then we have, or we could do our handwriting. Then we have snack. Then after snack we can play again. At snack, we have to, the teacher reads us a story. And then after that, we play again. And then after that we eat lunch, and then after that we take a nap. And then we take our reading jobs. And then after that, we go home."
"You have to put your things away. And then you can't play outside, you have to go inside. We have circle, and then we have reading jobs. Then we have free play time, have snack, then minigym. No, no, after reading jobs we have library. Then free play time, and then snack time, and then minigym. Then lunchtime, then rest time. Then it's time to go downstairs [for after-school day-care]."

TABLE 4
Kindergartener's Scripts During the Tenth Week of School

"I turn over my name. I do my handwriting. If I have time I do my art project. Then we have meeting time. Then we have math time. Then we have another meeting with snack. Then sharing if it's Friday. If not, story with snack. And sharing if it's Friday. After snack and story, minigym. Go to the bathroom, have lunch, then you get a little play time. And then we have Ron's [science class] or nap."
"I put my things away. Play. And then I turn over my name. And then I go to an activity until the teacher comes in. Play, meeting, reading jobs, meeting again, math jobs, snack. Then after, then minigym. And then lunch. And then we have, then we go home."

are presented in Table 1. Notice that the actions are not simply added to children's previous reports, they are incorporated into the temporal frame of the day's activities, and this temporal framework changed with increasing experience.

Temporal Organization. As mentioned earlier, even on the 2nd day of school children gave well-organized reports of the school day routine. They structured their reports in the timeless present tense and reported the component activities in their correct temporal order at all four interviews. However, the temporal organization of their reports did become more complex, as indicated by an increase in conditional statements from a mean of .40 conditionals reported on the 2nd day to 2.26 during the 10th week.

The children used two types of conditionals in their school day reports, enabling conditionals and temporal conditionals. An enabling conditional specifies a state that must be met in order for an act to occur. The best example is an if/then relationship, as in:

> "If it's time for meeting, go sit on the blue line."
>
> (Michael, week 4)
>
> "And then, if I have time, I do art project."
>
> (Tiffany, week 10)

As these examples demonstrate, children specify that particular actions will occur in the event sequence if a given condition is met. The second type of conditional is a temporal conditional. Examples are:

> "At snack, the teacher reads us a story."
>
> (Delali, week 4)
>
> "And when we ring the bell, that means it's clean-up time."
>
> (Lisa, week 10)

These conditionals do not specify whether or not an act will occur, but rather *when* in the event sequence the act can occur. Although reporting the component activities of the school day routine in their correct temporal order indicates an understanding of temporal succession in a beginning-to-end framework, children's ability to use temporal conditionals indicates a more sophisticated understanding of temporal relationships. If/then and when relations imply an understanding of causality. Not only is the event organized in terms of the daily routine of activities, but this daily routine can be modified by the presence of other causally related activities.

Another aspect of children's increasing temporal sophistication is their use of before and after statements:

> "But before I walk in the door, I put my sweater in the locker."
>
> (Michael, week 4)
>
> "And then we have lunch after meeting."
>
> (Emily, week 4)
>
> "Before snack we have reading."
>
> (Emily, week 10)
>
> "And after snack it's handwriting."
>
> (Robert, week 10)

This usage indicates an understanding of temporal reversibility. That is, events are not organized simply as sequential chains of action, where each act is linked only to the act that follows it. Rather, children are able to move back and forth in reporting the daily routine; they can insert forgotten activities in their correct temporal location. This is especially evident in children's self-corrections. The children often corrected themselves after making an error in reporting the temporal sequence of activities:

> "And after nap, lunch. No, lunch first. Then we have lunch, and after lunch, nap."
>
> (Ilana, week 4)
>
> "And then we have reading jobs. Then we have free play time, have snack, then meeting. No, no, after reading jobs we have library. And then free play time, and then snack and then meeting."
>
> (Christina, week 4)
>
> "Turn over our names. And the very first thing is put my things in my locker. I come in and turn over my name."
>
> (Ariel, week 10)

Self-corrections or temporal repairs are particularly interesting because they indicate that children are not simply reeling off well-rehearsed routines, but are monitoring their verbal reports. When they realize that they have made an error, they are able to go back over the report and either temporally reverse the reported acts or place the missing act in its correct temporal location between two previously mentioned acts. A particularly striking example of this process comes from one child's protocol from the fourth week. After reporting the morning's activities, she says:

> ". . . lunch, nap. What happens after nap? I can't remember. Oh yeah, social studies. No, social studies is in the morning. Oh yeah, that was after meeting. Then comes reading."
>
> (Roseanne, week 4)

In this example, the child momentarily forgets the routine and stops and questions herself. When she comes up with an answer, she realizes that it is wrong, and then goes back over the whole routine in order to place the newly remembered activity, social studies, in its correct temporal location. (A similar example can be found in the letter quoted at the beginning of Chapter 2. Similar findings are discussed more extensively in Chapter 6. See also French & Nelson, 1985.)

These examples clearly demonstrate that children represent events as temporal wholes. Moreover, as children gain experience with an event, this temporal organization becomes more complex and probabilistic.

Commonality. Another aspect of children's school day scripts was the high level of agreement, or commonality, among children in the reporting of acts. Certain acts, such as "meeting," "minigym," and "lunch," were mentioned by the vast majority of children. (Similar findings were reported in the studies in Chapter 2.) Inspection of Table 4.5, which shows the percentage of children mentioning particular acts at each of the interview times, indicates that children share a common representation of the school-day routine. Further, children interviewed only at the 10th week reported the same acts as children in the repeated interview group.

Why do all children mention the same acts when asked to report about the school day? One possible reason is that teachers tend to label activities in ways that make these acts particularly salient. The best example is "meeting," the term used for group discussions. When the teacher wishes to gather the children together to discuss some topic or to begin an academic activity, she calls a "meeting," and the children stop what they are doing and sit in the designated area. Because the teachers call this activity "meeting," the children also call it "meeting."

However, many of the activities that the teachers label all the time are not among those mentioned most often. For example, teachers label "clean-up"

TABLE 5
Percentage of Children Mentioning Particular Acts at Each Interview Time for the General School Day Question

Act	*Interview Time*				
	Day 2	*Week 2*	*Week 4*	*Week 10*	*Control Group*
come in/ put stuff away	50	37	42	32	50
ring bell/ turn name over	00	47	59	58	50
play	85	89	67	100	90
art project	15	16	33	21	20
meeting	35	68	58	100	100
work*	40	68	67	79	80
clean up	15	21	17	11	20
snack	20	42	58	58	50
minigym	20	53	42	89	70
lunch	45	63	50	84	70
rest	00	47	58	47	20
go home	40	58	67	63	60

*This includes children mentioning particular academic activities such as handwriting or reading, as well as general references to doing school work.

Note: From Fivush (1984). (Reprinted by permission of the Society for Research in Child Development.)

everyday, yet this is not a frequently mentioned act. A closer look at children's reports of the kindergarten routine revealed that the actions most often mentioned in common tend to be associated with a particular place; the activity begins with a movement from one part of the classroom to another, or from one part of the school to another, as in:

> "You have to clean up and go to lunch."
>
> (Delali, week 2)
>
> "After meeting, I always go to thc block area."
>
> (Michael, week 4)
>
> "We come to meeting."
>
> (Morocco, week 10)
>
> "We go back to playing."
>
> (Ariel, week 10)

The transition from one activity to another involves a change of location. Twice as many transitions between actions were associated with a change of place as not. This suggests that spatial cues may be one important way of defining when one activity ends and another begins. Activities that are clearly defined by their temporal and spatial slot in the routine are those acts mentioned most often and seem to serve a defining, or anchoring function.

Hierarchic Organization. One of the surprising findings of this research was that the children did not mention many academic activities in common. Although most children mentioned some form of academic activity, they did not mention the same activities. A possible explanation for this finding is that academic activities were conducted in the context of a meeting. When the teacher wants to begin an academic lesson, she calls the children together into a meeting and then one or more lessons can take place. Children may be subsuming academic activities under the category label "meeting."

Support for this explanation comes from the children's reports of two daily school activities, reading and minigym. Recall that the children were asked to report about these activities during the 2nd week and the 10th week interviews. Although the children gave well-organized event narratives when reporting the school day routine, when they were asked about these particular activities, they gave lists of examples of what these activities could comprise. For example, typical reports of what happens when you do reading were:

"Well, we read and find out letters and do riddles."

(Emily, week 2)

"We have to do it, reading. And then we, like, have to cut the thing out and paste it."

(Ian, week 10)

"We read. Sound out words. And sometimes we do some things like when she asks you what the letters are spelling. And sometimes we play this game. And if you read all of your cards, you get a check."

(Priscilla, week 10)

And for minigym, typical reports were:

"We go, and run around and play."

(Ayana, week 2)

"Play a lot. And Wilfredo chases us. Sometimes we play house. Sometimes I play by myself."

(Ayana, week 10)

"We play there. We run around. We play cops and robbers."

(Korun, week 10)

The children did not report these activities as organized sequences, but rather gave a list of possible actions that could be subsumed under this activity category. Thus, it seems that the school day is hierarchically organized, with the script forming the spatial-temporal framework of activities and each activity subsuming a collection of possible actions that the activity can consist of. Further, over time, children reported more possible actions for these activities, suggesting that the event becomes more hierarchically organized with increasing experience.

Schematization. Although the event is general from the outset, the representation seems to become more abstract, or schematized, with increasing experience. This process is evident in the protocols in Table 4.4. The children mentioned more activities during the tenth week of school, but they tended to include many fewer details. In fact, many of the reports were simply a list of the day's activities in their correct temporal order. The reported act became simply a label that encompassed a number of possible activities.

The increasing schematization can also be seen in how individual children report the same act over time. For example, following is a child's report about what happens on first coming into the classroom in the morning:

"We play with the blocks over there, and the puppet thing over there, and we could paint."

(Day 2)

"And then we could start playing."

(Week 2)

"We can play."

(Week 10)

We see that a whole set of activities has been subsumed under a shortened label. This is clearly related to the increased hierarchization of the event representation. As the representation becomes more hierarchically organized, the actions mentioned in the event narrative become more inclusive and schematic and come to act like superordinate category labels.

The Effects of Repeated Interviews. One could argue that some of the changes we see in children's verbal reports over time are attributable to our asking the same children to report about the same event over and over. However, comparisons between the reports of those children repeatedly interviewed and those children interviewed only at the 10th week showed no differences. Their reports were similar, both quantitatively and qualitatively. There were no differences in the number of acts mentioned, the types of acts mentioned, or the hierarchical organization of the reports. This indicates that the changes in the reports over time were the effect of changes in the underlying event representation rather than simply changes in reporting style.

Summary. Although the event representation is organized as a spatial-temporal framework from the first experience with the event, there are important changes in the representation with increasing experience. The children's representations not only become more elaborate; the increase in conditionals suggests that the representations also become more probabilistic and more temporally complex over time. The representation also seems to become more schematized and hierarchically organized; each component action seems to become more abstract and subsume a larger collection of possible activities with increasing experience with the event.

Changes with Age

The findings of the previous section indicate that there are important and dramatic changes in children's event representations with increasing experience with the event over the short run, yet there are still substantial differences in how children of different ages report about events. Regardless of which event is being reported, older children (from about age 5 on) mention more component actions than younger children (3- to 5-years-old) and more complex types of actions (see Nelson & Gruendel, 1981 and Chapters 2 and 3 of this book for reviews). In this section, we discuss several studies documenting some of the changes in event representations that can be attributed to changes with age or to more global aspects of cognitive development.

Age vs. Experience. As noted in Chapter 3, Slackman & Nelson (1984) conducted a study specifically designed to assess the effect of age and experience on the development of an event representation. They asked preschool, first-grade and third-grade children to recall script-like stories about visiting a friend.

The first part of each story was structured similarly, but the particular details, or variables, changed. For example, in all three stories one character travels to another character's house; but in one story, the character takes the bus, in a second story, the character drives, and in the third story, the character takes a train. Further, the actions within the first part were logically constrained sequences. An example of a constrained sequence is getting ready to leave home, traveling to a friend's house, and greeting the friend. These actions are constrained, in that they must occur in the presented order for the sequence to make sense. In the second part of the story, the particular acts varied across stories, and the sequence was arbitrary. An arbitrary sequence is, for example, playing a game, drawing a picture, and having a snack, all activities that may occur when visiting a friend but do not necessarily occur in any particular order. Finally, some of the story actions were general and some were specific, as determined by adults' ratings. An example of a general action was "They watched T.V.," and a specific action was "Martin's mother read them the story of Hansel and Gretel."

A different story was read to the child on each of 3 consecutive days, and the child was asked to recall it each time. On the 4th day, children were asked to recall all three stories. Visiting a friend was chosen as the event because preliminary research suggested that children do not have an elaborate representation for this event. Thus, we can assume that changes in the organization or content of recall over the course of the study were due to increasing experience with the event, where experience is defined as the number of stories heard.

Children at all three age levels organized their story recall accurately; they recalled the component story actions in their correct temporal order, although recall of the logically constrained sequences was somewhat better than the variable sequences, especially for the younger children. More interesting, for all three age groups, the nature of the story recall appeared to change with increasing experience from reproductive to reconstructive. That is, when children were asked to recall each of the stories again on the 4th day, they tended to recall general items better than specific items and variable acts and items tended to be confused between stories. Confusion of variable options suggests that the event representation becomes more general and less inclusive of particular details over time. This pattern suggests that the representation becomes more schematic, or abstract, as was found in children's developing scripts for the kindergarten routine. (See also Chapter 5 for further discussion of these effects on memory.) Thus, children of different ages showed similar changes in their event representations with repeated experience with an event.

However, there were also differences between children of different ages. First, in the delayed recall, older children were more likely than younger children to intrude in recall general items rather than specific items. Older children were also more likely to confuse the actions presented in the story with other actions that were consistent with the event but that had not actually been presented. This evidence indicates that constructive processing associated with more abstract schematic representation was more characteristic of older children than of younger children.

Second, younger children's difficulty in abstracting a general event representation from the variable activities in these stories apparently hindered their story recall. In particular, younger children had more intrusion errors than correct acts among the variable acts of the story; this was not true for the older children. This finding suggests that younger children have greater difficulty than older children in forming an internal representation based on verbal presentation of variable acts. They appear to depend instead on previously organized schemas of events for interpreting such material.

Script Dependence. If young children are dependent on their own internal representations of events to provide the organization and structure for other cognitive activities, then they should have difficulty performing tasks that violate the organization of their event representations. Several studies show this to be the case.

In one study, also discussed in Chapter 3, Hudson and Nelson (1983) asked 4- and 6-year-old children to recall script based stories presented either in their canonical order or with several misordered actions. While children at both ages organized their recall in qualitatively similar ways for the ordered stories, they performed differently with the misordered stories. Older children either restored the misordered actions to their canonical order or transformed the misordered action to make sense in its presented location. For example, giving presents at the end of a birthday party was transformed to getting party favors before going home. Younger children, in contrast, simply omitted the misordered actions from their recall. This suggests that older children were able to use their knowledge about familiar events in more flexible ways to understand and organize the misordered stories, but younger children relied more directly on their underlying representation. When a mismatch occurred between their representation and the presented material, they simply relied on their representation and ignored the conflicting information.

Sequencing was also examined in a study by Fivush and Nelson (1982). In that study, 4-, 5- and 7-year-old children were asked to give scripts, select pictures, and then tell stories about going to a restaurant or a birthday party. In a follow-up study, children were asked to sequence pictures of these two events. Seven-year-old children performed well on all tasks. They gave well-sequenced scripts and well-sequenced stories and were easily able to sequence pictures of the events.

Five-year-old children had some difficulties when pictures were introduced into the experimental situation. Although they could sequence event narratives verbally when no pictures were present, they had difficulty constructing narratives with pictures. In this task, children were asked to select script-related pictures and then tell stories using the selected pictures. The pictures were laid out in front of the children in the order that they had selected them. Some children selected pictures in their correct temporal order, and thus had a temporally sequenced picture series in front of them for the story narrative task; others did not select pictures in their correct temporal order. Those children who faced a randomly ordered picture series could not tell a well-sequenced story narrative.

Yet in the follow-up study, when they were asked simply to put a set of pictures into the correct sequence, five-year-old children performed quite well. Thus, when allowed to rely on their own internal representation of the event, as in the script elicitation task, they performed well. They also performed well when the organization of the task did not conflict with their internal organization, as in telling stories with coherently sequenced pictures. Even when the internal representation and the external organization conflicted, if they could physically reorganize the external organization to match their internal representation, they could still perform well, as in the picture sequencing task. However, when the task requirements did not allow them to change the external organization, their performance was disrupted; they had difficulty telling a well-organized story in the presence of misordered pictures.

The performance of 4-year-old children was even more striking. Although they gave well-organized scripts, as soon as pictures were introduced into the task situation, they were unable to perform the task at all. It appears that their knowledge about events is quite rigid and inflexible. When reporting the event, they seem to be essentially "reading off" their internal representation; and the representation being well organized, their reports are well organized. A similar effect was reported in Chapter 2, Study 6, in which 4-year-old children reported simple scripts when asked to tell a story about an event, apparently because they were unable to use the script to construct a novel episode. Apparently, when young children are required to use their event knowledge in any explicit way, as in selecting pictures about events, telling stories, or sequencing pictures, they have difficulty performing the task.

One final study addresses this issue. Hudson and Fivush (1983) asked 3- and 5-year-old children to recall a script-based story under two presentation conditions. In an alternate condition, children listened to the story and recalled it, and the procedure was repeated. In a successive condition, they listened to the story twice and then recalled it twice without hearing the story again between recall trials. For both presentation conditions, 3-year-old children's recall was extremely well organized and stable across recall trials. When asked to recall the story, they recalled each action in its correct temporal sequence and did not recall additional material when probed.

Five-year-old children, however, improved the organization of their recall over trials. Even when they did not hear the material again between trials in the successive condition, 5-year-old children recalled more and organized their recall better on the second trial. Like the 3-year-olds, the 5-year-olds gave the component actions in their correct temporal sequence on the first trial; but, when probed, they were able to go back over the organization and recall additional material. On the second recall trial, this additional recalled material was integrated into the temporal organization of the story. Thus, whereas younger children appeared to be "reading off" their internal representation and recalled essentially the same material in the same way on both recall trials, older children were able to use their event representations strategically as a deliberate retrieval guide.

These studies indicate that older children are able quickly and easily to reorganize their event knowledge to meet the demands of the task at hand. They can both reorganize the external organization of the task materials, as in the picture sequencing task, and reorganize their internal representation, as in the story tasks. Younger children, in contrast, can use their event knowledge only in its canonical form. When the task allows them to rely on this canonical organization, they perform quite well, as in the script elicitation tasks and recall of correctly sequenced stories. However, when the task requires some reorganization of their event knowledge, they perform poorly. This is really a two-sided argument: one, younger children depend more on their internal representations to provide the organization for task performance; and two, because of this dependence, they are unable to use their event knowledge flexibly. That is, they are unable to take advantage of the organization of the task itself, and so are bound to the organization of their representations. Younger children have implicit knowledge about events; with increasing age, their representations seem to become more explicit and flexible.

Scripts as Cognitive Context. Although the research reviewed here focuses on the limitations of young children's event knowledge, it must be recognized that their scripts are nonetheless a very powerful representational system. Even the very youngest children assessed have well-organized knowledge about real world events. Although they do not seem to be able to use this knowledge in the flexible and explicit ways that older children do, the organization of their event knowledge does provide the essential cognitive context for performing many other cognitive activities. Because children are able to bring a rich organizational scheme to the situation, they are not bound to the here and now context of the task. Thus, in situations that allow them to rely on the organization of their event knowledge, young children perform quite well. Among the activities that are facilitated by the cognitive context provided by an event representation are language and conversation (see Chapters 7 and 8 of this book), an understanding of temporal sequencing and reversibility (Chapter 6), and the development of categorical organization (Chapter 10).

However, these cognitive activities are embedded within the implicit organization of an event representation. Thus, although children may not be bound to the task context, they are bound to their internal representation. It is the representation that supports performance on the task. That is, young children do not display cognitive skills in the abstract; they rely on the organization of the event representation to organize their activity. In this way scripts allow children to perform cognitive tasks that they may not be able to perform without the organizational framework. This interpretation may explain the large discrepancies in young children's performance on various cognitive tasks under different circumstances (see, for example, Donaldson, 1978). Further, it allows for a developmental continuity of various cognitive skills. Skills and processes that are originally embedded within a familiar event routine may be abstracted and generalized with increasing experience with that event and other events, as well as with increasing age. (See Fivush & Mandler, in press, for more evidence on this point; also French & Nelson 1985; Nelson 1985.)

Summary

In this section we tried to determine the effects of age and experience on the development of event representations. The research we reported in the first part indicates that, with increasing experience with an event, children's scripts became not only more elaborate, but also more temporally complex and hierarchically organized. Thus, it seems that some of the differences found between children of different ages can be attributed to varying amounts of experience with the event. As children's experience increases, the event representation also becomes more schematic. However, age seems to have an important influence on this process as well. Even with similar experience with an event, older children's representations seem to be more abstract. Another difference that may be attributable to changes with age, or to general cognitive development, is the growing flexibility of event knowledge. Younger children seem to be more dependent on the organization of their event representations to organize the task at hand.

GENERAL CONCLUSIONS

Not surprisingly, scripts develop both as a function of increasing age and increasing experience with an event. Before we discuss our conclusions, however, we must emphasize that age and experience can be separated only for purposes of discussion. Not only are age and experience interwoven in the real world, but they clearly interact in complex ways in the process of script development. Still, the empirical findings allow us to draw some tentative conclusions about the relative influences of each of these factors. First, a general event representation appears to be constructed on the basis of the first encounter with an event. Even after one experience, children's reports are general and well organized. Children structure their narratives in the general timeless present tense and include little idiosyncratic information. Further, there seems to be relatively little intrusion of information about other, similar events in children's reports of new events. However, little is known about the effects of previous experience and prior expectations on the formation of a new event representation. We are reasonably sure that this kind of information influences the comprehension and organization of newly encountered events, but there is as yet no available systematic research aimed at investigating these influences.

Two areas of further research are suggested here. First, before they experience a new event, children should be interviewed about their expectations with respect to it, and this information should be compared to their representation of the event after the first experience. In addition, it would be important to control the amount and type of verbal explication children are exposed to while encountering new events, and to determine how what children are told about events influences their subsequent representations of those events.

Whereas the generality of children's reports after the first experience is certainly impressive, children's event representations continue to develop with increasing experience with the event. Not only do children report more component acts over time, but the temporal and hierarchic organization of the representation becomes more complex as well. In particular, the increase in conditional statements over time suggests that the representation is not organized in a strict sequential chain, but rather as a temporal whole, where the occurrence of any one action can modify or dictate whether or when other actions may occur. The use of conditionals further indicates that young children have at least a beginning understanding of causal relations and temporal reversibility.

The increased hierarchic organization over time appears to be related to the increased schematization of the representation with increasing experience. The event representation is from the outset organized as a spatial and temporal framework, which seems to become more skeletal with increasing experience. At the same time, each of the actions incorporated into the framework seems to subsume a growing collection of possible activities that can comprise that action. Thus, many of the changes that seemed to be related to increasing age in the first studies appear to be attributable to increasing experience with an event. Of course, this must remain a tentative conclusion until more research on the development of scripts is conducted and expanded to include other types of events.

One aspect of script development, however, seems to be associated with increasing age rather than experience. Younger children appear to be more dependent than older children on the organization of their underlying event representations. Scripts provide a rich cognitive context for young children that allows them to transcend the "here and now" of the task context, but they are not apparently able to transcend the organization of the underlying representation. Young children do not perform well on tasks that require them to explicitly manipulate their knowledge. Older children, in contrast, seem to be able to use their knowledge about events flexibly and explicitly.

This developmental difference relates not to a particular event representation but across all event representations. That is, although the development of the representation of a particular event seems to be similar across children of different ages, the ability to use event knowledge differs. Further, abstract cognitive skills may develop from skills originally embedded within the organization of an event representation. With increasing experience with that event and all events, these skills may become decontextualized. For example, as the research on sequencing previously discussed demonstrates, the concept of temporal succession seems to be implicit in younger children's scripts but later comes to be understood in a more explicit way. Probably the most exciting area for future research is to try to trace the development of these kinds of abstract cognitive skills with increasing age and experience. Preliminary research suggests several cognitive skills and abilities that seem to emerge from the organization of event knowledge, including temporal sequencing and reversibility (Fivush & Mandler, 1984; Fivush & Nelson, 1982; French & Nelson, 1982), causal and logical relations (Carni & French, 1984), and the development of taxonomic categories (Lucariello & Nelson, 1985; see Chapters 6 and 9).

Finally, one important aspect of script development has not yet been systematically investigated. Scripts are presumed to be organized around goals, and in Schank and Abelson's (1977) theory, they derive from plans to achieve those goals. The goals of the children's scripts that have been studied thus far are set by adults (e.g., eat dinner, buy food, get dressed, learn to read). The degree to which children share these goals may influence their acquisition of the script. Alternatively, children's scripts may not depend on goals for their acquisition; or they may be organized around different goals. Moreover, it seems unlikely that children's scripts evolve from plans; rather the relation is likely to be the other way around: that plans are formed from available scripts. These speculations await confirmation in further studies.

In conclusion we emphasize that although older children's knowledge seems to be more flexible than that of younger children, the process of script acquisition and development appears to be qualitatively similar across children of different ages. Not only do young children have well-organized knowledge about routine and familiar events in their world, but this knowledge is constructed and organized in similar ways across a relatively long developmental time span.

5 Memories are Made of This: General Event Knowledge and the Development of Autobiographic Memory

Judith A. Hudson

> The memory is sometimes so retentive, so serviceable, so obedient; at others, so bewildered and so weak; and at others again, so tyrannic, so beyond control! We are, to be sure, a miracle every way; but our powers of recollecting and forgetting do seem peculiarly past finding out.
>
> Jane Austen, *Mansfield Park,* 1814

The processes that control retention and recall of autobiographic memories seem random and unsystematic. How can we account for the fact that particular incidents from early childhood are vividly recalled, yet remembering the first day of last semester or even lunch last Tuesday can be an extremely difficult enterprise? A 3-year-old can astound us by recounting at length and in detail an incident long forgotten by adult participants. The same child becomes silent and unresponsive when asked, "Remember what we did yesterday?" or "What did you do at school today?" We may draw a blank when asked, "Don't you remember the time that we . . . ?", but with a few more details, images of the event suddenly come to mind in abundant detail. At other times, vivid memories impose upon our consciousness without warning, triggered by a chance word, image, taste, or smell.

Despite the richness of our day-to-day experience filled with a variety of people, places, activities, and interactions, we remember astoundingly little of these details. Of course, not remembering much of our experience is extremely adaptive. To organize memory for details of every day's events would consume so much mental effort, we would have little left to devote to any other mental activity. Indeed, the focus of this volume is on how we can represent experience without relying on memory for specific experiences. Yet we all retain a corpus of autobiographic memories for some specific events. The challenge of a theory of autobiographic memory is to discern the principles by which this corpus is organized and that can account for why and how some memories are retained over long periods of time while others are forgotten almost as soon as the moment has passed.

This chapter presents a model whereby autobiographic memories are conceived of as the products of constructive memory processes, drawing not only from details of specific past experiences, but also from general knowledge about events organized as generalized event representations (GERs). GERs can therefore influence the encoding, storage, and retrieval of autobiographic memories. The developmental implications of this relationship between general event knowledge and autobiographic memory are explored in three studies comparing children's scripts and autobiographic memories.

A MODEL OF GENERAL AND SPECIFIC EVENT REPRESENTATION

Autobiographic memory and general world knowledge or semantic memory have been considered as separate memory systems since Tulving's (1972) classic paper. In this taxonomy, autobiographic memory is considered a type of episodic memory. The distinguishing feature of this type of memory is that it is stored and retrieved in terms of temporal and spatial information. In contrast, conceptual knowledge, of which generalized event representations, i.e., scripts, are one type, was thought to be stored and retrieved through separate processes. (See Tulving 1984, for an undated version of this dichotomy.)

This chapter presents an alternative formulation for the organization of autobiographic memory. In this view, general knowledge about events and memory for details of particular experiences can be thought of as two forms of event representation—general and specific—that are intimately linked in the memory system. Autobiographic memories are conceptualized as specific event representations, organized in memory not by spatial and temporal tags, but in terms of their relationship to GERs. In this formulation, routine episodes that do not deviate significantly from an expected sequence of events are not attended to and are forgotten, absorbed by the GER. That is, because the GER already represents information about possible instantiations (e.g., lists of people and objects that can fill slots, optional actions, and alternative pathways) a single episode that matches in its details what is included in the GER contains no new information and is not stored separately as an individual autobiographic memory. (See also Nelson & Hudson in press.)

Mundane episodes may be quickly forgotten, but what happens when a novel event is experienced or when something unusual or unexpected occurs? Studies of adults' recollections from childhood show that novel and one-time events tend to be remembered better than recurring events in long-term autobiographic memory (Hanawalt & Gebhart, 1964; Potwin, 1901; Waldfogel, 1948). These memories may also be linked in memory to GERs, tagged, or indexed by their unusual or distinctive aspects. For example, in recalling a specific dinner, we might remember one of the following: a dinner that was especially good or bad; a dinner that was distinguished by the absence of typical slot fillers or the inclusion of unusual slot filler instantiations; or a dinner at which an unexpected action occurred or an expected action either did not take place or transpired in an unusual manner. Thus, the GER provides the background against which particular occurrences are experienced as novel or typical and, therefore, memorable or eminently forgettable.

If what is initially experienced as a novel event or an unusual variation is subsequently repeated, details of a specific occurrence that are initially tagged in memory as a specific episode can be incorporated or *fused* into the GER as an alternative action or optional pathway. In this way, attention to and memory for details of particular experiences are important for modifying general event knowledge. This fusion of specific event representations into the GER accounts for the "schematization" of episodic memories over time and repeated encounters (Slackman & Nelson, 1984). Linton (1975, 1979, 1982) describes this process as a transition from episodic to semantic memory, whereby the strength of episodic memories weakens as typical features of the event are abstracted. The end result is that all that can be remembered about "what happened" is "what must have happened" given general knowledge about the event.

Thus, what is recalled as an autobiographic memory can actually include both details of specific episodes and information drawn from general event knowledge. For example, we might be able to recall some details of a particular dinner at a particular restaurant but not others. However, without necessarily drawing on memory for the details of a single occurrence, we could infer some information, for example, that a waiter or waitress took the orders and served the meal and that the check was paid, on the basis of general knowledge about that event. If we are able to recall particular details of those actions, our recall may be guided by the knowledge that those activities must have occurred. In this way, GERs can also serve as retrieval guides to direct memory search for specific episodic information and can help to fill in memory gaps.

Although GERs can assist the reconstruction of autobiographic memories, they also contribute to inaccuracies and distortions in recall. When reconstructing "what must have happened," details from separate individual experiences can become confused in recall. We may be able to remember particular foods eaten at a particular restaurant, but we may confuse the participants with those present at a different meal. In a study of her own long-term recall of daily events, Linton (1975, 1979, 1982) reported that she was acutely aware of these processes of fusion and confusion when trying to reconstruct a specific episode. For example, details surrounding the mailing of a "final" draft of a textbook to the publishers were relatively easy to remember, but after three "final" drafts, she could not distinguish one episode from another.

At other times, inaccuracies in recall are apparent only when there is a veridical record of the experience to refer to. For example, Barclay, Wellman, & Abrams (1982) reported that subjects sometimes confused actual descriptions of "what happened" recorded by themselves a year ago with event descriptions that were consistent with "what could have happened." In the case study of individuals' autobiographic memories, Smith (1952) found that subjects sometimes did not realize that an event they recalled as a single experience had actually been repeated, and that their recall included particulars from more than one episode. Checking John Dean's testimony to the Senate Watergate Committee against transcripts of the actual conversations in the Oval Office of the President, Neisser (1981) found that Dean often confused separate conversations in his recall. In recalling a meeting from March 13, 1979, Dean reported a discussion of "hush money." Although this topic was raised in conversation, it was not brought up in the March 13 meeting. It was, in fact, part of a discussion on Marsh 21, but Dean's recall of the March 21 meeting made no reference to this topic.

This last example is interesting because, unlike remembering day-to-day experiences that consist largely of routine or repeated experiences, Dean was recalling momentous conversations that had extreme legal and historical repercussions, and he was under great pressure to recall the conversations accurately. The distortions in recall are minor; he does not distort the truth or gist of the activities that transpired. But, because the cover-up plans were laid in the context of repeated meetings and conversations, inaccuracies in recall reflect fusion and confusion between similar experiences. Neisser argues that Dean's recall of these meetings is more "repisodic" than "episodic;" although they are not completely accurate with respect to the actual details of each occurrence, they represent the gist of what occurred. Moreover, they serve the function for Dean of organizing memory for details of similar experiences and representing his participation and involvement in the architecture of plans and projects that evolved over the course of repeated episodes.

Experimental studies also have demonstrated how general event knowledge can direct and distort episodic recall. This line of research dates back to Bartlett's (1932) original studies of how schemas organize story recall. The model of general and specific event representation outlined here is similar to Bartlett's "schema plus correction model" whereby schemas organize long-term memory and special attention is paid to information that violates the schema. More recent models of the relationship between general event knowledge and memory for particulars of individual experiences include the "script pointer + tag hypothesis" of Graesser and his colleagues (Graesser, Gordon & Sawyer, 1979; Graesser, Woll, Kowalski & Smith, 1980), Reiser's (Reiser, 1982; Reiser, Black & Abelson, 1982) "context-plus-index" model, Schank & Abelson's (1977) script model, and Schank's (1983) characterization of "failure driven memory." Experimental data demonstrating the relationship between general event knowledge and memory for particular episodes are available from story recall studies and studies of the effects of cueing on autobiographic recall.

Story recall studies have shown that memory discrimination is better for atypical actions in a passage than for typical actions, and typical actions are poorly discriminated (Graesser et al., 1979; Graesser et al., 1980). Because unexpected or unusual actions in a familiar event sequence are "tagged" in memory, they are easily discriminated. In contrast, actions that are expected to occur are recalled as part of the story even if they have not been explicitly stated.

In a study of effects of cueing on autobiographic recall, Reiser et al., (1982) timed how long it took subjects to remember a specific autobiographic memory when they were given different types of cues. *Activity* cues referred to larger events (e.g., going to a movie); *action cues* referred to specific actions from the event (e.g., paying at the ticket booth). According to this model, action cues produced shorter response latencies because autobiographic memories are tagged in memory in terms of distinctive actions. By identifying an event and a particular action, the search process was narrowed to an optimal number of specific episodes. Action cues that included expectation failures (e.g., not finding a seat) resulted in longer response latencies because they constrained subjects' memory search to a much smaller category of episodes. Subjects' spontaneous search processes were therefore interrupted when the cue was too restrictive. In addition, Reiser (1982) found that cues referring to infrequently performed actions or low saliance actions slowed down subjects' recall of particular episodes because subjects had greater difficulty accessing the general event representation with these cues.

These descriptions of the relationship between general and specific event representation are inherently developmental in that they describe a memory system with the potential for constant modification as a result of any new experience. However, it is not clear from this research that children's autobiographic memory system actually operates in this way. Some evidence, in fact, indicates that young children's autobiographic memories are not organized in the same way as the adult system. The question arises, then, whether there are changes in the organization of autobiographic memory with age.

AUTOBIOGRAPHIC MEMORY DEVELOPMENT IN CHILDREN

One line of inquiry suggesting that the autobiographic memory system may undergo significant changes during childhood is the research on adults' recollections of childhood. One of the major findings from this research is that adults have almost no recall for their first 3 years, they experience difficulty recalling events from the years 3 to 5, and recall increases significantly for the years 5 to 8 (Crovitz & Quina-Holland, 1976; Crovitz & Schiffman, 1974; Dudycha & Dudycha, 1932; Robinson, 1976; Rubin, 1982; Waldfogel, 1948). This phenonenon was first identified by Freud (1905/1953) as infantile amnesia: "the peculiar amnesia which in the case of most people, though by no means all, hides the earliest beginnings of their childhood up to their sixth or eighth year" (1953, p. 173). According to Freud, early memories are forgotten in order to survive the tumultous period of the Oedipal years, fraught with violent and incestuous desires that must be denied and repressed. He invoked the notion of screen memories to account for the infrequent and rather banal memories that survive into adulthood. These screen memories stand in for the emotionally charged memories that are repressed (Freud, 1916–1917/1963).

White and Pillemer (1979) report that Freud's "blockade" model was subsequently modified to account for recollection studies by Henri & Henri (1898) showing that adults often had vivid memories of emotionally significant events occurring in the years 3 to 6. In his later "selective reconstruction" model, Freud proposed that children younger than 6 or 8 remember experiences as traces, fragments, or images and not as full experiences. In recalling these years, narratives of full episodes are constructed from the memory fragments, but the constructions are not actual memories.

More recent cognitive reconstruction models propose that cognitive developments that take place during childhood result in a restructuring of the autobiographic memory system (Neisser, 1967; Piaget, 1962; Schactel, 1947; White & Pillemer, 1979). According to Piaget:

> There are no memories of early childhood for the excellent reason that at that stage there was no evocative mechanism capable of organising them . . . The memory of the two or three year old child is still a medley of made-up stories and exact but chaotic reconstructions, organised memory developing only with the progress of intelligence as a whole. (1962, p. 187).

Thus, in this theory memory for the years 0 to 3 is nonexistent and memory for the preschool years becomes lost to adult recall because we no longer operate with the same organizing structures or schemas that are necessary to locate and retrieve those memories. Other interpretations of infantile amnesia have emphasized changes in sensory input as a result of physical growth, brain maturation, growth spurts, central nervous system changes, and increases in information processing capacities during childhood. (See White & Pillemer, 1979 for a review.)

Yet empirical data does not support this characterization of young children's autobiographic memory. Diary studies provide evidence of autobiographic memories in children as young as two (Hurlock & Schwartz, 1932; Nelson & Ross, 1980). Other research indicates that preschool children are able to produce organized narratives about past episodes, either spontaneously (Umiker-Sebeok, 1979), or in response to experimenters' queries (Menig-Peterson & McCabe, 1978; Todd & Perlmutter, 1980); in contrast, other narrative genres, such as story production, are not mastered until later. (See Seidman, Nelson & Gruendel, Chapter 8 in this volume for a discussion of scripts, episodic recounts and story production.) It is possible that conversations with adults about shared past experience are instrumental in teaching children how to talk about the past. Indeed, conversations about past episodes seem to occur frequently in mother-child interactions during the years 1 to 3 (Eisenberg, 1982; Engel, Kyratzis & Lucariello, 1984; Ratner, 1980).

There is little evidence to support the claim that preschool children's autobiographic memories are qualitatively different from those of older children and adults. However, research on constructive memory processes suggests that developmental differences in children's use of schemas in memory may characterize changes in the relationship between children's GERs and autobiographic memories with age. Studies of the effects of story and event schemas in memory have found that both children and adults use schemas to direct their recall of particular story episodes (see Mandler, 1983 for a review). Although story schemas specify categories of story information and relationships between those categories, this organization is content free. GERs, on the other hand, specify content as well as organization.

The effects of GERs on the structure and content of recall of script-based stores have been demonstrated for both children and adults (Bower, Black and Turner, 1979; Hudson & Nelson, 1983; McCartney & Nelson, 1981; Slackman & Nelson, 1984). Generalized event representations dynamically organize recall by providing a framework of expectations to guide retrieval. Reliance on this framework can also produce distortions in memory. When the material deviates from the expected structure, it may be "corrected" in recall to conform to expectations. Information that is expected to occur, but that is not explicitly given, may be falsely recalled.

A consistent finding in research on children's use of story schemas and GERs in recall is that younger children tend to rely more heavily on schematic structures in memory than do older children and adults. These types of effects are stronger for younger children, presumably because they use general knowledge structures automatically but are less able to attend to and accommodate deviations (Hudson & Fivush, 1983; Hudson & Nelson, 1983; Mandler, 1978, 1979; Mandler & DeForest, 1979; see also discussion in Chapter 4).

What does this phenomenon imply for children's recall of autobiographic memories? Because younger children's recall is more schema-bound, they may be more influenced by general event representations in recalling particular experiences than older children. To the degree that distortions in autobiographic memory are a result of using general event schemas to guide retrieval, more distortions would be predicted in younger children's autobiographic recall. If this is the case, preschool children who can easily demonstrate general event knowledge should have relatively poor recall for specific episodes. This would explain Linton's (1979) finding that preschool children had difficulty answering questions about specific past experiences and tended to provide general information (e.g., "We always visit my grandmother on Saturday") instead of episodic descriptions. This characterization of preschool children's autobiographic memory is in direct opposition to the belief that young children's memory consists of unorganized fragments.

The following studies explore the relationship between GERS and the development of autobiographic memory. The major issue of interest was the extent to which children's autobiographic memory is influenced by general event knowledge and whether preschool children's (ages 3–4) autobiographic memory is more schema bound than older children's (ages 5–7). In three studies, children's scripts for various types of events are compared to children's recall of particular episodes in terms of the amount of information provided, the type of information reported, and the level of specificity in children's accounts.

The first study by Hudson and Nelson compared 3- and 5-year-olds' scripts for two familiar events with their recall of particular episodes of the same events and also to their recall of novel episodes. A second study by Hudson and Nelson compared 3-, 5-, and 7-year-olds' scripts and autobiographic memories for events that varied systematically in terms of their familiarity to the child. The last study, by Fivush, Hudson and Nelson, is a minilongitudinal study of kindergarten children's memory for an unusual episode of a familiar event over time.

An important issue that is addressed in each of these studies is how familiarity with events affects children's recall of specific episodes. More experience with events should lead to more complex general knowledge about events; but does increased familiarity also result in more schematic processing in children's recall of particular episodes? Are older and younger children's autobiographic memory differentially affected by familiarity? Are novel events easier or more difficult for young children to recall? These questions are addressed in the first two studies. Study 3 investigates the possibility that memory for a novel occurrence of a familiar event could become incorporated into a general event schema.

A related issue involves effects of cueing on autobiographic recall. For example, is it easier to remember a familiar event that happened "one time" (i.e., any time) than what happened "yesterday" (i.e., one particular time)? This question is investigated in Studies 1 and 2. Study 3 examines the effects of increasingly more specific cues on children's recall of a novel event after a time delay of one year.

STUDY 1: "WHAT HAPPENED YESTERDAY?": RECALL OF RECENT EVENTS[1]

Although autobiographic memory organizes long-term memory for personal experience, memory for an experience may first be recalled after a brief period. This study explored the possibility that GERs affect how children at different ages attend to and retain memory for specific episodes of routine events one day later by comparing children's recall for "what happened yesterday" at snack at their summer day camp or during dinner at home with their scripts for the same events. (See Hudson & Nelson in preparation for an expanded version of this study.) Three- and five-year-old children were interviewed twice at approximately a one week interval. Half the children in each age group were asked the *general* questions, "What happens when you have snack at camp?" and "What happens when you have dinner at home?" in the first interview; and the *specific* questions, "What happened when you had snack at camp yesterday?" and "What happened when you had dinner at home yesterday?" in the second interview. The order was reversed for the other children.

Because the children were very familiar with these events, it was expected that they could provide general scripts for "what happens." It was also predicted, on the basis that young children rely heavily on schematic structures in memory, that they would have difficulty recalling yesterday's episodes. That is, they would recall little from the experiences, and the information they could recall would tend to reflect general event knowledge, not memory for details of individual episodes. If younger children's recall is more schema-bound than older children's, these effects would be greater for 3-year olds than for 5-year-olds.

For comparison to their recall of yesterday's snack and dinner, the children were also asked to recall episodes of more novel events—a field trip or birthday party at camp that had occurred in the last week and an event that was special for them. Less familiar experiences might be remembered better because there is less potential for general event knowledge to absorb the details of an individual experience. Alternatively, young children might have even less or no recall of infrequent occurrences because they do not have GERs available for organizing and retrieving memories of these unfamiliar experiences. This latter possibility was suggested by Nelson & Ross (1980) as an explanation for late appearing autobiographical memory.

Each protocol was first coded for the number of propositions, that is, the utterances containing an argument and a predicate. Each proposition was then

[1]This study was reported in Chapter 2 in terms of tense uses in response to each of these questions.

coded as either an act, an elaboration, a conditional, or a description. (These categories are exhaustive of all the propositions reported by the children in both accounts.) *Act* propositions are defined as any action reported in either a script or episodic event narrative, for example, "I just came running to snack" and "We played outside." *Elaborations* are defined as the repetition of a previously mentioned act with the addition of new information or changes in slot fillers (e.g., "We had juice for snack . . . We had orange juice."). *Conditional* propositions include both temporal conditions, referring to acts or states that follow or co-occur in a temporal sequence (e.g., "after we go swimming" and "when it was rest time"), and enabling conditions that specify conditions to be met in order for an act to occur (e.g., "if people are eating ahead of people" and "because I was at the park"). *Descriptions* include both physical characteristics (e.g., "He's bigger than me"), as well as affective statements (e.g., "Apple juice is one of my favorite drinks").

Prior research has shown that children's script reports consist primarily of acts and act elaborations, with some mention of conditionals but few descriptions (Fivush, 1984; Nelson & Gruendel, 1981). In contrast, episodic memories include relatively more descriptions, providing the specific background information to put the episode in context. Conditional propositions, however, can be used to report either general or episodic information.

A second analysis examined mention of qualifiers indicating that children were reporting general or episodic information. For example, the action of eating dinner could be mentioned in both types of reports, but this information might be included as "Sometimes we go out for dinner" in a general report or as "Last night we went to McDonald's" in an episodic report. To distinguish these types of statements, optional and particular qualifiers were scored. *Optional* qualifiers included "sometimes" and "usually," as in "We usually have the first snack on the roof," "Sometimes we order for some pizza," and in conditional terms such as "or" (e.g., "Then we go on buses or our mommy picks us up"). These qualifiers generally indicate optional or alternative acts in a script (Fivush, 1984; Nelson & Gruendel, 1981). *Particular* qualifiers refer to specific people, times, and locations, as in "I had to play with my friend, Alexander" and "Today I had some saltines." Adjectives, adverbs, adjective clauses, and adverbial clauses were also coded as particular qualifiers. Although this type of information is sometimes given in script reports, more could be expected to be included in episodic accounts.

Finally, each proposition was coded for present, past, future, or conditional tense. Whereas script narratives are usually given in the timeless present tense, the past tense should be used to describe specific past episodes (see Chapter 2). Future and conditional tenses were used so infrequently that these were excluded in the final analysis.

General and Specific Snack and Dinner Reports

The prediction that children would have greater difficulty recalling a specific memory than giving a script report was borne out. Children at both ages gave more information in response to the general question than to the specific question (see Table 5.1). Although older children gave more information than younger children, this tendency was apparent in both types of accounts. This finding is similar to Linton's (1979) finding that preschool children had difficulty providing episodic information when asked about specific episodes of familiar events, but readily volunteered general event information.

Further evidence that children have difficulty recalling what happened yesterday came from an analysis comparing the content of the children's general and specific event narratives in terms of number of acts, elaborations, conditionals, and descriptions mentioned. As shown in Table 5.1, there was no difference in the percentage of each type of proposition reported in the two event narratives. (Proportion scores were used in analysis to control for the fact that older children consistently reported more information than younger children.) The children reported mostly acts and act elaborations, with a few conditionals and descriptions, in both the script and episodic event reports. The children mentioned optional information only in response to the general question, but the difference in the proportion of particular reference in the general and specific narratives was not significant.

Thus, the content of the children's episodic recounts was very similar to their

TABLE 5.1
Means for Snack and Dinner Analyses, Study 1

	Question					
	General			*Specific*		
	Age 3	*Age 5*	$\bar{X}$	*Age 3*	*Age 5*	$\bar{X}$
Number of propositions:	5.48	11.25	8.37	4.26	8.78	6.52
Percentage of proposition types:						
Acts	61	52	56	63	47	56
Elaborations	19	24	22	24	25	24
Conditionals	9	13	11	4	13	9
Descriptions	11	12	12	9	15	12
Percentage of qualifiers:						
Optional	9	15	12	1	2	2
Particular	11	23	17	23	30	26
Percentage of use						
Present	82	88	85	25	26	26
Past	18	7	12	74	73	74

script accounts. The primary difference between the children's scripts and episodic recounts was whether children used the timeless present or the past tense. To some degree, tense use is an indication of whether the children responded appropriately to the two questions. The fact that the children used the correct tense to indicate past and timeless event information indicates that they reported general information in response to the general question and gave specific information about past episodes in response to the specific question. That they also gave less information in response to the specific question than to the general question and indicated optional information only in response to the general question suggests that they were doing more than just mimicking the tense used in the experimenter's question. Rather, the children were able to understand the two questions and to formulate appropriate narratives in response to each.

Children's difficulty in recalling yesterday's snack and dinner suggests the possibility that details of these episodes had not been retained in memory over the past 18–24 hours. If nothing out of the ordinary happened, nothing particular about yesterday's occurrence would have been encoded and there would be no particular information about yesterday represented in memory. In this case, the best approximation of a specific memory would be based on what usually happens, reported in the past tense, but few particular details would be provided. This is actually a good characterization of children's recall when they did respond to the question. For example, one 5-year-old gave the following account of yesterday's snack:

> Some children ate cookies. And then we finished snack and went to rest. And then after we rested, we had swimming. After we had swimming, we went back. And then after we went back, we went home.

If details were mentioned, they tended to be particular slot fillers, such as "apple juice," that might actually be quite common. Distinctive activities, that is, activities that stood out from the usual routine, were uncommon. For example, one child included what appeared to be a distinctive activity from last night's dinner:

> I started not to eat 'cause I wasn't hungry. But my mommy said I have to eat dinner. But I didn't eat dinner. So she sent me in my room.

However, his dinner script included the following:

> I don't like the dinner. And then she sends me into my room.

Another common response was, "Nothing." One child kept insisting, "Nothing. Nothing happened. We just had snack. That's all." Such a response illustrates directly that autobiographical memory consists in deviations from the expected routine.

These findings are consistent with the hypothesis that young children's GERs can absorb memory for details of particular episodes, although there was no evidence that this effect was more apparent for 3-year-olds than for 5-year-olds.

Special and Camp Episodes

At the end of the second interview, the children were also asked to recall a class field trip or a birthday party at camp, so that we could compare their recall of routine snack and dinner episodes with their recall of specific occurrences of less routine events (e.g., "What happened when you went to the Museum of Natural History?"). In addition, they were asked to recall "What happened when you did something really special?" to test whether novel events would be remembered better than daily events and familiar camp experiences. In response to this question, the children reported a variety of events, such as going to a ballet or movie, trips to the beach, zoo and circus, and family vacations. These data are shown in Table 5.2.

Again, older children reported more information than did younger children, but children at both ages provided more information in the special episode accounts than in the camp episode reports. Further, children at both ages mentioned a higher proportion of acts when they reported a camp episode than when reporting the special episodes. Although there were no significant differences in

TABLE 5.2
Means for Special and Camp Event Analyses, Study 1

	Event					
	Special			*Camp*		
	Age 3	*Age 5*	$\bar{X}$	*Age 3*	*Age 5*	$\bar{X}$
Number of propositions:	5.44	11.31	8.37	2.00	6.69	4.35
Percentage of proposition types:						
Acts	46	50	48	68	56	62
Elaborations	22	15	19	17	18	18
Conditionals	4	9	6	0	5	2
Descriptions	28	26	27	15	21	18
Percentage of qualifiers:						
Optional	0	0	0	0	4	2
Particular	39	42	40	41	36	39
Percentage of tense use:						
Present	22	10	16	9	14	11
Past	78	88	83	91	86	87

the proportions of conditionals and descriptions mentioned or in the proportion of optional and particular qualifiers used, there was a tendency for children to report more descriptions in the special episode reports. As in the episodic accounts of snack and dinner, there was virtually no mention of optional information, but here the children tended to include more particular information.

Thus, in contrast to their recall of everyday snack and dinner episodes, the children reported more detailed memories of less routine experiences. Still, recall of the camp episodes was shorter and included a higher proportion of acts than did recall of episodes that were personally significant. One interpretation of these findings is that, although birthday parties and field trips at camp are less common than snack, they are nevertheless relatively familiar activities; whereas the special episodes recalled may have been novel experiences. In fact, there was some indication that camp birthday parties are simply variations of snack, as illustrated in the 3-year-old's birthday party recall:

> She just ate the cake. And then we ate it. And then we sat down. And then we were done with our snack.

However, there was also a difference in the form of the specific questions. The children were asked to recall particular episodes for snack and dinner and camp events (e.g., "yesterday" and "Hilary's birthday party"); but the question about special events was phrased as "Can you tell me what happened one time . . . ?" Recalling what happened *yesterday* and recalling what happened *one time* may involve different search processes. If specific episodes are stored in memory in terms of their unusual characteristics and not in relation to temporal tags, even if something unusual had happened yesterday, the cue "yesterday" may not have provided enough information for children to retrieve those episodes.

Further, although some children reported relatively novel and probably one-time special episodes (e.g., seeing the Nutcracker Suite), some special episodes that children recalled in great detail may have been quite familiar, for example, visiting a friend. Thus, effects of cueing, novelty, and personal saliance overlapped in children's recall of special episodes. It is impossible to determine from these data whether one factor or all three were responsible for children's longer and more detailed memories.

Conclusions

The results from this study show that children can provide more information about "what happens" in general than they can remember about "what happened yesterday" in routine events. Whether details of yesterday's experiences were never recorded in memory or whether they were inaccessible through the cue "yesterday" is unclear. When given the opportunity to select any episode to report, children recounted longer and more detailed memories, providing further evidence that young children do indeed have rich autobiographic memories.

STUDY 2: "WHAT HAPPENED ONE TIME?": RECALL OF NOVEL AND FAMILIAR EVENTS

The goal of this study was to examine changes in children's scripts and autobiographic memories as a function of increasing experience with events. Although Study 1 found no evidence that younger children's recall was more schematic than older children's, recall of "what happened yesterday" may be uncharacteristic of children's autobiographic memory. To maximize their autobiographic recall, children in this study were asked to recall "what happened one time" for enjoyable events that varied systematically in terms of their familiarity. We were interested in whether familiarity with events differentially affected younger and older children's autobiographic memory. That is, are processes of schematization in recall of familiar events stronger for preschool children than for older children? Also of interest were the features of specific episodes that children recalled. That is, what makes some episodes more memorable than others?

Three-, 5-, and 7-year-old children were asked to provide either script accounts or episodic accounts for three events: an event that had been experienced more than five times, an event that had been experienced two to five times, and a one-time experience. Half the children in each age group were asked the *general* question, "What happens . . . ?" (e.g., "What happens when you go to the zoo?"), and the other half were asked the *specific* question, "What happened one time . . . ?" (e.g., "What happened one time when you went to the zoo?"). Familiarity was determined from a questionnaire accompanying the consent form in which parents indicated how many times their child had participated in a variety of enjoyable events such as birthday parties and trips to the beach, zoo, circus, and amusement parks. Particular events queried varied across children, and some events that were experienced only one time by some children were experienced many or a few times by others. Again, the children's narratives were analyzed in terms of the number of propositions reported, the proportion of each type of proposition reported, use of optional and particular qualifiers, and tense use.

The children's scripts and episodic reports for these events were considerably longer than their general and specific accounts of snack and dinner reported in the previous study. The mean number of propositions reported across scripts and episodic recounts were 6.03, 12.45, and 14.45 for 3-, 5-, and 7-year olds, respectively. Presumably, this is because they were asked about more personally meaningful events. Although there were significant age differences in the amount of information the children reported, there were no effects of either familiarity or type of question on the number of propositions children reported. These factors did, however, influence the content of the children's narratives, as is evident from the mean percentages of proposition types, qualifier, and tense use shown in Table 5.3.

First consider the overall differences between the two types of reports. The children reported a higher proportion of acts and a lower proportion of conditionals in the script accounts than in the episodic recounts. The majority of conditional propositions that the children reported referred to specific moments in time (e.g., "When the circus ended."), indicating a more temporally contingent type of reporting. Although the proportion of descriptions mentioned was consistently low across both types of reports, analysis of use of particular qualifiers indicated that the children provided more specific details in the episodic narratives than in the script accounts. Further, the children mentioned optional information only in the script reports. Finally, the timeless present tense was used predominantly in the script accounts, whereas the past tense was used to narrate specific episodes.

Familiarity with events also influenced the content of both types of reports, supporting the hypothesis that increased experience with events leads to increased schematization in memory. With increased experience, the proportion of acts mentioned increased while the proportion of conditionals mentioned decreased; mention of particular qualifiers decreased while use of optional qualifiers in the script accounts increased; and use of the present tense increased while past tense usage decreased.

In summary, the major finding from this study was that familiarity had a

TABLE 5.3
Mean Percentages of Proposition Types, Qualifiers, and Tense Use, Study 2

	Question							
	General				*Specific*			
	One	*Few*	*Many*	$\bar{X}$	*One*	*Few*	*Many*	$\bar{X}$
Proposition types:								
Acts	47	49	61	52	38	44	49	44
Elaborations	18	23	19	20	19	24	21	21
Conditionals	30	21	10	21	35	27	23	28
Descriptions	5	7	10	7	4	7	6	6
Qualifiers:								
Optional	3	9	9	7	0	0	0	0
Particular	29	18	17	21	37	36	31	34
Tense:								
Present	56	73	78	69	9	12	19	13
Past	40	21	15	26	90	84	80	84

strong effect on both general accounts and specific memories. After only one experience, both the general and the specific accounts were highly episodic in content. After repeated experiences, the children's narratives in both types of interviews included more general information and fewer particular details.

There was also some suggestion that the effects of general knowledge on children's autobiographic recall might be different for children at different ages. Three-year-olds were the only age group that had difficulty recalling particular episodes of very familiar events and sometimes provided script reports instead of autobiographic memories. For example, in recalling a day at camp, one 3-year-old reported:

> In summer you go to camp. Play. And play. Play in the sandbox.

When older children included general information in their autobiographic memories, it seemed to provide a context for highlighting episodic details. For example, in the following report of "what happened" at a birthday party, the child first mentioned that you (generally) play games and then indicated the particular game played:

> You play games . . . We played pin the tail on the donkey. And we had cake. And that's what all birthday parties happen to have. And you get party bags. (Age 5;9)

Age differences were found in all measures of elaboration and complexity in children's narratives. Older children (5- and 7-year-olds) not only reported more information than 3-year-olds but also mentioned a higher percentage of descriptions and both optional and particular information. Children at all ages differentiated general from specific narratives by their use of tense and by the percentage of acts and particular qualifiers they reported, but older children provided more elaborated narratives in both types of interviews.

These age differences must be interpreted with caution, however. Older children's memories may be more differentiated and less schematized than younger children's, but it is also possible that older children's recall simply reflects more developed narrative skills. For example, older children's episodic accounts may actually be 'repisodic,'' that is, based on general knowledge about events but given in the past tense with the inclusion of particular slot fillers that are likely to have occurred. Because children have mastered the formal characteristics of narrating episodes, this type of "repisodic" reporting would not be confused with script accounts. In contrast, 3-year-olds may not have achieved the same level of narrative skill and would give scripts instead of repisodic reports.

In addition, the children's scripts and episodic narratives at all ages were similar in structure, and the reports were equally affected by the amount of experience the children had had with the event in question. This finding provides support for the interpretation that age differences in children's episodic reports reflect older children's developing awareness of the stylistic features of different types of event narratives rather than developmental differences in the organization of general and specific event representations. It also supports the interpretation that GERs and specific autobiographical memories are part of a single memory system.

There was some evidence that the children confused similar episodes in recall. Trying to remember a trip to the zoo after a few visits, a 5-year-old recalled:

> I remember only a time that I went to the Israel one. There was a wolf there, I think . . . No, that was another zoo. There was no wolf . . . There was a duck. There wasn't no zebras . . . I think there *was* zebras, but I'm not sure.

Sometimes the children who were unable to produce extended narratives of a single episode reported fragments from more than one experience:

> I slept most of the way to Florida and back. And when we went to Holland, my brother spilled two glasses of soda on this person next to him (age 7;11).

What was it that distinguished the episodes of familiar events the children were able to recall? The children's introductory statements often provided clues to what had prompted their recall. Some episodes appeared to stand out because they were either very recent or they involved personally salient people and particular places:

> I went to the circus a couple of days ago. I went on the 6th of May . . . (age 8;0)

> I went to Cousin Ruth's house and I went to the beach . . . (age 3;2).

A few recounts mentioned atypical or unexpected occurrence:

> It was just at my birthday party . . . Somone cried there and she ruined my whole party . . . (Age 5;3).

> Well, once I went to the beach and a storm was coming up . . . (Age 6;8).

> Well, I was in California and we went to the San Diego Zoo. And my mother really loves penguins. And we expected to see at least three species of penguins. And we were really disappointed to see only one . . . (Age 7;11)

These findings suggest that, like adults' autobiographic memory, children's memory for episodes of recurring events is organized around general event schemas, but that specific episodes may be tagged in memory in terms of distinctive slot fillers, that is, particular people, places, and props, as well as deviations from the script. Further, there was no strong evidence that familiarity differentially affected children's autobiographic memory at different ages although children's scripts and episodic narratives became more complex and differentiated with age.

STUDY 3: "WHAT HAPPENED AT THE JEWISH MUSEUM?": MONITORING THE FATE OF A PARTICULAR EPISODIC MEMORY

The first two studies suggest that experiences with recurring episodes are better predictors of changes in autobiographic memory organization over time than of age-related changes in memory organization. They also provide evidence that GERs can guide encoding and retrieval of children's autobiographic memories. The next study examined effects of GERs on kindergarten children's memory of an unusual variation of a familiar event: a class trip to an archeology exhibit at the Jewish Museum in New York City. (See Fivush, Hudson, & Nelson 1984 for a complete report.)

Although it was expected that children could remember details of this excursion immediately afterward, we questioned whether these details would be remembered after 6 weeks or after 1 year. If "what happened" at the Jewish Museum was sufficiently different from "what happens" when you go to a museum, information about the particular experience should be retained as an autobiographic memory. On the other hand, if the trip represented only minor variations of the typical museum trip, these variations could become incorporated into the GER as options or alternatives. To chart the fate of this particular autobiographic memory, changes in the children's episodic recall as well as changes in their museum scripts were monitored over 1 year.

All the children in this kindergarten class lived in New York City and had been to museums, both natural history museums and art museums. Two weeks before the trip, all the children were asked to report, "What happens when you go to a museum?" On returning to school on the day of the trip, half the children were asked, "What happened when you went to the Jewish Museum today?" After 6 weeks, half the children were asked to report, "What happens when you go to a museum?" and half were asked, "What happened when you went to the Jewish Museum?" Then all the children were interviewed 1 year later and were asked, "What happened when you went to the Jewish Museum?"

That this trip was not a typical museum trip was apparent when children's museum scripts were compared to their descriptions of the visit to the Jewish Museum. As shown in Table 5.4, other than going, leaving, and seeing things, there was no overlap in the content of the children's responses to the two questions. (All actions shown in this table were mentioned by at least two children and account for 88% of the total output.) Nor did this variation on the typical museum trip affect children's museum scripts at 6 weeks. Not one child

TABLE 5.4
Percentage of Children Reporting Individual Acts for Each Type of Question, Study 3

	General Question	
Act	*Pre-trip*	*6 weeks*
Go there	38	43
Enter	50	57
Get ticket/Pay	44	43
Find exhibit	31	14
See X/Look at X	94	71
Be quiet	19	14
Leave	25	00

	Specific Question		
Act	*Immediate*	*6 weeks*	*1 year*
Went there	22	25	38
Talked with guide	78	50	46
Dug/Found things	100	100	85
Made clay models	89	75	38
Walked upstairs	56	38	23
Saw X	56	38	54
Went back/Left	67	38	46

mentioned any of the specific activities that occurred in the trip to the Jewish Museum.

The children's memory of the trip after 6 weeks was as accurate and detailed as their immediate recall. After 1 year, the children's recall was less complete but equally accurate. The primary difference in the children's recall at 1 year was that children required more specific cues to recall the same information that had easily been recalled before. Whereas only 7% of the children were able to recall the trip when asked the original question, "What happened when you went to the Jewish Museum?", 53% remembered activities when they were asked, "Do you remember you learned about archeology?" Although the children had been to many exhibits at different kinds of museums, this was the only archaeology exhibit they had been to. This cue provided distinctive enough information for the children to distinguish this one occurrence from all other occurrences of the event.

This study demonstrated that an unusual occurrence of a familiar event was not incorporated into the general script and therefore was accessible to recall even 1 year later with almost no intrusion of general information. The only difference between immediate recall and recall 1 year later was that the children required more specific cues in order to access their autobiographic memories.

Because this was an unusual occurrence, specific cues were available that could effectively differentiate this trip from any other museum trip.

GERS AND AUTOBIOGRAPHIC MEMORY: WHAT DEVELOPS?

This chapter has been concerned with the relationship between children's general event knowledge, organized in the form of general event representations, and the development of autobiographic memory. The three studies discussed here suggest that the relationship between GERs and autobiographic memories that characterizes adult memory is also apparent in 3-year-olds' recall. That is, GERs can automatically guide constructive processes in autobiographic recall, resulting in schematization in recall of specific episodes of familiar events. Although there was no clear evidence for age differences in effects of schematization in autobiographic memory, this research does suggest that there are changes in autobiographic memory associated with increasing experience with events. In Study 1, children had difficulty recalling particular episodes of very routine events. Study 2 showed that increased familiarity with events leads to the inclusion of more general event information in the autobiographic recall. In Study 3, an unusual episode of a familiar event that was *not* incorporated into a general event schema was remembered accurately after one year.

This research also demonstrates effects of cueing on autobiographic recall. Although routine occurrences may be absorbed by general event representations, some distinctive episodes are retained in memory and recall of these memories may depend on the match between the distinctive features of episodes and the cues given for recall. Temporal cues such as "yesterday" used in Study 1 may not be effective, but the "one time" used in Study 2 seemed to enhance recall by allowing children to recall any distinctively tagged episode. In Study 3, the children who could not remember an unusual episode of a familiar event after a year were able to do so when given a cue that referred to a distinctive action from that episode.

These findings suggest that issues of cueing and familiarity could also account for the phenomenon of childhood amnesia. It may be that adults lack the appropriate cues for recalling events from early childhood. Our earliest memories may be irretrievable because the cue, "earliest memory," is ineffective. In addition, because adult activities and social contexts are different from those experienced by children, cues that are distinctive to children may not be distinctive to adults. Returning to a childhood home can therefore revive "forgotten" childhood memories, as observed by Hall (1899). However, if experiences that are novel to a young child are later repeated, individual episodes can lose their distinctiveness and become fused into GERs. These experiences may be permanantly lost to recall as individual, autobiographic memories.

This interpretation is similar to the cognitive reconstruction theories considered earlier (Neisser, 1967; Piaget, 1962; Schactel, 1947; White & Pillemer, 1979). The important difference is that this interpretation does not attribute loss in cue effectiveness or changes in organization of autobiographic memory to more general cognitive developments during childhood. Rather, changes in autobiographic memory organization are viewed as a natural result of increased real world experience that leads to richer and more elaborated representation of both personal and historical events. These changes are not specific to childhood but are also characteristic of knowledge development in adults (Winograd & Killinger, 1983).

Of course, there are other dimensions of autobiographic memory that are not captured by their relationship to GERs. Autobiographic memories are more than just representations of specific past experiences; they constitute individuals' personal autobiographies or life histories and are mediated by personality factors and systems of self-knowledge (Barclay et al., 1982; Neisser, 1981; Purcell, 1953). It has also been shown that historically significant events, such as hearing news of the assassination or attempted assassination of the President, are retained in memory in great detail over long periods of time (Brown & Kulick, 1977; Colegrove, 1899; Pillemer, in press; Winograd & Killinger, 1983; Yarmey & Bull, 1978). Neisser (1982) argues that these are retained not so much because they are novel or significant, but because they are frequently rehearsed. Certainly rehearsal must play an important role in the long-term retention of autobiographic memories, and personally meaningful or socially shared memories are most likely to be rehearsed.

The proposed model of autobiographic memory, in which recall of particular episodes is viewed as a constructive process, drawing not only from memory of individual experiences, but also from general knowledge structures, is not inconsistent with other influences on autobiographic memory. Research on adults' autobiographic recall and the three studies discussed in this chapter indicate that GERs are particularly powerful forms of cognitive representation used by children and adults to organize memory for specific episodes of real world events.

6 The Language of Events

Lucia A. French

In this chapter, we focus specifically on the language of children's event descriptions and the cognitive competencies that can be inferred from this language.[1] In other words, here we are less concerned with the *content* of children's event representations than with the *form* in which that content is expressed. The close relationship between language and cognition provides an opportunity for discovering facts about underlying cognitive ability and representation through analysis of the language forms used. Cognition forms the concepts that can be expressed verbally; whereas language provides a window, albeit often quite opaque, on cognitive abilities and representation.

As the previous chapters have demonstrated, children's event knowledge appears to constitute one of their earliest, most complex, and most stable forms of representation. The language children use to describe this event knowledge also appears to be more complex and in many ways more advanced than the language they use in other situations. It seems probable that children's well-established and complex general event representations provide a crucial cognitive context for the development of an appreciation of temporal, causal, conditional, and disjunctive relationships; and that it is therefore within the context of describing these event representations that children's use of language expressing these concepts is first apparent.

According to current literature, the acquisition of certain syntactic forms and certain classes of vocabulary items seems to be delayed relative to other complex language constructions, that is, to develop after age 3, sometimes considerably

[1]This chapter is based on data described in more detail in French & Nelson (1985).

later. These later acquisitions have tended to be considered "special cases," distinct from language acquisition in general, and the delay has been explained in terms of their having as prerequisites certain late-developing cognitive abilities. Thus, the relatively late acquisition of the passive voice (Beilin, 1975) and of temporal terms such as *before* and *after* (Ferrerio & Sinclair, 1971) have been accounted for in terms of their reliance on the attainment of reversibility, a characteristic, within Piagetian theory, of the stage of concrete operations. Similarly, and also within Piagetian terms, McNeill (1979) has accounted for the late production of "timeless" speech in terms of its reliance on the attainment of temporal decentration. Clark (1971) accounted for the acquisition of *before* and *after* in terms of a semantic feature model, with the implication that the features governing these terms are cognitively more complex than those governing vocabulary items that are acquired earlier. Similar componentially based arguments have been made regarding the acquisition of *but* (Kail, 1980) and *because* and *if* (Emerson, 1979; 1980).

There is much to recommend the view that later language acquisition is dependent on the attainment of relatively advanced levels of cognitive functioning. At a very simple level, it is obviously impossible for children to genuinely acquire vocabulary referring to concepts and relationships they are incapable of understanding. At a different level, it is certainly plausible that there are developmental parallels between the acquisition of certain syntactic forms and the attainment of particular cognitive operations. Finally, it is undeniably true that language and cognitive ability are tightly intertwined; what children say and what they comprehend both rely on and provide evidence for their level of cognitive functioning.

It is perhaps inevitable that the obviously close relationship between cognitive level and language ability might lead to circular explanations: That a word or syntactic form is not used until relatively late suggests its dependence on advanced cognitive functioning; this "prerequisite" cognitive functioning is then offered as the explanation for the late language acquisition. Once such a connection is posited it is not difficult to propose a plausible account for *why* the linguistic ability should require a relatively advanced level of cognitive ability. Imagine, for example, the advanced levels of understanding that could be proposed as prerequisites for the acquisition of the concept "nurturant female parent" if, instead of being one of the child's first words, *mama* was not acquired until age four.

The difficulty of obtaining independent evidence for particular causal relationships between language and cognition is further complicated by the fact that many advanced cognitive abilities either cannot, or traditionally have not, been measured nonverbally. For example, measures of both reversibility and decentration have typically relied on the child's comprehension of an adult's verbal questions and the production of verbal responses. It is plausible that the causally interpreted correlation between the attainment of a particular cognitive ability and a particular linguistic ability actually reflects the attainment of an unspecified higher order ability that governs a variety of performance variables. It is also plausible that many such correlations are purely coincidental. In short, although in general there is a close relationship between cognitive development and advanced language acquisition, specific appeals to the relatively late acquisition of a particular cognitive ability to account for the relatively late acquisition of a particular linguistic form are often based more on intuition than on empirical evidence.

Most attempts to relate advanced language acquisition to cognition have relied on Piagetian theory. However, in recent years that portion of Piagetian theory dealing with the cognitive abilities of children between the ages of 2 and 7 has received heavy criticism (e.g., A. Brown, 1976; Donaldson, 1978; Gelman, 1978). Piaget's critics have cast considerable doubt on his claims about the cognitive limitations of preschoolers; they provided a number of demonstrations that, given a "maximally supportive" experimental setting, preschoolers do exhibit many of the cognitive abilities—such as an appreciation of causality, of conservation, of transitivity, and of another's perspective—that Piaget regarded as defining features of the stage of concrete operations, which he claimed was not achieved until about age 7.

The difficulty of accounting for the relatively late acquisition of certain aspects of language in terms of prerequisite cognitive development is therefore further complicated by the numerous findings that Piagetian theory, to which most such accounts appeal, seriously overestimates the age at which certain cognitive abilities are initially displayed. It is inevitable that the revised profile of preschoolers' cognitive competence that is emerging must eventually lead to a reconsideration of how later language acquisition is to be explained. This chapter reports data showing that, just as preschoolers' cognitive abilities have been underestimated, so too have their linguistic abilities. It is further argued that similar factors are responsible for the underestimation of preschoolers' abilities in both cases.

Central features of the research that has challenged Piaget's description of preschoolers' cognitive competency have included a decreased reliance on verbal measures, embedding tasks in familiar and therefore more meaningful contexts, and an attempt to reduce or eliminate task components that may pose cognitive demands extraneous to the cognitive ability purportedly being measured. Thus, by and large, those who have challenged Piaget's description of the preoperational period have attempted to develop procedures that are equivalent to the traditional procedures in terms of the target ability being assessed, but are less dependent on the child's ability to deal with secondary task demands that are essentially independent of the target ability.

Supporters of Piagetian theory have claimed that, by changing the traditional procedures, Piaget's critics are not measuring the same abilities that Piaget was measuring and that it is therefore neither surprising nor relevant to Piagetian theory that their findings are not the same as Piaget's. This objection, however, begs the real questions: What abilities do preschoolers have? How do these relate to later abilities? Why is it that apparently insignificant changes in task variables may have such a strong effect on their demonstration of these abilities? ''What develops'' between the time a child is able to demonstrate an ability in certain situations and the time he or she exercises control of the ability in a variety of settings?

Because basic abilities seem to emerge earlier than previously believed and because context seems to play such a major role in determining whether preschoolers exhibit particular cognitive competencies, it has been posited that much of ''what develops'' during the preschool years is the ''decontexualization'' of basic abilities, that is, an extension of their range of application to situations in which the degree of contextual support is minimal (e.g., Carni & French, 1984; Donaldson, 1978; French & Nelson, 1982). Under this interpretation, basic abilities initially emerge within limited contexts and only gradually come to be applied beyond those contexts. One plausible explanation for the disparity between Piaget's findings and those of his critics is that Piaget's methods tapped abilities that had become largely context independent, whereas the more context-sensitive methods adopted by recent investigators tap abilities that are still highly dependent on the particular context in which they were initially acquired.

''Context'' has generally been discussed in terms of such factors as experimental setting and experimental stimuli. However, as argued in Chapter 1, the child's representation of events provides the essential ''cognitive context'' for interpretation of tasks (see also Nelson & Gruendel, 1981; Nelson, Fivush, Hubson & Lucariello, 1983). Previous chapters of this book have dealt with event knowledge per se, including the indications of knowledge of causal-temporal relationships revealed in children's event descriptions. The present chapter is concerned with the context that event descriptions provide for the display of linguistic and cognitive ability, and with a detailed description of the data relevant to preschoolers' competencies in dealing with rational concepts that are to be found in their descriptions of familiar events.

Although we discuss here both cognition and language, our data are primarily verbal protocols. It is often possible to infer with confidence the presence of certain cognitive competencies on the basis of these linguistic data, but in most cases we do not have independent measures of cognitive ability. Please note that we do not make any claims with regard to whether or not the cognitive abilities demonstrated in the verbal protocols could be readily tapped using other measures.

The event descriptions provide evidence that preschoolers control many of the linguistic forms and possess many of the cognitive competencies that previous investigators have concluded they lack (French & Nelson, 1982; in press). The Piagetian and psycholinguistic explanations advanced to account for these presumed incompetencies on the part of preschoolers become, in light of the data contained in the event descriptions, possibly erroneous and certainly inadequate. These data and their conflict with previously posed explanations raise two questions. First, what is it about previous investigators' methods and underlying assumptions that led them to conclude that preschoolers lack competencies that the event descriptions clearly show them to possess? Second, how can previous research and conclusions be integrated with the data derived from the event descriptions to provide a more adequate account of the development of preschoolers' linguistic and cognitive competency?

This chapter describes the data derived from preschoolers' descriptions of familiar events, illustrates how these data conflict with conclusions and predictions that are derived from previous investigations, and suggests how these apparently contradictory lines of evidence may be integrated to yield a richer and more complete description of language acquisition and cognitive development.

INTERVIEW SETTING

A description of the ways in which event descriptions were elicited from preschoolers is available in Chapter 2. We provide here only a summary description of the procedures used. Event narratives were elicited by asking general initiating questions, such as "What happens when you go to a restaurant?" or "Can you tell me about getting dressed in the morning?" Nondirective follow-up probes, such as repeating the child's last statement with rising intonation or asking "Anything else?" or "Can you tell me more?" were provided when the child paused. These probes were continued until the child indicated that he or she had nothing else to say about a particular topic.

This standard procedure in collecting data is important to the interpretation of the analyses reported here, because it did not give the children any indication of how the description should be structured or what syntactic and semantic forms might be appropriate. All the children were asked to do was to reflect on their event knowledge and produce a description, which presumably was supported by their event representations. In other words, the procedure is nondirective in terms of both the content of the output and the linguistic means for expressing that content. As is apparent in the examples that follow, children did not always produce complete narratives, although typically they produced descriptions with general narrative structure. We emphasize again that the children were able to draw on their ER's to provide event descriptions despite the absence of any nonverbal context to support such descriptions.

EVENT DESCRIPTIONS AS A DISCOURSE FORMAT

Exposition, that is, explaining to someone what you know about something, is a discourse form unlikely to be called for frequently in the daily life of preschoolers because they are seldom regarded as experts on anything that their conversational partners might be interested in learning about. Our sense is that, although parents often ask their preschoolers about particular experiences (e.g., What happened at nursery school today?) they rarely ask them for general descriptions of frequently experienced events. Nevertheless, whether or not they are practiced with this discourse form, preschoolers seem to find it reasonable to be asked to describe familiar events and they respond quite facilely. Their adoption of this discourse form results in some uses of language that are of special interest because they do not typically occur in the usual contexts for studying children's language.

Most investigations of preschoolers' language ability involve one of two basic procedures. In naturalistic studies, children's speech during free play or participation in everyday activities is recorded. In experimental studies, the experimenter typically says something and judges from the response whether or not the child understands a particular word or syntactic structure contained in what was said. The response required from the child varies across different paradigms and includes such things as selecting from among a set of pictures, sequencing pictures, making a grammaticality judgment, enacting a statement with a set of toys, or repeating or paraphrasing what was said.

In both naturalistic and experimental contexts, the children's attention, and therefore their spontaneous speech, tends to be focused on the immediate environment. Because most of the recorded speech of young children concerns the "here-and-now," there is a widespread assumption that preschoolers talk only about the here-and-now (e.g., Clark & Clark, 1977). By implication young children are assumed to be *unable* to escape the influence of the immediately perceptible environment and speak about events removed in time and space, that is, about the "there-and-then." Responding appropriately to requests for event descriptions necessarily involves talking about the there-and-then, and the event descriptions in our studies thus contradict the "common knowledge" that preschoolers either are unable to talk about or at least are unskilled in talking about anything that is not immediately perceptible (see also Sachs, 1983).

Preschoolers' event descriptions rely on an ability to represent events mentally and to access these representations without concrete contextual cues. This indicates that preschoolers possess a greater ability for abstraction from present context than many psychologists and psycholinguists have in the past credited them with and suggests the need for further reevaluation of the cognitive competencies of preschoolers. The youngest children from whom we have elicited event descriptions were around 3 years old, and there is good reason to believe that children quite a bit younger are able to talk about the there-and-then (see Chapter 7). In fact, the ability to represent the there-and-then mentally may precede the development of sufficient productive control over language to describe such representations. For evidence that still younger children engage in displaced reference, see French, Lucariello, Seidman and Nelson, in press; Lucariello, 1983; Lucariello and Nelson, 1982; Nelson, 1984.

Although preschoolers' ability to talk about the there-and-then is itself of great theoretical interest, their adoption of an expository discourse mode also results in related linguistic phenomena that are not usually present in the discourse settings in which linguistic data are typically collected. As described in previous chapters, preschoolers' event descriptions are typically given in *general* rather than *specific terms*. Because young preschoolers' were generally held to be deficient in abstraction ability, the initial expectation was that they would tend to report more specific experiences and that only as they got older would they give generalized event descriptions (e.g., Nelson, 1978). However, even the youngest children providing descriptions have described their event knowledge in general terms. These general descriptions also require the use of syntactic and lexical forms not usually noted in preschoolers' language.

SYNTACTIC FORM

As described in Chapter 2, there are several linguistic corollaries of the generalized nature of children's event descriptions. These include the use of the general, impersonal pronoun forms *you* and *we*, and timeless present verb forms. *You eat and you drink*, a statement made by a child of 2;11 in response to a request to tell "what you do at a restaurant," contains both the general *you* and timeless present verbs. The use of timeless present verbs is of theoretical interest because the speech samples collected from Adam and Sarah in Brown's (1973) landmark longitudinal study were found not to contain timeless expressions until age 4 (Cromer, 1968). Accepting Cromer's findings as generally valid, McNeill (1979) interpreted the relatively late appearance of what seems to be a very simple grammatical construction in terms of cognitive limitations. Specifically, McNeill claimed that not until about age 4 do children attain a level of cognitive development that permits them to decenter sufficiently to formulate timeless expressions. Our data indicate that, in contexts in which it is appropriate for them to do so, children produce timeless expressions as early as the beginning of their 3rd year. Such expressions are, however, appropriate only within a limited range of discourse contexts, and we suspect that Adam's and Sarah's speech was not sampled in such contexts. Because the youngest children who were asked for event descriptions provided timeless generalized accounts, we have no basis for assigning a lower age limit for these abilities. It is not implausible that the cognitive bases for providing generalized, timeless accounts are in place before productive control over such language use is achieved.

A final noteworthy syntactic correlate of the generalized nature of the event descriptions is our subjects' choice between the definite and indefinite articles. They frequently used the definite article, *the,* to introduce nouns that, although they have not been previously mentioned, referred to elements that were intrinsic to the event being described. Examples include *the teacher* when describing school, *the fire escape* when describing a fire drill, and *the cake* when describing a birthday party. The indefinite article, *a,* was appropriately used to introduce nouns referring to elements that had not been mentioned previously and that were not intrinsic to the event being described. Examples include *a funny noise* (referring to whistle received at birthday party), *reading a story* (referring to a possible activity if one arises before one's parents), and *a hole* (referring to what might happen in case of a real fire). The children's appropriate selection of *a* or *the* indicates that they recognize which elements are intrinsic to an event and which are not.

OPTIONAL PATHWAYS

Just as the displaced reference and generalized nature of the event descriptions lead to the use of linguistic forms that are infrequently observed in the speech of young children, the nature of events themselves leads to language use that is interesting in light of earlier claims regarding preschoolers' linguistic and cognitive abilities. As the structural analyses in earlier chapters have shown, although events are composed of core acts, they are seldom invariant across all possible individual occurrences. For example, although certain core components of getting dressed remain largely invariant across individual instances, there are a large number of optional components, depending on season, plans, mood and, as one of our informants pointed out, which clothes happen to be clean. Such options are acknowledged in young children's event descriptions, which offer one of the few sources of evidence that young children are aware of optional pathways and coordinate classes and are capable of conditional and/or hypothetical reference.

The terms most frequently used to mark optional possibilities in the instantiation of an event are, *or, if,* and *sometimes.* The examples below illustrate how our subjects have used these terms.

And then we buy some stuff and then we go home or go to school or go to Stuart's. (Grocery, Age 4;0)

Pay money to go, or else if you don't, you'll get in jail. (Restaurant, Age 4;8)

You put on pants or shorts or a dress or if you went to a wedding you would wear a long dress. (Getting Dressed, Age 5;4)

Well, if they have one here for real, you have to crawl or roll to get the fire out. (Fire Drill, Age 5;1)

Sometimes there are clean clothes I don't like to wear so my mom wants me to wear what I have clean. (Getting Dressed, Age 4;8)

But if you have time you get your coat on and run, run, run. But sometimes you don't even have time to put your shoes on. (Fire Drill, Age 5;6)

Sometimes I get a Tootsie Roll, then I pay them, then I eat, my daddy lets me have it, or my mommy does. (Grocery, Age 5;6)

The statements that contain *or* can be interpreted as showing an awareness of coordinate classes. In natural language, *or* generally links mutually exclusive items that are members, at equivalent levels of specificity, of the same subordinate category (Ford, 1976). It is clear that the children using *or* were sensitive to this natural language restriction and were expressing the possibility of choices among "equivalent" alternatives (French & Nelson, 1982, 1985). The statements containing *if* indicate an appreciation of conditional relationships, that is, that optional components may be linked to one another in such a way that one component establishes a condition for the occurrence of another. Statements containing *sometimes* indicate awareness that the component mentioned is a possible but not obligatory aspect of the event being discussed.

The view that preschoolers are incapable of hypothetical thought was recently challenged by Kuczaj's (Kuczaj, 1981; Kuczaj & Daly, 1979) study of preschoolers' spontaneous production of and responses to hypothetical statements. Kuczaj restricted his definition of hypothetical statements to those referring to past or future time and involving explicit marking with a modal auxillary. Because our subjects' descriptions were predominantly timeless, they did not contain reference to past or future and so could not be considered hypothetical under that definition. This definition may, however, be overly restrictive; statements such as those above do indeed have a hypothetical quality. The multiple possibilities for instantiating a particular event, and the contingent relationships that may hold among event elements, provide a basis for talking about alternative and conditional relationships that, because they are formulated in a general timeless context, may assume a hypothetical status.

It is not possible to describe alternatives and conditionals in the absence of a conversational topic that involves such relationships. It is probably for this reason that most samples of preschoolers' speech do not reflect their ability to describe these complex relationships. A more theoretically interesting question is how preschoolers acquire their initial knowledge of conditionals and alternatives. Repeated encounters with an event should lead to an awareness of which elements are constant, which are optional, which depend on optional conditions, and which do not co-occur. Such repeated encounters may constitute the child's first systematic experience of alternative and conditional relationships and so seem a likely source for the development of an understanding of such relationships (see Chapters 3 and 4). Parallel arguments, to the effect that an understanding of temporal and causal relationships arises from experience with routine events, are made later in this chapter.

TEMPORAL STRUCTURE

The structure of their event descriptions offers important insight into preschoolers' cognitive organization and cognitive ability. The standard interpretation of the Piagetian position has been that the construction of temporal sequence relies on the attainment of temporal reversibility and therefore is not within children's cognitive capabilities until the onset of concrete operations at around age 7 (Ferreiro & Sinclair, 1971; Fraisse, 1963; Piaget, 1971; see French & Nelson, 1985, for a fuller discussion of the Piagetian position).

Piaget's view has been challenged by a number of more recent findings. Stein and Trabasso (1982) reanalyzed some of the data on which Piaget (1955) based his claim that preschoolers were unable to sequence stories appropriately and found that, although Piaget's subjects had omitted a number of events in their retelling of stories, they did appropriately sequence those they recalled. A. Brown's (1976) research indicated that preschoolers may understand temporal sequences prior to being able to express this knowledge in the context of expository tasks such as those that Piaget relied upon. Clark's (1973) investigation of preschoolers' spontaneous speech in free-play settings revealed that, when children began to form sentences that describe more than one event, they sequence them in the actual order of occurrence.

Although these findings have challenged the traditional Piagetian view, they do not adequately assess the question of whether preschoolers can form stable internal representations of personally experienced events. Both Piaget's and Brown's subjects recalled stories rather than personally experienced events, and pictorial cues were provided to the subjects in Brown's studies. Clark's subjects were commenting on ongoing activities, and their sensitivity to temporal structure may have relied on perceptual information rather than on an internal representation of temporal sequence. Thus, none of these lines of investigation has addressed Fraisse's (1963) claim, apparently based on his interpretation of Piaget's position rather than on independent data, that "the memories of young children are completely jumbled up, for they have not learned to reconstruct their past. . ." (p. 254).

The data derived from preschoolers' event descriptions address the issue of children's memory for personally experienced sequences, the stability of these internal representations of sequences, and children's ability to carry out temporal reversals. As discussed in Chapter 2, children questioned about the same event on two separate occasions were found to be highly consistent in terms of both the event elements mentioned and the sequencing of those elements.

Children could, of course, have a stable but idiosyncratic representation of the ordering of acts within an event. However, this is not the case; rather, the order in which they describe acts reflects the order in which the acts occur. An analysis of a set of descriptions of going to a restaurant that were produced by 40 children ranging from 2;11 to 5;6 (French & Nelson, 1981; in press) found that the majority of those children mentioned two or more elements having an invariant real world order (e.g., ordering, followed by being served, followed by paying, followed by leaving) and virtually always ordered these elements appropriately. These same children were responsible for producing nearly 700 protocols (each child was queried two or three times about each of six events) containing several thousand individual elements; these protocols contained only 19 instances in which the correct order of elements having an invariant real world sequence were misordered. Furthermore, these misorderings were primarily cases in which either the conventional means of expression violated the actual order of occurrence, as in "I put on my shoes and socks," or in which an element was mentioned two times, once in an incorrect, then in the correct position, as in "You just sit, you come in and sit down." As noted earlier, there was nothing in the methods of elicitation to cue the children to structure their descriptions according to the temporal structure of the events; this structure was spontaneously imposed and indicates the speakers' sensitivity to the temporal organization of the events they described.

The preschoolers' ability to engage in temporal reversibility was revealed when they recalled an element after the point in their event description at which it should have been mentioned. According to the conventions of discourse, it is inappropriate simply to mention such omitted elements at the time they are remembered. Rather, the speaker must indicate where the element fits into the sequence being described. Some examples of these adjustments, which we have termed "temporal repairs" (French ' Nelson, 1981, in press), follow:

She gots something out to bake muffins with. But first she has to buy some things for muffins. (Making cookies, Age 2;11)

You know what I do is, I just blow off the candles and eat it. And before I eat it, I just take out all the candles (Birthday party, Age 4;1).

And um, the person will open it. And take off, take off the ribbon before they open it, and they'll find out what's inside (Birthday party, Age 4;7).

You make the dough, eat them, but only when they're baked (Making cookies, Age 5;4).

Such temporal repairs indicate that, in addition to having a mental representation of the temporal structure of the events being described, the speaker can move bidirectionally within that representation. (See also the discussion of this point in Chapter 4.) These two factors meet Piaget's criteria for the attainment of temporal reversibility (e.g., Ferreiro & Sinclair, 1971), an operation he claimed did not emerge until the onset of concrete operations around the age of 6 or 7.

There is no reason to believe that the children responsible for the temporal repairs were precocious; and although these temporal repairs offer convincing evidence for temporal reversibility, it seems likely that this "advanced" cognitive skill is highly domain specific. We suggest that temporal reversibility is fostered by, and initially develops in the context of, personal experience with events that have readily apparent and invariant temporal/causal structure. Under this interpretation, it would be only later, after its initial development within meaningful and experientially supported contexts, that children would be able to abstract a more general concept of temporal reversibility and apply it in a relatively context independent manner. Again, then we are arguing that young children's general event knowledge provides the basis for the initial emergence of what will later become abstract, operational skills.

RELATIONAL TERMS

Words such as *before, after, because, so, if, or,* and *but* conjoin propositions, and, in doing so, report the relationship between the events described in those propositions. These relational terms lie at the intersection of logic and language because they provide the means for expressing logical relationships linguistically. The acquisition and comprehension of these terms has been extensively studied by investigators with a number of different interests—cognitive development, language acquisition, the relationship between language and thought, and the relationships among formal logic, informal logic, and natural language.

Virtually all investigations of the acquisition of relational terms have concluded that the terms are acquired relatively late compared to many other linguistic forms, with a lower age limit of about 5 proposed for the acquisition of *before* and *after* (Clark, 1971) and an upper limit of high-school age for the acquisition of *or* (Neimark, 1970; Neimark & Slotnick, 1970). *Because* and *if* were found to be comprehended only at about age 8 (Emerson, 1979, 1980). Research on the acquisition of relational terms offers a prime example of the circular explanatory process described earlier. That is, the late acquisition of the terms suggests their reliance on late developing cognitive abilities, and then these late developing cognitive abilities are invoked to account for the late acquisition of the terms.

With few exceptions (e.g., Ferreiro and Sinclair's, 1971, study measuring linguistic and cognitive ability within the same subjects), such explanations have generally been imprecise, with the investigator studying the acquisition of relational terms by either relying on Piaget's account of cognitive development or simply inferring the lack of requisite cognitive abilities on the basis of the limited language ability. As noted previously, reliance on Piaget's age norms has become problematic in light of recent demonstrations that he tended to underestimate preschoolers' cognitive abilities. Inferring the lack of cognitive abilities on the basis of limited language ability and then using this cognitive inability to account for the linguistic inability is obviously circular. In addition, the possibility is always open that the subjects *did* have the linguistic ability but that the investigators failed to tap it adequately.

Although it is not logically valid to infer the absence of a particular cognitive ability on the basis of a child's failure to demonstrate lexical knowledge, it is generally legitimate to reason in the opposite direction, that is, to infer the existence of cognitive competency on the basis of a demonstration of genuine understanding of the appropriate vocabulary. There may be reasons other than cognitive inability for failure to use or understand a particular relational term; however, when the term is correctly used and comprehended under appropriate assessment conditions, this generally may be taken as evidence of an understanding of the relationship expressed by the term.[2]

Our subjects' event descriptions contained numerous productions of the relational terms—*before, after, because, so, if, but,* and *or*—that previous investigators had concluded preschoolers are unable to comprehend. Furthermore, these terms were almost always used appropriately, with no indication that the children possessed the types of "partial knowledge" of the terms that many investigators have proposed. For example, there was no evidence that *after* was interpreted as if it meant *before* (Clark, 1971), that *but* and *or* were interpreted as if they meant *and* (Kail, 1980; Paris, 1973), or that the "causal" component of *because* and *if* was understood but the "order" component (that is, whether the term appropriately introduces the antecedent or consequent clause) was not (Emerson, 1979, 1980). Bloom and her colleagues have also reported the accurate production of various relational terms in preschoolers' spontaneous speech (Bitetti-Capatides, Fiess & Bloom, 1980; Bloom, Lahey, Hood, Lifter & Fiess, 1980; Hood & Bloom, 1979).

There is simply no way that children could consistently use such relational terms appropriately without an understanding of the relationships they express. The appropriate use of *before* relies on an understanding of temporal relations, the appropriate use of *but* on an understanding of adversative relations, and so forth. In short, preschoolers' spontaneous and appropriate production of relational terms appears to discredit the "cognitive deficit" accounts of late acquisition, as well as the late acquisition itself, proposed by previous investigators. Leaving the matter at this would be unsatisfactory; however, it is necessary to account for the discrepancy between these findings and the conclusions reached by others.

One obvious difference between our results and those of previous investigators is that we are relying primarily on production data whereas others have relied on comprehension measures. Clark (1983), in discussing the acquisition of deic-

---

[2]There is a general point to be made here, which is that conclusions of general incompetency based on performance in a single setting (or even a limited number of settings) are quite likely to be erroneous, and should be interpreted very cautiously (see French, 1985a, for a detailed discussion of this point as it applies to research on lexical development).

tic terms, states that, "Observations of misuse in spontaneous speech are rare, mainly because it is always possible to construct an appropriate interpretation" (p. 814). This statement is used to support the suggestion that, at least within the realm of deictic terms, comprehension may be a more sensitive measure of acquisition than of production. An argument that our subjects' productions of relational terms only "appeared" to be appropriate was considered carefully and rejected. There were a few individual productions for which we were unable to determine that a term had been used appropriately to express the intended meaning, but in the vast majority of cases it was quite clear that each of the seven relational terms we considered was in fact used unambiguously and appropriately (see French & Nelson, 1985, for a complete set of these productions).

Another possible account for the disparity between our subjects' appropriate productions and other investigators' findings that preschoolers fail to comprehend relational terms is that production precedes comprehension. Not only is it generally accepted that the nature of language acquisition is such that nonformulaic production derives from and assumes comprehension; but, even if it were reasonable to assume that in some cases production precedes comprehension, it is extremely implausible that it should do so by several years.

We have no reason to question the validity or replicability of other investigators' research, and we suggest three possible explanations for the different profiles of preschoolers' cognitive and linguistic abilities offered by our data and those of other investigators. First, it seems that, in the limited case of children's comprehension of *or,* investigators (e.g., Neimark, 1970; Neimark & Slotnick, 1970; Paris, 1973) have often been insensitive to the distinction between the ordinary language and the formal logic meanings of *or* (Ford, 1976), and so have confounded these two aspects in both their measures and their conclusions (French 1985a; French & Nelson, 1985).

Second, as noted earlier, the interpretation of task failure is always problematic because it is not clear whether the subject lacks the ability purportedly being assessed or whether the experiment does not adequately tap an ability that does exist and could be tapped by other means. Successful performance on comprehension tasks involves not only comprehension of the term being assessed but also an understanding of and compliance with a variety of secondary task demands. Successful performance requires that the subject cooperate, listen carefully, and realize that he or she should respond as accurately as possible. Such "test-taking" attitudes are unlikely to be well developed among preschoolers. In addition, all comprehension tasks involve several components in addition to comprehension of the target word. The enactment task typically used to assess comprehension of *before* and *after* requires that subjects realize they are and to act out two events rather than just the one in the main clause. Grammaticality judgment paradigms involve metalinguistic skills, and the ability to reflect consciously on and judge language is clearly of a higher order than linguistic knowledge per se. Selecting pictures to match a statement requires exhaustive scanning of the options. Children who lack either the appropriate attitude or component skills required by a particular task may perform poorly on a comprehension task even if they comprehend the words that are the main focus of the task.

The third factor that may account for the difference between the competence with relational terms that our subjects demonstrated in production and the lack of competence that other investigators have found has to do with context, or more specifically, sentence content. We claimed previously that it is possible to infer knowledge of temporal, causal, and other relations on the basis of consistently appropriate use of relational terms. Rephrased, the claim is that knowledge of these relations is necessary in order to use these terms appropriately. The spontaneous productions of relational terms occurring in our data involved describing a relationship that was already known to the speaker. Comprehension, on the other hand, involves forming a mental representation of the relationship based on what someone else has said. Though obviously related, these processes are quite different.

In general, spontaneous production requires simply using language to report an already known relationship, whereas there are at least two different types of relational statements that one might be asked to comprehend. If the relationship being expressed is already known to the listener, the speaker's sentence simply evokes a pre-existing mental representation. "I'm going to put soap on the washcloth before I wash your face" would be an example of such a sentence. If the relationship being expressed is unknown to the listener, she must use the linguistic input as the sole source for creating a novel mental representation. A sentence such as "The boy went upstairs before the girl got in the car" is an example of this sort of sentence. These two different types of sentences obviously place very different cognitive demands on the listener, and there is evidence to suggest that they are understood at different ages (e.g., Carni & French, 1984; French & Brown, 1977).

In accord with Nelson's (1974) and Macnamara's (1972) claims that language acquisition is highly dependent on the nonlinguistic context, French and Brown (1977) suggested that it would be impossible for the child to learn the meanings of the terms *before* and *after* except by hearing them used in situations where the nonlinguistic context (either the immediately perceptible environment or prior knowledge) provided information redundant with the meaning of the terms. They proposed that children would understand these terms at an earlier age when they referred to sequences whose temporal structure they already knew than when they established arbitrary sequences for which no prior mental representation could exist. French and Brown (1977) and Kavanaugh (1979) offered evidence in support of this hypothesis when they showed that preschoolers could enact two-event logical sequences conjoined by *before* and *after* earlier than they could enact arbitrary sequences. However, in both of these studies subjects could have relied on their prior knowledge of the logical sequences rather than on the meaning of the temporal terms in order to enact them appropriately, and so these studies did not provide unequivocal evidence that the terms themselves were first understood in "logical" contexts.

In a study testing the same prediction, Carni and French (1984) devised a different measure of comprehension to assess 3- and 4-year-olds' comprehension of *before* and *after* when these terms referred to familiar or novel event sequences. The procedure involved telling the children stories describing five events whose temporal order was either arbitrary or had a real world fixed order, and then asking what happened either before or after the third event. All stories were about activities familiar to young children. The stories having a real world fixed order were about familiar, "scripted" events. In contrast to the enactment paradigm used by French and Brown (1977) and Kavanaugh (1979), this procedure assured that above chance performance could result only from comprehension of the temporal terms. Four-year-olds responded with a high level of accuracy to questions about both sequence types. Three-year-olds' performance was similar to the older children's in response to questions about sequences having a real world invariant order, but close to chance in response to questions about the arbitrary sequences.

These data were interpreted as showing that rather than being an all or nothing affair, comprehension of *before* and *after* proceeds in a context-sensitive manner. Comprehension is initially highly dependent on semantic context, with the child relying on prior knowledge to support interpretation of these terms. In addition, comprehension, or at least the ability to display comprehension, is dependent on the particular paradigm being used. Secondary task demands were minimal in the Carni and French (1984) study. Carni (1982) subsequently used various paradigms, including that developed by Carni and French, to assess preschoolers' comprehension of *before* and *after*. Within each of these paradigms, she varied content so that it either did or did not tap the children's prior mental representations of fixed real world sequences. She found that both the content of the sequences and the assessment paradigm contributed to the children's ability to display comprehension of *before* and *after*. The use of sequences with which the children were already familiar was not, in and of itself, sufficient to guarantee the display of comprehension.

Given the finding that 3-year-olds do understand *before* and *after* when two conditions are met (i.e., the terms refer to sequences for which they have a prior mental representation and the secondary task demands are minimal), we can conclude that it is not basic lexical knowledge that develops between ages 3 and 4. Rather, "what develops" during this period is the ability to extend the basic lexical knowledge to a wider range of contexts. With age, the child's ability to demonstrate comprehension of *before* and *after* becomes increasingly less dependent on prior knowledge of the sequences and less affected by the demands associated with various assessment paradigms.

At this point, *before* and *after* are the only relational terms for which we have shown that comprehension is context sensitive and can be elicited at a very early age. However, our data are in accord with Ford's (1976) demonstration that preschoolers can comprehend the term *or* when task demands and sentence content are adjusted to comply with natural language conventions. The implications of Carni and French's (1984), Carni's (1982) and Ford's (1976) studies can be generalized to other relational terms, that is, preschoolers typically fail to demonstrate their comprehension of such terms because they either cannot comply with secondary task demands or have not yet achieved the ability to comprehend the terms independently of context. This interpretation of the data on children's comprehension and production of relational terms suggests that there is no mysterious "comprehension lag" to be accounted for and highlights the fact that context must assume a major role in accounts of language development, just as it does in accounts of congitive development (see French, 1985a, for a fuller discussion of these issues).

SUMMARY AND CONCLUSIONS

In the introduction to this chapter, the complex interrelationship between cognitive development and language acquisition was discussed, with special attention to the problems inherent in attempts to infer lack of cognitive ability from poor performance on measures of language ability. These problems by and large disappear if one focuses on competencies rather than incompetencies and interprets linguistic ability as reflecting underlying cognitive ability. The bulk of this chapter consists of such an analysis. The verbal protocols provided by preschoolers when they were asked to describe familiar events were used as evidence of both their linguistic ability and their cognitive ability.

Evidence was presented for preschoolers' ability to rely on mental representations rather than the immediate environment in speaking, to decenter from present time, to abstract the general features of events, to form mental representations of temporal sequences, to engage in temporal reversibility, to recognize hypothetical and optional possibilities within events, and to understand the logical relationships expressed by the terms *before, after, because, so, if, or,* and *but.* All of these abilities would be unexpected on the basis of previous research, and it is obviously important to understand why they emerge so readily in the context of describing event knowledge yet remain so elusive in other contexts.

Generalized event representations are one of the most highly "contextualized" forms of knowledge. They derive from repeated personal experience, are highly stable, provide the framework for interpreting novel experiences, and seem to be among the first complex cognitive representations the child forms. They thereby provide an ideal context for the acquisition of the cognitive abilities discussed here. We believe it is because these cognitive abilities are based initially on event representations that our data portray the preschooler as having a high level of cognitive competence. All the available data seem to suggest that it takes some time for the child to extend these abilities into less familiar, less well represented domains. One very important direction for future research is to attempt to understand how this process of extension takes place and what factors encourage or retard it. These issues are considered further in Chapter 11.

7 Event Representations, Context, and Language

Joan Lucariello
Amy Kyratzis
Susan Engel

The previous chapter analyzed the language that children use in describing their event knowledge revealing an interdependence between the representation of events, the understanding of relations within events, and the acquisition of linguistic terms for referencing those relations. In this chapter we are concerned more generally with the issue of how event knowledge may support language development and, reciprocally, how learning language in a situation may support the acquisition of event knowledge.

Theoretical and empirical attempts to trace the process of language acquisition (beyond whatever specific linguistic abilities may be involved) have led in two general directions. These directions have been viewed as mutually exclusive, resulting in an apparent partitioning of the child. One direction emphasizes the cognitive foundations of language; the other, the social foundations of language.

In the cognitive direction, for example, some investigators working within a Piagetian framework have sought a relation between object permanence attainment and vocabulary acquisition (e.g., Bloom, 1973; Corrigan, 1978). Others, such as McCune-Nicolich (1981) and Gopnik (1982), have explored how early relational terms express general object relations of the type assumed to be established during the sensorimotor period, involving temporal, spatial, and causal notions. Still others have suggested that the child's first two-word utterances reflect in language the concepts and relations, such as actions, objects and causes, that come to be understood at the end of the sensorimotor period (e.g., Brown, 1973; Edwards, 1973).

Another version of the cognitive approach to the child's linguistic and communication skills is derived from adult cognitive research, as exemplified by Shatz's work (1977, 1983). Shatz (1983) argues that the importance of adult cognitive research lies in two areas: the nature of the representations and the process by which those representations are utilized in the production of behavior. As to the nature of the representational systems, as yet little is conclusively known. Regarding the process of using representations, two concepts are essential. One is the constraints on the capacity of the processing system that must solve communication tasks, involving integration of information from a variety of sources in real time. The second concept concerns the executive function that sets the goals for communicative behavior and selects means of achieving them.

Cognitive approaches to early language delineate a role for cognition in the language acquisition process. However, one major problem with these approaches is their failure to take account of the child as a social being who interacts with a social world virtually from the outset of life. Accordingly, the role that the *interactive context,* that is, the mother-child engagement, plays in language acquisition has usually been either ignored or downplayed by cognitive approaches.

However, the child does operate as a social participant in various interactive contexts throughout the language learning period, and this has led some investigators to move in a second direction in trying to discern the foundations of language acquisition. Following the tradition of Mead (1934) and Vygotsky (1978), theorists have posited a social basis for language.

There are several versions of interactional approaches. For example, Halliday (1975) studied the functions to which his son Nigel put language and reported that interpersonal or pragmatic functions developed prior to ideational ones. Dore (1983) has proposed that the necessary component of language emergence is the dialogue *between* caregiver and infant. He states, "First words will be seen to emerge in the infant as consequences of dialogical functions of affective expressions across members of an intimate dyad" (p. 168).

An interactional approach to the study of language acquisition is evident also in the work of Snow and her colleagues (Snow, Dubber, & De Blauw, 1981; Snow & Goldfield, 1983). Here the emergence of child language is studied within highly routinized interactive contexts involving mother and child, such as prelinguistic games, instructional games, and book reading. It is thought that routines enable the child to deal with complexity, and enable the insertion of fillers more complex than could be dealt with elsewhere into the slots created by them. Bruner and his colleagues have similarly studied the interactive context (see Bruner, 1983 for review). Bruner (1983) has proposed that the "arranging" of early speech interactions requires routinized and familiar settings, or formats, for the child to comprehend what is going on. These routines constitute what Bruner calls a Language Acquisition Support System. He has analyzed the structure of early game formats between mother and child in terms of their constituent acts and act sequences, their rules, their goals, and their interchangeable roles. He has found gamelike structures to be imposed on indicating and requesting formats and argues that such structures are essential to the development of these communicative functions.

Although social-interactional approaches recognize that the child is a social being and have pointed to the importance of the interactive context in the language acquisition process, they generally have not explored the child's cognitive support for this process. Thus, the role that the child's conceptual system may play in early language is not well specified in these accounts.

However, a synthesis of cognitive and social-interactive approaches to the study of language can be achieved if we assume that the child forms cognitive representations of social-interactive events. In the consideration of the role played by event knowledge in child language learning, the child can be conceived of as both a social participant and a cognitive being. The child is seen as engaging in social interaction and as a competent participant in interactive contexts throughout the infancy period. Insofar as the child must represent the roles of others and reciprocate with appropriate actions in order to participate competently in these interactive formats, it can be said that representations have been built up to guide interaction in these exchanges. Event representations, then, can be thought of as the cognitive counterparts to formats or routines. There is ample evidence that during the infancy period the child has a number of event representations that guide action and interaction in familiar routines (e.g., Ashmead & Perlmutter, 1980; Bruner, 1983; Nelson, 1978; Schank & Abelson, 1977; Snow et al., 1981; Snow & Goldfield, 1983).

These event representations can be thought of as comprising a *cognitive context,* as formulated in Chapter 1, for the young language learning child. This cognitive foundation for language relates to the social-interactive world in three ways. First, the social-interactive contexts in which mother and child participate constitute the bulk of event knowledge for the child during the first years of life. Second, such knowledge is considered social by virtue of its being *shared.* Finally, shared event knowledge can affect social-interactive behavior, both verbal and nonverbal.

In this chapter we present research that explores the relation between *interactive* and *cognitive contexts* in language acquisition and use within the framework of the event representation. The first section reports an experiment by Lucariello and Nelson that examines mother-child language across interactive contexts. This work demonstrates that interactive contexts differ in the cognitive context support provided the child by event representations. When mother and child both *possess* and *share* event knowledge for the interactive context, the child's competence in using language is greatly enhanced.

The second section of this chapter presents a study by Engel, Kyratzis, and Nelson that explores the decontextualization of word meaning. A single mother-child dyad is observed in a highly familiar and routine interactive context for which both members of the dyad have presumably formed an event representation. Here, mother and child share event knowledge of the interactive context, and this knowledge enables the mother to confer pragmatic meaning on the child's first words, thus enabling the child to grasp and adopt that meaning for her words.

In the third section of the chapter an experiment by Kyratzis, Lucariello, and Nelson is discussed. This research explores how interactive context participates in the establishment of cognitive context. Here the role played by the mother in the mother-child dyadic interactive system and the role played by language in the formation of shared event knowledge were studied. Several mother-child dyads were observed repeatedly in an interactive context that was novel at the outset, and the process by which *shared* event knowledge comes to be established is described.

THE EFFECT OF DIFFERENT INTERACTIVE CONTEXTS ON LANGUAGE USE

The study reported here examines the varied effects on mother-child language exerted by interactive contexts for which the mother-child dyad share event knowledge, as compared with interactive contexts for which there is no shared event knowledge. There are three possible ways in which *Event Contexts,* defined as *situations* for which each member of the dyad has, and thereby shares, event knowledge, can be expected to facilitate or enrich mother-child use of language. (Event Context is henceforth capitalized in this chapter in order to emphasize its technical meaning in this sense.) First, in such contexts mother and child share knowledge of the immediate situation. Nelson and Gruendel (1979) argued that shared event knowledge facilitates discourse among preschool peers and this proposal has been supported in studies by Seidman (1983a, 1983b) and Boynton and French (1983). (See also Chapter 8.) It is proposed here that such knowledge should exercise the same effect on mother-child discourse.

Second, child speech may be more enriched in an Event Context by the role that mothers play in their child's acquisition and use of language, a role that may vary with context. The facilitative role played by mothers in formatted, routine, or Event Contexts has been well documented by the work of Bruner and his colleagues (Bruner, 1978a, 1978b, 1983; Ninio & Bruner, 1978; Ratner & Bruner, 1978). Bruner (1978b) has described three strategies that the mother employs on her side of the dyad through formats. One is *scaffolding,* which provides a model of the expected dialogue from which the child can extract selectively what is needed for filling his or her role in discourse. Second, mothers engage in *extension,* enlarging the scope of the situations in which, and the functions for which, different utterances can be used. Finally, the mother plays *communicative ratchet:* as the child makes a forward step, a communicative acquisition, she prevents a backslide and assures that the child goes on with a new construction, thereby developing a *next* platform for the *next* launch (Bruner's emphasis).

To Bruner's list we propose the addition of a fourth facet of the maternal role that we believe to function in Event Contexts. This facet involves the role of the mother as *catalyst,* by which we mean that the mother can set the child's (nonlinguistic) knowledge into action, enabling the child to use all kinds of knowledge in the service of language (e.g., use memory to converse on the past). Most of these maternal behaviors have already been found in Event Contexts, and we propose that they are more likely to occur in Event than in non-Event Contexts. Thus, the multifaceted role played by mothers in Event Contexts should enable the fullest expression of the child's linguistic potential in such settings.

A third reason to expect more sophisticated child speech in Event Contexts relates to the information processing approach to children's linguistic skills presented by Shatz (1977, 1983). Shatz argues that children's linguistic performance can be degraded when a task makes heavy processing demands, and conversely, that skills are more readily revealed when other cognitive demands are minimized. In Event Contexts representations can be instantiated to guide action and interaction, and thus dealing with the ongoing scene or activity becomes a light workload situation in comparison to contexts for which no representation is available. Accordingly, more processing capacity of the limited information processor (the child) can be allocated to language related behavior.

In order to explore the issue of contextual variation in mother-child language, ten mother-child dyads with children aged 2;0–2;5 were audio- and video-recorded at home in three contexts. The Event Context was a highly familiar, well-conventionalized, routine situation chosen on the basis of information gathered in a preliminary interview with each mother. A routine was defined as any activity of approximately 15 minutes' duration that involved mother and child only and that occurred at least 3–4 times per week. Of the ten dyads, five were observed in a lunch routine, three in a morning routine of bathing and/or getting dressed, and two in an evening routine of bathing and getting ready for bed.

Language was observed also in two 15-minute non-Event situations, that is, situations for which the dyad did not share event knowledge. One of these was the *Novel* context, in which the pair was presented with a model castle and associated figures. Here it was ascertained that the child was completely unfamiliar with the actual physical materials, and with the "castle" scenario.

The second non-Event Context was a Free Play situation, in which the pair were presented with five common toys: a hand puppet, a tea set, a shape register, a stack-toy dog, and a pull-toy train. Here it was confirmed that no child had precisely these toys in his or her own collection; thus no particular sequence of actions or distribution of roles could be readily anticipated by the child on the basis of event representations formed in prior play experiences with the mother. This situation differs from the Novel context in that no particular scenario is involved, and the toys, although unfamiliar, are of the type usually offered to children of this age.

A single situation was audio- and video-taped in each home visit, with the entire series concluded within a 2–3 week period. Transcripts of these sessions were analyzed in terms of a number of aspects of language use, particularly pragmatics, discourse, and semantics. For the purposes of this chapter the results of only subsets of some of these analyses are presented. The complete data analysis will be reported in full elsewhere (Lucariello & Nelson, in preparation).

Among the discourse features examined were child question-answering ability and the functions of maternal questions (Lucariello & Nelson, 1982). With respect to child question-answering ability, it was found that children were significantly better at answering questions in the Event Context than in either of the non-Event Contexts. Two factors may be responsible for this. First, as noted earlier, in the Event setting the child can allocate more processing resources to attending to and responding to incoming linguistic information contained to maternal utterances because an event representation can be instantiated to deal with the procedural aspects of the situation. Second, the child can utilize knowledge of the present situation in the Event Context to answer questions about the ongoing scene, such as "What do you want for lunch?" or "What do you do when we wash your hair?"

Analysis of maternal questioning behavior indicated that the mother was operating as catalyst in the Event Context. There was no difference in the number of questions asked by mothers across the three contexts, but there were significant differences in the function of maternal questions across the contexts. Real questions, that is, questions that genuinely seek information from the child and call on the child to generate a linguistic response were used significantly more often in the Event Context than in either of the other contexts. Such questions accounted for more than one third of maternal questions in the Event Context and were the most frequently used question type in this context. The real question type is distinct from the "test question" for which the mother already has an answer and assumes that the child has also. This was the type least utilized in the Event Context. These question types are also distinct from directive and attention-focusing questions, which simply attempt to control the child's nonverbal behavior. It is not surprising that directives and attention focusers were more common in the non-Event Contexts, than in the Event Context; in non-Event Contexts, event representations cannot be instantiated to guide behavior, and maternal questioning behavior assumes this function. Thus, in the Event Context, mothers require more of their children in terms of answers or responses to questions. The real questions they use call for linguistic responses that are not already available to the child. The children have to rely on or utilize their knowledge base to *formulate* an answer. For example, in answer to the question "What do you want for lunch?" the child has to conjure up lunch foods as well as his or her own reactions to them.

For the study of semantic aspects of speech, the transcripts were analyzed into conversational units (see Lucariello, 1983). A conversation was defined as a segment of the discourse in which the dyad demonstrated communicative *and* semantic contingency. Communicative contingency meant that the utterances of each person were directed to and responsive to the utterances of the other. Semantic contingency meant that a communicative set of utterances shared a common topic, that is, the partners were talking about the same thing. A minimum of four turns were required to constitute a conversation. These conversations were then analyzed to determine the semantic topics they contained. A list and brief definition of topic types can be found in Table 7.1.

One index of the semantic richness of conversations is their breadth, or *number* of topic types covered within them. Almost half (48%) the conversations in the Event Context included more than one topic type, and of these, approximately one third contained three or more topic types. In the play context, approximately 20% of the conversations contained more than one topic type, and in the novel context approximately 35% contained more than one topic type. The difference between the Event and each non-Event context was significant and indicates that semantic breadth was greater in Event Context conversations than in conversations held in the non-Event Contexts.

TABLE 7.1
Description of Semantic Topics

1. OBJECT TALK - Utterances that:
   A. Draw attention to objects.
   B. Name or identify objects.
   C. Describe aspects of objects.
   D. Refer to actions with objects, e.g., "put man in castle."
2. FANTASY TALK - Utterances that express fantasy play activity.
3. CULTURE TALK - Utterances that refer to information mediated through language and other symbolic forms, e.g., knowledge of television characters, behavior rules.
4. SPATIAL DISPLACEMENT TALK - Utterances that refer to objects, persons, or places not in the immediate context.
5. PAST TALK - Utterances that refer to any activity which occurred at any time prior to the recording situation.
6. FUTURE TALK - Utterances that refer to any activity that will or may take place at any time after the recording situation.
7. LANGUAGE TALK - Utterances that have a linguistic referent:
   A. Language routines, e.g., songs, book reading.
   B. Language instruction, e.g., politeness expressions, word pronunciation.
   C. Language games, e.g., mother playing game about child's name.
8. CHILD BIOGRAPHY TALK - Maternal reference to child's habits, abilities, or possessions, e.g., "You don't eat many sweets," "You know how to put your head under water."
9. EVENT-RELATED TALK - Utterances that refer to aspects of the event situation in which participants are currently involved. This talk can involve reference to actions that are not currently being performed but that comprise the present event, e.g.,

   M: (taking child's sleeper off)
   First we'll take your sleeper off
   C: No diaper change

   This topic applicable to routine context only.

A second index of the semantic richness of conversations is the *kind* of topics contained within them. Four topic types are considered here: Object Talk, Spatial Displacement Talk, Future Talk, and Past Talk. These topic types are considered because they represent two salient features of language. Object Talk represents one of the most basic uses of language, that is, to refer to the immediate scene. "Here-and-now" talk is very pervasive in the speech of young children (Bloom, 1970; Brown & Bellugi, 1964; Sachs, 1983) and in the speech of adults interacting with young children (Phillips, 1973; Snow, 1979). The use of language to refer to displaced topics, however, represents a more advanced, semantically complex use of language. Displacement may involve the spatial domain with reference to objects or persons that are not in the immediate environment, or the temporal domain with reference to the past or future. According to Sachs (1983), linguistic skills for displaced reference, particularly temporal displacement, are just being acquired at the age of the children studied here.

More than half the conversations in the non-Event Contexts contained object talk only, as compared to fewer than 20% of the conversations in the Event Context. This finding reflects the predominance of "here-and-now" conversational talk in each of the non-Event Contexts. Object talk tended to be very repetitive. The following conversational excerpt involves the placement of shapes in the shape register and illustrates talk involving "actions with objects" in the play context:

M: (Referring to C's inserting shape in slot) Doesn't go in there/
C: (Tries new slot) In there?
M: Not in that one either/
C: (Tries another slot) In there?
M: Not that one/
C: (Tries another slot) In there?
M: Not that one/
C: (Tries another slot) In there?
M: That's right/
That's good/

(Male, 24 months, 22 days)

For displaced topics, the story is reversed. These topics were present to a considerably greater extent in the Event Context conversations than in either of the non-Event Context conversations. Of the conversations in the Event Context, 17% contained spatial displacement talk, as compared with approximately 4% in each of the non-Event Contexts. The vast majority of the displaced object references in Event contexts were to Event-related objects. For example, in the lunch routine, there were many menu negotiations involving nonpresent foods and beverages. These references indicate that the dyad is not tied to the immediate interactive context, that is, to this particular lunch, but rather to a representation of the lunch Event, which includes knowledge of situationally appropriate items, including ones not present. Event-related object talk accounted for 89% of the spatially displaced talk. The following excerpt from a conversation occurred as the dyad was preparing for the child's bathtime. The bathroom was not visible to the dyad and the conversation involves reference to non-present toys that will be put in the non-present tub:

M: (standing with C in living room) We'll get your big boat and put it in the tub/
C: Yeah/
M: Okay/
. . . (conversation continues)
C: Dinosaur/
M: Dinosaur/ (walks to other room) Well your dinosaur's down here/
M: (returns with toy/gives to C) Here/ Take your dinosaur/
C: Take/ In/ The bathtub?

(Male, 27 months, 2 days)

Future and past talk were virtually absent from the conversations in the two non-Event Contexts, whereas, in the Event Context, 15% of the conversations contained future talk and 13%, past talk. The percentages are not large, no doubt because children are just beginning to acquire relevant linguistic skills at this age. Nevertheless, the findings indicate that Event Contexts provide a forum for the emergence of linguistic skills, the context for their acquisition. The following excerpt from a conversation between the dyad while having lunch illustrates reference to a future activity:

M: I think Elmer* would like to come in/
C: Should we take Elmer to the park?
M: Should we take Elmer to the park?
C: Yeah/
M: Well Maybe/

(Male, 26 months, 9 days) *Family dog

In summary, these data on conversational topic types and on conversational breadth indicate that, in the Event Context, conversational talk encompasses greater semantic complexity and breadth than in the non-Event Contexts. These conversations indicate that children have the knowledge of the past and future to converse on displaced topics, as well as the capability to converse on a number of topics within a given conversation. Why do they do so primarily in the Event Context? It appears that the mother is the catalyst for this. The semantic topics were introduced to the conversation largely by the mother. In addition, those topic statements not pursued, that is, not responded to by the partner, were introduced by the mother. This finding indicates that these mothers never failed to pick up on a topic introduced by the child. The factors of mother as catalyst and the allocation of processing capacity to linguistic behavior on the part of the child may combine to make these conversations possible in the Event Context. The following conversational segment illustrates some critical features of the maternal role. It occurred while the dyad was having lunch, and it involves the discussion of a past activity:

M: What'd the baby squirrel eat for lunch today?
C: Um/ Um/
M: What did Chris feed the baby squirrel?
C: What?
M: You remember?
C: What? What?
M: What did she feed the baby squirrel?
C: What?
M: Remember it was in the bottle? Was it water?
C: No/
M: Was it apple juice?
C: No/
M: What was it?
C: (pointing to cup) Here's apple juice/
M: Right/ But what was in the bottle?
C: Milk/
M: Right!

(Male, 26 months, 9 days)

The mother persisted in her attempt to get the child to converse on the past topic. She played "communicative ratchet," in Bruner's terms, knowing that the child could handle this conversational topic and not letting him get by without contributing. In addition, scaffolding was evidenced by her providing the child with useful bits of information, by modelling in her contributions to the conversation the kind of information the child was being requested to supply (i.e., types of beverages). These forms the mother modelled enabled the child to make an eventual contribution.

Conclusions. Taken together, these data indicate that a critical factor in mother-child language behavior is whether interactive context has a counterpart cognitive context. Thus, both *interactive* and *cognitive* context must be taken into account in attempts to describe child language. Additionally, these data support the hypothesis that the three factors—event knowledge, maternal role, and processing capacity—operate within an interactive context conjoined by cognitive context, that is, an Event Context, to bring about enriched child language use.

THE DECONTEXTUALIZATION OF WORD MEANING WITHIN AN EVENT CONTEXT

This section reports a study that explores how the cognitive context shared by mother and child affects the learning and development of first words. More specifically, the process of the decontextualization[1] of early word use was studied within an interactive context for which the dyad shared event knowledge, that is, within an Event Context.

The decontextualization of first words is a phrase often used to describe the finding that children frequently use words only in highly specific behavioral contexts before using them in a contextually flexible manner (Barrett, 1983; Bates, 1979; Bloom, 1973; Gopnik, 1982; Nelson, Rescorla, Gruendel, & Benedict, 1978; Piaget, 1962). More recently, Nelson (1985) and Nelson and Lucariello (1985) have viewed contexted and decontexted word use as indicative of different aspects of lexical meaning; and have attempted to account for the shift from contexted to decontexted word use in terms of cognitive development during the second year of life.

In this study the acquisition of particular pragmatic functions (e.g., requesting, initiating, narrating, planning) for referential (object) words within an Event Context was examined. These different functions are related to the ongoing event-based action in varying degrees. It was proposed that these functions are acquired in order of their increasing distance from the action, an order determined by the process of decontextualization.

Central to this decontextualization process is the mother-child interaction as it occurs within a situational context for which the dyad share event knowledge. In the earliest phase of word use, the child uses words in a "functionless" or "meaningless" way. However, because the dyad share a cognitive context, the mother can assign or attribute appropriate pragmatic functions to the child's words and does so by interpreting them in specific ways (e.g., as requests, or initiations). Eventually, the child comes to adopt these interpretations as his or her own and uses words functionally within the Event Context.

The culmination of the decontextualization process is reached when words take on conceptual status, that is, when they can enter into relations with other

[1]This use of the term decontextualization is in accord with its use by others in reference to early word learning. The term has also been used to refer to developments taking place during the preschool period. In this regard a different interpretation of the term has been proposed by Nelson (1985); the two interpretations do not refer to the same processes.

words, can be used to highlight a particular aspect of the referent (e.g., a property of it, such as color), and/or can be used to invoke a particular fact about the referent in the service of some conversational topic. It is proposed that at this point the child has acquired the "invoking" function of words. Now words can be used by both mothers and children as context-establishers for talking about virtually any known topic. Words are no longer "purposeful" solely as they relate to the ongoing Event Context in particular ways.

In this proposal, the mother[2] is essential to the decontextualization process. She models the invoking function before it is assumed by the child. Although the invoking function does not involve word use in relation to event knowledge, it is hypothesized that event knowledge supports, or enables, the use of the invoking function. We suggest that only after some understanding and use of the word is achieved by the child through its relation to the Event Context is this more sophisticated "cognitive" use acquired.

In order to study how shared event knowledge between mother and child helps the child to realize both the pragmatic and invoking functions of language, we carried out a longitudinal study of one little girl, Rachel. Once a week for 8 months, beginning when Rachel was 16 months old, Rachel and her mother were audiotaped in their morning routine of getting dressed and having breakfast. This routine constituted the Event Context. These months spanned the period in which Rachel moved from one-word to three-word utterances and in which she acquired a substantial productive vocabulary. Her mean length of utterance (MLU) at the beginning of the study was 1.11 and at the study's end, 1.54. Rachel came from a white, middle-class, urban family; her parents were separated, and her mother cared for her full time.

All words that showed up consistently as part of Rachel's productive vocabulary were traced from their first appearance in the transcripts until their last appearance. The following information about the context of the use of each word was recorded: the part of the Event that the mother and child were engaged in at the time of the utterance, the action that was being performed, what mother and child had said both immediately prior to and subsequent to the child's utterance of the word. These histories are called "word evolutions." On the basis of this contextual information, the use of each word over time was described. As an example, for the purposes of this chapter, the evolution of the word "juice" is presented. (For descriptions of the uses of other words see Nelson, Engel, and Kyratzis, in press.)

During the early occurrences of "juice," only the mother used the word and only in the context of offering juice to Rachel at the breakfast table. The mother's use of the word was embedded in the eating breakfast action sequence. She

[2]Although the present discussion is phrased in terms of mothers, there is no implication on the part of the authors that *only* mothers can and/or do play the described role in dyadic interaction.

would typically say, "Would you like some juice?" and immediately bring Rachel a cup of juice.

Next, Rachel used the word "juice" herself. Her earliest uses, as in the example below, occurred only within the context of actually eating breakfast, that is, they were embedded in the action. She would often use the word in a diffuse manner, apparently without having any particular meaning or function for it. In the example, although the mother interprets the child's utterance as a request for juice, it is not clear that the child's use encompasses that function. The mother conferred meaning on the child's talk and followed up on that interpretation with appropriate language and action.

(R in high chair as M brings food)
R: djees/du/djees/
M: Would you like a little juice?
R: Yah/
M: Okay (pours R juice)

(16 months, 28 days)

A little later, a shift in the *mother's* use of the word occurred when she began to discuss what Rachel should or should not do with juice. This represents an early modelling of the "invoking" function of word use. At this point, however, the child could not participate in the use of this function. The mother pulled the word "juice" into a conversation not directly related to the Event Context as follows:

M: Wait a sec/ Tell me what you want/ Want me to put some milk in here for you? Please?
R: Pees?
M: Okay/
R: Ahh/ de/ peeh eeh eeh of doos/ (pours juice in cereal bowl)
M: No, juice doesn't go in there sweetheart/ juice goes down your throat/

(17 months, 20 days)

This segment illustrates the shift from completely action-embedded language to language that is distinct from action. The mother talked about what one does with juice, in effect presenting a functional definition of the word.

The next important shift occurred when Rachel acquired the "initiating" function for her word "juice." This is the first example in which Rachel used the word with clear intention, and this represents a further step in the decontextualization process. Here the word was used by the child immediately *before* the action sequence pertaining to the eating of breakfast, and in fact, it initiated that sequence of actions.

(R runs and climbs into her highchair, M puts bib on her)
M: Oh, all of a sudden you are in a terrible hurry/
R: Yeah, Djoos/
M: Just a minute, I'm gonna get you some juice, you want some juice with breakfast?
R: Yeah/
M: Yes, what?
R: Djoos/

(18 months, 13 days)

In this example, "juice" was also used as a request for action. The mother made this interpretation and elaborated on it by practicing the request function with the child. The mother's pedagogy here involves meeting what Bruner (1983) has termed the affiliative condition of requesting, that is, the child's having to respect the mother as an ally. The mother attempts to introduce a politeness form (e.g., "Yes, what?") into the child's "nominal displaced request" (Bruner, 1983).

In the next example, Rachel not only used language to comment, regulate, or affect the sequence but could also use language to refer to more abstract aspects of the sequence, such as ownership. The mother once again modelled the "invoking" function, but here the child was able to participate in this kind of word usage as well.

R: Djoos/
M: You have your juice, that's my juice/
R: My djoos/

(19 months, 20 days)

Such examples suggest that Rachel might be developing an articulated concept of juice, distinct from ongoing action, which included the notion that juice can belong to (or be associated with) different people.

The last stage of Rachel's use of the word juice was marked by the mother and child discussing juice while in the bedroom. At this point, the word was clearly disembedded from the action sequence that normally surrounded the use of the word (e.g., going to the kitchen, getting in the highchair, having the bib put on, opening the juice, drinking from cup). In this example, the "invoking" function is realized by the child for her word "juice." This is evidenced in two ways. First, the concept of juice evidently includes the notion of an item that can be eaten for breakfast and is associated with other breakfast items. Second, "juice" is now embedded in a conversational context, not in the context of the action sequence of eating breakfast. It is within this conversational context with both parents that the word takes on a planning function in relation to the action sequence.

(R in bedroom with father and M)
M: Okay? You ready to go downstairs and have some breakfast?
R: Dadd?
F: Yeah/ I'm coming too/
R: Yeah/
F: What are you going to have for breakfast?
R: Cereal
F: Yeah/
M: What else?
R: Toast/ Milk/ Juice!

(22 months, 24 days)

In summary, the word "juice" was initially used as an integral part of an action sequence belonging to an Event Context: having breakfast. The mother interpreted Rachel's utterance of "juice" as a request to get the juice. The first major step in the decontextualization process came when Rachel could anticipate or deliberately initiate the action sequence with her use of the word "juice." Next, Rachel began to use the word to refer to more abstract features of the event sequence. Finally, the word "juice" could be used to plan the action sequence from another place and time altogether in the larger Event Context: getting dressed. This indicates that the child has a representation of the event that includes the total activity sequence and can refer to objects within that representation. Additionally, the word took on the "invoking" function by which it enters into relations with other words and aspects of the referent can be discussed, and by which the word can be used to contribute to a conversational context divorced from the event itself. The changing status and use of the word "juice" emerged as part of the interactive process between mother and child as it occurred within an Event Context. Shared cognitive context enabled the mother to confer meaning on her child's words and enabled the child to adopt that meaning.

Conclusions. Shared cognitive context is essential to the child's acquisition and use of word functions. The actual process of meaning acquisition operates through mother-child interaction as it occurs within an Event Context. Shared event knowledge enables the mother to supply meaning and the child to adopt meaning. After some Event-related functions are acquired, the way is ready for the acquisition and use of the "cognitive" or "invoking" function.

THE ROLE OF INTERACTIVE CONTEXT IN ESTABLISHING COGNITIVE CONTEXT

In this section we present a study by Kyratzis, Lucariello and Nelson that examines the process by which the child acquires event knowledge through participation in an interactive context with the mother. The acquisition and development of event knowledge was discussed in Chapter 4 in relation to changes in children's script reports. Although the present study is clearly relevant to the issues discussed there, its focus is on the process by which the child utilizes the interactive context—and specifically the information provided in the mother's language—to acquire event knowledge and to take part in the evolving event structure.

This research falls within the tradition of theory and research that explores the social origins of cognitive processes (e.g., Bruner, 1983; Wertsch, 1978, 1979; Wood, 1980), a tradition originating with Vygotsky (1978). Vygotsky proposed that any function in the child's cultural development appears first between people as an interpsychological category and then within the child as an intrapsychological category. Wertsch and his colleagues, for example, have applied this approach to the study of goal-directed problem solving, involving mother-child dyads in constructing a physical object in accordance with a plan. They have documented a shift from other-regulation in connection with crucial strategic behavior, such as gaze behavior. Before the child is able to function as an independent (i.e., self-regulated) problem solver, the adult in the adult-child dyad functions to plan, regulate, and reflect on the problem-solving task.

In considering the social origins of event knowledge, that is, the role played by the mother in the child's acquisition of event representations, we must first briefly review the nature of the acquisition. As outlined in Chapter 3, event knowledge involves knowledge of cultural events, such as shopping, birthday parties, and the school day. This knowledge specifies the ordered sequence of actions that are appropriate to a particular spatial-temporal context organized around a goal. It includes knowledge of the objects that complement the actions, that is, the objects that fill the slots created by the action, as well as knowledge of other props, actors, and roles (see Chapters 3 and 4 of this volume.) It is evident from the work reported thus far that at some point children acquire event knowledge as their own and operate with that knowledge as independent social and cognitive agents.

Based on the theorists mentioned earlier, it can be hypothesized that, to some extent, experience of the world, and thus knowledge of the world, comes to the child not directly but via the mother. The implication of this hypothesis is that the event structures that the child comes to represent are mediated through the mother's structuring. There are many ways in which mothers can mediate event structure. For example, mothers can impart knowledge (e.g., goal information) of culturally-determined event structures, such as restaurant and shopping, and regulate their children's behavior within such settings. Additionally, mothers can create and organize event structures themselves, as when they establish caretaking routines or game formats, and regulate their children's behavior in these situations. Another way in which mothers can mediate event structures (culturally-determined or self-created) is by selectively emphasizing or de-emphasizing elements or aspects of the structure, perhaps enabling the child to make distinctions such as "central acts" or "basic level acts" (see Chapter 3). This list of maternal mediating possibilities is not meant to be exhaustive, but rather to demonstrate how mediation of event structure can occur. It can be further hypothesized that *language* is the primary means by which mothers mediate event structure.

Whatever the kind of mediation, such an approach to the child's acquisition of "cognitive context" emphasizes the influence of the social/cultural world. Thus, in our view, one of perhaps many possible ways in which the child acquires event knowledge is characterized by a shift from other-regulated participation in "mediated" contexts in dyadic interaction with the mother, in which language plays a major role, to possessing this mediated knowledge, using it to operate in a more self-regulated way in social situations, and using it cognitively to generate other forms of knowledge. In this sense our conception is similar to Vygotsky's (1978) conception of a move from interpsychological to intrapsychological knowledge. In terms of the child's behavior throughout the acquisition process, as it relates to any specific event, Wertsch's (1978, 1979; Wertsch, McNamee, McLane, & Budwig, 1980) conception of a shift from other-regulated to self-regulated behavior can be applied and serve as an index of knowledge acquisition by the child. Mothers regulate their child's behavior within mediated interactive or event structure contexts until the child acquires knowledge or mental representations for these mediated contexts. Such representations enable the child to regulate his or her own behavior in such settings.

To study this proposed process of event knowledge acquisition we followed six mother-child dyads over time in an interactive context that was novel at the outset of the study. The context consisted of presenting the dyad with an elaborate circus scenario toy and requesting them to "play circus." The toy contained a circus ring with bleachers, a circus tent, a ticket booth, a band, a cage, circus people (e.g., trainers and ringmaster), audience people, and six animal acts with props—items associated with "real" circuses. Children were aged 2;4–2;9 and had no prior experience with a circus. The dyads were audio- and video-recorded in the home for six sessions of the "playing circus" situation. Sessions took place once a week and lasted approximately 20 minutes. The present description is based on preliminary analyses of transcripts from three dyads. Transcripts of each experimental session were analyzed into episodes. An episode was defined as all the verbal and nonverbal behavior, organized around a specific set of objects in the circus toy set. For example, an episode would consist of verbal and nonverbal behavior related to the elephants, their trainer, and their props. All the episodes across experimental sessions related to a particular set of props were termed units. Units were examined whose episodes were fairly consistent across experimental sessions. That is, three episodes within the unit had to share at least three acts in common.

Episodes were subjected to an act and goal-act analysis. An act consisted of a specific verbal and/or nonverbal behavior within an episode, such as giving the audience children a ride on the elephant or leading the elephant around the ring. Act knowledge might incorporate role knowledge (e.g., "bring lion tamer" or "lion tamer comes in here"), or prop knowledge (e.g., "Well, those are little stools that they put in here with the lions").

The definition of goal-act was based on the view that event representations embody goal hierarchies, consisting in a goal for the entire event, as well as subgoals (Bower, Black, & Turner, 1979). Within an episode, goal-acts were defined as statements such as "The lions are gonna do tricks now" or "The lions are gonna perform," which subsume acts such as the lions going into the ring, or the lions jumping through hoops.

The present analysis examines the best unit that evolved over the six sessions for each of the three dyads. The best unit was defined as the unit in which the child contributed the greatest number of different component-acts and goal-acts. Three episodes of the best unit were selected from the experimental sessions to represent the process of event acquisition. "Maternal Introduction" episode refers to the episode in which the mother introduced the unit and delineated the majority of its components for the child.[3] The "Intermediate" episode refers to the first episode in which the child was able to contribute at least *one* component. This episode usually occurred within one or two episodes subsequent to the Maternal Introduction episode, suggesting that the child acquires some knowledge of the unit relatively quickly. "Later" episode refers to the episode with the greatest number of child-contributed components occurring after the Intermediate episode.

The progression of knowledge acquisition was as follows. In the Maternal Introduction episode, the mother introduced the unit for the child, imposing an eventlike organization. The mothers utilized goal acts, which reference as a whole the different behaviors comprising the episode, (e.g., "This is the lion act" or "Let me show you what the lions do at the circus"). In this episode, the mother introduced the majority of the component-acts of the unit to the child, accompanying her naming of them with demonstrative action; in later episodes she sometimes introduced additional components. Moreover, she specified the acts according to the culturally-specified sequence for "acts" as they occur in the real world event of circus (e.g., "lion-act"). Because acts designate appropriate relations among actors, actions, and objects, role and object information appropriate to the circus event was incorporated as well. Because mothers were imposing event-like organization on the units, henceforth units are referred to as *event*-units.

Thus, at the outset, the mother in the mother-child system was seen to be organizing interactive context by organizing the circus materials and regulating

---

[3]The Maternal Introduction episode did not always represent the first occasion within the experimental sessions in which the dyad interacted with the particular set of props. It was the first episode of behavior enacted for the props whose content and structure was adhered to across a minimum of two subsequent episodes with at least three acts in common.

the child's behavior in relation to the materials. In this episode, mothers contributed almost all (91%) of the acts, and two kinds of maternal mediation can be identified. One is the creation and organization of event structure context in terms of a play routine for these experimental sessions. However, because the play routine set up by the mother in the sessions conforms or corresponds to the culturally-defined circus event, the second kind of maternal mediation involves imparting knowledge to the child of this cultural event.

By the Intermediate episode the children had acquired some knowledge of the event-unit, being able to contribute approximately 36% of the total number of components. By the Later episode the degree of knowledge the children had acquired was relatively high, children contributing a mean percentage of 62% of the components. Thus, the acquisition of event knowledge enabled a shift from other- to self-regulated behavior in these experimental sessions, with the child coming to organize the circus materials somewhat independently of the mother.

A second analysis was carried out in order to examine the kind of components contributed by mothers in the Introduction episode and by children in the Intermediate and Later episodes. The presence or absence of goal-acts was noted, and acts were categorized into four types: general, specific, relational, and circus-inappropriate. General acts were those that would pertain to any circus event-unit. Included in this category were such acts as putting the animals and trainers in the ring. This type could be attributed to a general scheme for toy playing (e.g., put everything in the middle). Specific acts were those that pertained to particular event-units only. The seal blowing a horn on a stand and the lion going through the tamer's hoop are examples of this type. Relational acts were those that related the particular event-unit in question to the larger Event Context—the circus. Examples of this type of act included references to the audience reaction or reference to the band playing. Circus-inappropriate acts included actions such as having the elephant jump off the bandstand or climb the ladder to the bandstand.

When the mothers introduced the event-unit to the child in the Maternal Introduction episode, it consisted of all types of *appropriate* components. Each mother used goal-acts, comprising approximately 10% of the episode-components. In addition, all the mothers contributed each of the three appropriate act-types with means of 23% general, 46% specific, and 20% relational.

In the Intermediate and Later episodes, the children also contributed all appropriate component act types. The children's contributions were, therefore, not limited simply to general knowledge of where objects could be placed, but reflected a conceptualization of the specific event-unit, with specific acts accounting for means of 33% and 43% in the Intermediate and Later episodes respectively. In addition, a conceptualization of the larger event—the circus—of which the specific event-units are a part, was evidenced by the contribution of relational acts (33% and 24% in the Intermediate and Later episodes respectively). Only one child in one episode contributed an idiosyncratic or circus-inappropriate act; and all children incorporated goal-acts in either the Intermediate, or the Later episodes. Thus, the children's component contributions included the full range of types, as did their mothers'.

Finally, the origin of the child-contributed components was investigated. Independent components were those that had not been specified by the mother as constituent of the event-unit in any former episode; dependent components were those that had been so identified. Child contributions in the Intermediate and Later episodes were predominantly dependent (71% and 80% respectively), indicating that the child's conceptualization of the event-unit's content and organization was derived mainly from the mother's delineation of it. Thus, it was clearly the "mediated" event structure that became represented in the child's conceptual system. The children were, however, able to contribute a small number of independently derived components. These independent components included goal-acts, as well as general, specific, and relational acts. These findings indicate that, whereas the conceptualization of the event-unit was derived largely from the mother, the child's cognitive system also operates independently on event knowledge, incorporating new components not directly derived from the mother's contributions, and placing components independently within the larger conceptual framework of the circus event. Thus, the child operated as an independent cognitive agent, utilizing, adding to, and reorganizing newly acquired knowledge.

In illustration of these results, Tables 7-2 and 7-3 contain excerpts of mother-child dialogue from two episodes—the Maternal Introduction episode and the Later episode—of the most extensive event-unit for one dyad, involving the lion act. The episode in Table 7.2 contained a goal-act, together with three general, six specific, and two relational act-components. All 12 components were contributed by the mother, a strong index of other-regulated behavior. The episode in Table 7.3 contained a total of nine components, eight contributed by the child, of which five were derived from the Maternal Introduction episode. The child's contributions include a goal-act, and three general, three specific, and one relational act. This episode reflects the shift from other- to self-regulated behavior. With the acquisition of event knowledge, the child assumes the primary role in organizing the materials.

All the data indicate that, by the Intermediate and Later episodes, the child had come to share in the mother's knowledge of the cultural event of circus. We feel justified in terming the child's knowledge of the unit *event* knowledge because it manifests the main characteristics of event representations, that is, temporally organized schemas specifying the sequence of acts, as well as the objects and roles to be expected in a particular spatial/temporal context and incorporating knowledge of the goal of the event. All mothers in the transcripts analyzed here specified some kind of goal-act in the Maternal Introduction episode for the series of acts that they delineated in that episode. All the children also used goal-acts, indicating that the children grasped the goal of the event. Additionally, children contributed a large percentage of acts and act-knowledge

TABLE 7.2
Maternal Introduction Episode

Code	*Component*	
M, G	M:	And the lion tamer brings the lions right out here into the middle of the circus (Makes sweeping gesture with arm to indicate ring)
	C:	(Puts lion tamer into ring)
M, G	M:	Bring the lion tamer. And bring the lions right out into the middle of the circus
	C:	(Puts a lion into the cage)
M, S	M:	(Puts cage into ring)
		And the lions . . . They don't want the people to be too close to the ree-al lions, so they put this cage in
M, Goal	M:	And the lion tamer comes in here and makes them do tricks
		--------(Discourse Continues)
	M:	Okay, what kind of tricks should you make the lions do?
	C:	(Reaches for stools)
		What? . . . Whatta thee-eese?
M, G	M:	(Puts the stools in the middle)
		Well, those are little stools that they put in here with the lions
	M:	(Makes ''cracking'' movement with her arm) and the Ringmaster says to
M, S; M, S		the lions, he snaps his whip, and he says to the lions, ''up.'' And the lion
M, S		goes like that (Puts a lion on a stool in the ring)
M, S		(Sits back)
		He climbs up on the chair. So you be . . . you be the lion tamer, you tell the lion, ''up!''
	C:	(Takes lion out of middle. Holds it up high) ''Up!''
	M:	And what does the lion do?
	C:	(Puts lion atop the other stool)
		--------(Discourse Continues)
	M:	That's right. And the lion gets right up on the stool. And the people in the
M, R		audience all say ''Yeay!''
		-----(Discourse Continues)
	M:	You know . . . You know what else he has them do? You see what he's holding? This red thing? And he makes them jump through the hoop. He
M, S		says ''jump,'' and the lion comes . . . jumping . . . right through the hoop
M, S		(Passes lion through tamer's hoop)
	C:	(Spots elephants. Brings them over to himself)
		A elephant! . . . We have a baby elephant!
M, R	M:	A baby and a mommy? Should we bring the elephants in the circus now and put the lion away and let the elephants come in and do some tricks?
		(MALE, 28 months, 16 days)

Key
M, C Mother or Child
G General
S Specific
R Relational

TABLE 7.3
Later Episode

Code	Component	
	C:	(Scoops the lions up off the floor and throws them into cage)
C, Goal, D		They not going to do tricks today[a]
M, R	M:	No tricks today! Oh, the children are going to be so disappointed!
C, G, D	C:	(Scoops lions out of cage and puts them into ring)
C, G, D		The which lion's performing[b]
---	M:	What kind of tricks will they do?
	C:	No lion man!
C, G, D		(Picks up tamer and puts it into ring with lions)
C, S, D	C:	(Cracks the tamer's whip against floor of ring)
---	M:	What do the lions do?
C, S, D	C:	He doesn't want to do the hoops today[a]
C, S, D		(Throws the lions back in the cage)[b]
		He's going sleep; he's resting
C, R, D.	C:	No one's performing today[b]
		(29 months, 28 days)

Key
M, C Mother or Child
G General
S Specific
R Relational
I Independent
D Dependent
--- (Repetitions and fillers not included)

[a]Variations by the child (e.g., negation), on act knowledge that had been contributed by the mother were not coded as independent contributions by the child.

[b]These acts were coded as dependent because although they were not contributed by the mother in the Maternal Introduction episode, they were contributed by her in a subsequent episode.

that assumes understanding of the relations among actors, actions, and props (e.g., putting lion through tamer's hoop or having lion tamer crack his whip). That children had acquired organized event knowledge was apparent also in the fact that they introduced almost no intrusions, that is, circus-inappropriate acts, to the event-unit episodes.

That the mother's language was essential to the establishment of event knowledge for the child was evidenced in several ways. First, the mother conveyed knowledge of the circus event to the child through language. All event-unit components—acts and goal-acts—were delineated in language, with action only as a complement to the verbal narration. Second, maternal language referred to a diverse series of acts with a goal label, thus emphasizing the organization of acts around a goal. For example, putting the lions in the ring, placing their trainer and stools next to them, putting the lions on the stools, and having the lions go through the tamer's hoop, were referred to with a goal-act statement, such as "the lion act," or "what the lions do in the circus." Referring to diverse acts by a goal statement presumably helped the child to consolidate them into an event. Mother's language can be seen to relate to the process of event acquisition in a third way, through the use of *fantasy*. The lion doesn't just get placed in the ring, he "comes in." He isn't just placed on a stool or through the hoop, he "sits on a stool" or "jumps through the hoop." These are instances of animate attributions, whereby language is used to attribute feelings, actions, or abilities to lifelike objects. Maternal language was also used to refer to imaginary objects that were appropriate to the activity, as, for example, when the mother referred to the figures' buying *hot dogs* and *tickets* (both nonexistent objects) at the concession booth. The imaginary nature of some event-unit components points to the necessity of using language, in particular its *nonliteral* usage, in the process of imparting event knowledge to the child by the mother.

Conclusions. This study demonstrated that "cognitive context" is acquired by the child through participation in interactive contexts with the mother. For the child this is a process of *participatory interaction*. The mother's use of language in the interaction is essential to the child's formation of a representation for the culturally specified event. In demonstrating the role of the mother and of her language in the child's acquisition of event knowledge, we emphasize the social/cultural factors that operate in the child's acquisition of event knowledge.

GENERAL CONCLUSIONS

This chapter began by referring to a dichotomy that has existed in the study of language development between those emphasizing the cognitive basis for language and those emphasizing its social basis. The event representation provides a means for conjoining cognitive and social-interactional emphases. The event representation is a cognitive entity; cognitive processes operate in its formation, and it is a constituent of the conceptual representational system of the individual. Yet, it is also a social entity, formed in part through social-cultural processes, as the third study demonstrates. Additionally, the events represented are social, that is, they involve interpersonal interaction, and for the young language-learning child this often involves mother-child interaction. This knowledge is social also because it is shared, held in common by more than one speaker of the language. Finally, such knowledge may be considered social because it impacts on the social world by affecting social-interactive behavior.

In this chapter, we have explored the relation between event representations and language in two ways. The first two sections documented how established event representations support mother and child use of language; the third section explored the use of language in mother-child interaction in establishing such representations. Thus we have revealed the interdependencies between the child's language and event knowledge.

8 Make Believe Scripts: The Transformation of ERs In Fantasy

Susan Seidman
Katherine Nelson
Janice Gruendel

The previous chapters have documented the ways in which ERs function in memory and in discourse, including the production of narratives about events and conversations within events. In the present chapter we examine some of the ways that ERs function as the source of imaginative productions in stories and play. Children's story productions and their play have in common the possibility of creating novel fantasies that have not been experienced in real life. At the same time, both can be seen to have roots in the child's own experience. However, unlike recounting episodes or producing scripts, that is, specific or general memory (Chapter 5), story and play need not stick to the facts; they allow for free flights of imagination if children are able to take advantage of this opportunity. One of the interesting questions that the script analysis raises is the extent to which children use their ERs as a basis for constructing fantasy.

Memory for stories has been used as a tool for the evaluation of script structure in both adults (e.g., Bower, Black & Turner, 1979) and children (e.g., Hudson & Nelson, 1983; McCartney & Nelson, 1979; Slackman & Nelson, 1984, see chapters 3 and 4). In the studies with children, script-based stories have generally been very closely modelled on the GER, with only the introduction of specific characters and a specified past time. Problem resolutions, the hallmark of story schemas (Mandler & Johnson, 1977; Stein & Glenn, 1979), usually have not been introduced. Thus, the child's task in remembering such stories is very close to that of producing a script based on an underlying ER. These are very boring little stories; that children can reproduce them indicates a good deal about their script-based knowledge but very little about their understanding of story structure. Of course, children may be able to use story schemas in comprehending and reproducing stories, as Mandler and others have shown, even though they are not able to use the schema to produce their own stories. Although we are interested here in children's story productions as a possible reflection of their scripts, we expect to find evidence for such a relation in story content, not necessarily in story structure. The distinction between a story schema and a script schema, and the possible ways that they may each enter into story productions, must be considered in this connection.

Symbolic play resembles story telling in that both require working through an episodic sequence for which there is little or no support from outside the child's own imaginative resources. Both must draw on what we have termed cognitive context. At the same time, play may have its own script; or, rather, different types of play may have different scripts. Moreover, because fantasy play usually involves more than one child, it also involves the sharing of scripts for play and scripts for events that form the basis for the play. Event-based play has been the topic of considerable research in recent years, and we briefly review some of that research and its most important findings in this chapter.

Following the discussion of script-based stories and event-based play, this chapter concludes with a consideration of some of the developmental questions relevant to event schemas that this research has brought out.

SCRIPT-BASED STORIES[1]

Story Structure

Scripts and stories have both been characterized as schemas with many characteristics in common (Mandler, 1983). Both have temporal-causal structure, and both seem to function in memory in similar ways through a top-down process in which activation of the schema provides the individual with expectations about subsequent acts in the event. However, there are also important differences between scripts and stories that can best be appreciated by a consideration of the basic characteristics of the constituent structure of stories (e.g., Botvin & Sutton-Smith, 1977; Kintsch, 1974; Mandler, 1983). There is wide agreement that in a single episode story the minimally acceptable set of constituents includes: A formal device or node that marks the narrative as a "story," for example, "Once upon a time . . . ," and provides stative information about the character(s), the time, and the locale of the story; several nodes that present the problem or focus of the episode, the actions (mental, emotional, or physical) of the characters, and the outcome(s) of the action; and a formal device indicating the end of the story, for example, "And they lived happily ever after." Stories are constructive,

---

[1]The research on stories reported here is based on Janice Gruendel's unpublished dissertation (Gruendel, 1980).

fictional accounts that are told in the past tense and rarely include reference to the storyteller.[2]

In contrast, children's scripts are general timeless accounts told from the point of view of the narrator without necessarily specifying other characters, times, or locales; seldom specifying mental or emotional states, actions, or motivations; involving no problems to be solved but only a routine to be followed. Whereas the same event structure may form the basis for both a script and a story, the narration of one or the other will be very different. Scripts will be produced in the timeless present tense, in the order in which actions occur, and without details of time, place or characters. Beginnings and endings will be very simple (e.g., "First you . . . ," "That's all"). Stories are told in the past tense, provide specific characters, present a problem and its resolution, and often have conventional beginnings and endings.

Previous research has provided information on how children's story productions compare with the canonical constituent structure outlined above. Ames (1966) and Pitcher and Prelinger (1963) asked children ages 2 through 5 years to "tell a story" and accepted all responses as instances of story constructions. According to this definition—that a story is what a child tells when asked to tell a story—even a child of 2 or 3 years is able to produce what is, in the child's view, a story. From a more formal perspective, however, the productions of many of these children lack some of the basic constituent units of a story. Analyzing the structural complexity of episodes in children's stories, Botvin and Sutton-Smith (1977) reported that the productions of 3- and 4-year-old children lacked even the simplest story structure, the statement of a problem and its resolution. Instead, the children's stories were described as a series of events linked in loose associative fashion, for example, "The little duck went swimming. Then the crab came. A lobster came. And a popsicle was playing by itself." In this study, by the age of 5 years, 60% of the children produced stories with a single episode; and by age eight, 50% produced stories with two or more well-developed episodes linked in a temporal series.

It appears from the Botvin and Sutton-Smith (1977) study that before the age of 5 children cannot use a story schema in their own story productions, if indeed they have a schema for what constitutes a story. Confirming this finding, Pradl (1979) re-examined the Pitcher and Prelinger (1963) story productions. In an analysis of the opening narrative strategies of the children, Pradl found that only 20% of the 2-year-olds' stories began with a formal opening device, whereas by 5 years, 73% did. The younger children's stories began with an immediate action ("The eency weency spider jumped out of the window and hurt himself") 65%

[2]These general characteristics of children's stories ignore the complexities of narrative devices found in adult narratives, such as the contrast between past and present tense uses. The description is not meant to apply to stories in general.

of the time. There was a similar trend toward increased use of conventional story endings over the period from 2 to 5 years.

Rather than being narratives with canonical story structure, some young children's productions are characterized as descriptions by Botvin and Sutton-Smith (1977). A similar characterization was put forth by Appleby (1978) based on his reanalysis of the Pitcher and Prelinger (1963) data and on a series of interviews with children about their story understanding. Appleby reported that the stories generated by young children are often expressive accounts of events "bound up closely in the world of the child" (p. 38). Ninety-seven percent of the narratives produced by the 2-year-olds were set "in the immediate world of home and family," and, within that setting, the majority of actions depicted were ones with which the children were also familiar (eating, sleeping, crying, spanking). By 5 years, the locale of only one third of the children's stories was in or near the home. As late as 6 years, according to Appleby's research (see also Friedson, 1953; Harms, 1972), children are still strongly committed to the view that stories depict true and real events. Thus it may be that young children do not distinguish between ERs for actual events and stories.

The Botvin and Sutton-Smith (1977) and Appleby (1978) studies suggest that there may be both functional and structural relations between children's scripts and their story productions. It appears that at least some of the narratives produced by children asked to make up a story derive from their ERs for familiar events in the same way that scripts do; that is, event knowledge functions in place of story knowledge. Moreover, in the absence of knowledge about the constituent structure of stories, children's story productions may resemble scripts.

The Developmental Relation between Scripts and Stories: An Empirical Study

As described in Chapter 2 (Study 6), stories were gathered from 20 children at each of three age groups—4, 6 and 8 years. Children were asked to "Tell a make-believe story about ______," with the blank being filled in with one of four events: having a birthday party, planting a garden, making cookies, or building a campfire. Each child told all four stories, which were tape-recorded for analysis. After an interval of 3 weeks, the experimenter returned and asked the children to "Tell me again what you told me last time, just the same as last time," explaining that the tape recorder had not caught the words clearly. Thus, each child told two stories about each of the four events.

Stories were first classified into the three main types of narratives described in Chapter 2: episodic (making reference to a particular event occurrence), script, and story. Stories were distinguished from scripts by the following characteristics: (a) opening statements signalling a story, describing the scene and introducing the protagonist(s); (b) at least one episode in which a problem arises and is resolved; and (c) a concluding statement.

According to these criteria, only 7% of the story productions by 8-year-olds and none of those by the 6- or 4-year-olds were true story constructions. Rather, when given the instruction to "make up a story," the children produced descriptions of actual events in the form of scripts and episodes, and three types of story-like constructions.

One type of story variant can be characterized as *elaboration,* in which the protocols included a story beginning, end, and/or protagonist but with an internal script act sequence rather than a story episode, or in which the protocol was based on a script embedded in a larger event description. An example of the first type of story elaboration is the following by a 6-year-old:

> Once there was a little boy and he was 9 years old. He wanted to plant a garden. And . . . then he planted pumpkin seeds and watermelon seeds and watermelon seeds . . . uhm . . . potato seeds and . . . and then they watered them and then they grew. And then you wait . . . you don't open them until when they're all finished growing, then you pick them and uhm . . . bring them inside and then you cut them.

In this story, although the child's response was basically a script for planting a garden, he was able to adhere to the task instructions by employing a story-beginning marker, "Once there was . . . " and by designating the actor in the story as a boy of 9. Two-thirds of the way through his narrative, however, the child returned to the "you" as subject and present tense verb, which are typical of script accounts.

An example of an elaboration that occurs through embedding a script within a specific event description from an 8-year-old is as follows:

> Three stooges hike . . . go hiking in a woods and then probably make a tent and make a fire. Then probably cook their food. . . Probably goes back in the tent and go to bed or something.

Here, building a campfire is embedded in the larger context of camping trip. Although the child designates a nonpersonal protagonist (three stooges), he describes the action in the present tense. (Although the present tense may be used by adults for narrative effect, children rarely display command of tense alterations in narrative and almost always use the past when recounting episodes or telling stories.)

A second type of story variant was the *transformation,* in which a script was varied by changing or violating some act or outcome within it. Examples of transformation stories usually accompanied by laughter include the following:

> . . . You . . . uhm . . . like make little holes or put like that. And then put seeds and when . . . like you put jelly beans in and in like a zigzag line and then it goes up and jelly beans come off the leaves and the little rows at the top. (6 year old)
>
> You throw in the chocolate chips, burn the cookies until they're black. . . Then . . . uh . . . blow the oven up . . . and that's it. (8 year old)

Transformations provide evidence that children have come to know something must be done to scripts to transform them into stories. The transformation is not as superficial as the elaborations in which the basic script is untouched. Rather, in transformations an obvious and often dramatic alteration is made in either the objects, actions, or outcomes in a typical script. Whether the change results in a list of violations, an unusual object, or an unpredicted outcome, the children who produce transformations appear to know that a story about an event is different in structure from a script about an event. What they lack, however, is the knowledge of how to construct the most appropriate transformational device, a problem-resolution structure, from their basic script knowledge.

The third type of story variant most resembled a proper story, for it included at least one *problem-resolution* structure and often included several other formal story characteristics as well. This type of story variant is illustrated by the following:

> First these people came along, and they made a big tent. And then the fire came out of a big campfire . . . so their mother could cook dinner. While she was cooking it, the fire went out and the father had to make another fire. So then the mother could finish cooking her supper. (8 year old)

In this example, the problem-resolution episode is extremely simple and even predictable from script knowledge about building a campfire: the fire goes out and someone must rebuild it.

In the next example, several levels of problems are introduced and resolved:

> There was a lady and she was going to bake cookies. She had everything out. She rolled out every cookie. And then when she got to put the flour in, she didn't have any flour. And then she went to start her car and it stopped and her car wouldn't start. So then she had to borrow some flour from another lady and she didn't have any flour! Then . . . and then she had . . . she got her car started and went to the store. (8 year old)

First, the lady lacked the necessary object, flour; then the means of obtaining the object—the car to go to the store—was unavailable; and, finally, an alternate resolution to the problem through the use of a neighbor is also unavailable. Resolution was achieved by the young storyteller, however, as the car is made to work and the would-be cook goes to the store to purchase the missing flour.

A final example of a story constructed by an 8-year-old illustrates the full development of story structure based on everyday event knowledge.

> One day a girl asked her mother if she could make cookies. And the parents said NO. She was really mad about it and everything. She went upstairs and cried and cried and cried. And they finally said OK. But when she started making them, the electric beater, it fell off down into the batter. The cookie batter was really thick, the girl had never made cookies before. So she put them in for the wrong amount of time and everything, she watched them pop up and everything. And they turned out really good! The end! (8 year old)

Using these definitions of story variants, the protocols for each age group (a total of 160 "stories" at each age) were classified into types. Even under these weak criteria, only 8% of the 4-year-olds' productions were found to be story variants, the remaining 92% being actual event descriptions (episodes or scripts). Story variants accounted for 38% of the 6-year-olds' productions and 50% of the 8-year-olds'. For these groups as well, all nonstory productions were actual event descriptions. Most of the nonstory actual event descriptions were classified as scripts rather than as scripts with partial embedded episodes or episodic recounts, although the preschoolers produced more episodes (about 30% overall) than either the 6- or 8-year-olds (less than 10%). It appears from this finding that some of the younger children might have interpreted "story" to mean "recount." Still, overall the production of scripts was the most frequent response type, with 63% of [illegible] 4-year-olds, 60% of the 6-year-olds, and 47% of the 8-year-olds produc[illegible]m when asked to tell a story.

An analysis of [illegible]n's verb tense and person of subject in stories is presented in Table 8.1. [illegible]nalysis reveals that, although even the 4-year-olds distinguished their story narratives by using the past tense more frequently than in script recounts (compare Table 2.7), and by using third person subjects rather than "I" or "You," there was an increase with age in both of these factors, consistent with the greater command of the story structure by the older children. Additionally, the use of formal story markers to begin and end the story variants increased from 38% to 42% to 83% for the 4-, 6-, and 8-year-olds, respectively. Thus, the largest increase in the use of formal marking devices occurred from the ages of 6 to 8 years, during which the use of such markers nearly doubled.

In addition to the increase with age in overall frequency of story or story variant responses, there was also a trend toward the production of more complex narratives, as shown in Table 8.2. The percentage of story variants that were elaborations, which relied heavily on script structure, declined, while problem resolution structures increased. Transformations, which varied components of the script, often with dramatic or humorous results, remained at about the same proportion at each age. Thus, with increasing age came the ability not only to

TABLE 8.1
Percentage of Verb Tense and Subject Reference in Stories by Age

	Age		
	4	*6*	*8*
	(n = 8)[a]	*(n = 31)*	*(n = 40)*
Verb Tense			
Present (timeless)	65	39	30
Past	35	56	68
Future/Conditional	0	5	2
Person Reference			
First (I, we)	18	2	5
Second (you)	41	14	13
Third (proper names, third person pronouns, other definite and indefinite referents)	41	85	82

[a]"n" refers to number of stories analyzed for each age group. See text for explanation.
Note: Based on Table 3, Gruendel, 1980.

produce stories when asked for stories, but also to construct narratives whose internal characteristics more closely conformed to canonical story structure.

As these analyses suggest, the youngest children in this study had great difficulty producing story constructions; in their place, the children produced actual event descriptions, mostly in the form of scripts. The uniformity of the 4-year-olds' performance regardless of task—scripts being produced whether one asked for actual event descriptions (see Chapter 2) or for stories about events—

TABLE 8.2
Percentage of Story Protocols by Response Type and Age

	Age		
	4	*6*	*8*
	(n = 8)[a]	*(n = 31)*	*(n = 40)*
Response Type			
Elaboration	63	68	37
Transformation	37	26	35
Problem-resolution	0	6	28

[a]"n" refers to number of stories analyzed for each age group. See text for explanation.
Note: Based on Table 2, Gruendel, 1980.

suggests either that children had no schema to guide story construction and relied instead on the structural information they did have (i.e. script structure) or that their existing story schema was not under complete operative control and thus could not compete with the better-established GER structure as a production guide. Further, although both script and story schemas are structured, the script is content-based as well and thus may be easier to use as a production guide.

Progress in the development of and/or productive control over the story schema, and hence reduced reliance on scripts for structural and content information, was evident by the age of 6 years, as children became better able to produce story-like constructions when asked to do so. Although the story productions at this age were mostly of the simplest type, that is, elaborations, they mark clear progress in the children's developing knowledge that stories have a structure that differs from that of scripts. Progress in story generation continues to 8 years, as the number of children producing story variants increases still further. It is also evident that scripts continue to exert a competing influence, at least in a task situation in which children are asked to generate stories about specific events; even at 8 years of age, 35% of the children produced predominantly scripts when asked for stories.

Thus, overall, the findings from this study indicate that the ability to produce stories according to the requirements of a story schema improves between the ages of 4 and 6 years, but even at the oldest age studied a large minority of the "stories" were simple scripts. The low occurrence of real story constructions is in apparent contradiction to the previous research showing that children of similar ages can generate stories (Botvin & Sutton-Smith, 1977) and use a story schema to facilitate recall of story material (Mandler & DeForest, 1979).

One explanation for the present findings is that the youngest children simply had not developed a story schema and hence could not use it to guide story construction. An alternative explanation that fits the findings of Mandler & DeForest is that while some of the children may have developed a story schema, it was not under complete operational control, and stories were therefore not readily produced. This is a variant of the "comprehension precedes production" argument, in that, although 6-year-old children appear to have a story schema that aids them in story recall, the schema being useful in comprehension and memory tasks, it is not available in a task requiring the use of the schema in production.

Another possible explanation for the failure of children in this study to produce stories is that requiring children to make up stories about familiar events may encourage the production of scripts rather than stories. The reasoning here is that asking for stories about particular common events may create a competition of sorts between the story schema, which may not yet be well developed, and script structures, which are event based and easily produced by young children; or it may be that the content available in ERs may simply lead the child to rely on that structure rather than the more abstract story schema. Asking specifically for event-based stories may thus increase the probability that scripts will be produced.

Whatever the correct explanation for the low frequency of story production among the younger children, it is possible to outline a progression in children's ability to generate stories on the basis of scripts. The earliest stage involves the ability to generate a script about an event, an ability apparent among 4-year-olds. At this stage children tend to produce scripts about events even when asked to generate stories. A second stage is marked by children's use of story markers, including beginning and ending formalisms and the past tense, to indicate that a story format is intended. This early period of story development, here identified as "elaboration," is still heavily reliant on script organization for the internal structure of the narrative. At a third stage, children recognize that the internal organization of the script can be modified to change it into a story, resulting in script transformations in which particular acts or outcomes of scripts are altered or violated in an attempt to produce a story. Finally, the story structure becomes fully evident in production as children employ story markers, the past tense, specification of a protagonist, and at least one problem-resolution episode in the narrative. The greatest progress in constructing stories was evident here between the ages of 6 and 8. Further development in this direction would include the ability to produce sequences and episodes that are increasingly hierarchical in organization and abstract in nature.

In general, then, this study provided evidence of a close relation between scripts and stories and revealed the possibility of conflict as well as confluence between them in children's narrative productions. A final observation on the story production task may help to illuminate both positive and negative effects of one on the other. The story production task is in some ways an odd and certainly demanding one where the child is asked to construct on the spot an imaginative, presumably novel, episodic narrative. The resources children have at their disposal for accomplishing this task presumably include script structures, episodic memory, the recounts of others' experiences, standard stories, vicarious experience through TV, and perhaps a general story schema. There was some evidence in the data that younger children interpreted the request for a story (specifically "make-believe") as a request for a personal experience; and some examples seemed as though they may have been based on personal experiences, although no inquiry was made as to whether or not this was the case.

Nonetheless, it is striking that given the varied sources that they might call on, children appear to base their story attempts overwhelmingly on the GERS, in that most of their stories are indistinguishable from script narratives and have the same format. Story variants, as discussed previously, were transparently based on scripts. It appears that children use the script structure to produce a new possible variant on that structure; but their first attempts are unsuccessful, and it appears that the script actually gets in the way, taking over from the attempt to specify a novel happening.

All in all, these results suggest that greater attention to the developing form of children's stories may uncover more details about how general structures such as story schemas and scripts work in guiding production as well as comprehension.

THE USE OF SCRIPTS IN PLAY

Children's fantasy play has much in common with story production, requiring the construction of an imaginative event sequence, but there are also important differences between the two modes. Play is more open ended, there being no single canonical form or schema underlying it. It may be structured as the child or children see fit. Play also involves nonverbal action as well as verbalization. For these reasons using event knowledge in play may be easier than constructing stories on this basis. However, when play involves more than one child, it requires the children to establish shared knowledge (Nelson & Gruendel, 1979) or shared meaning (Brenner & Mueller, 1982), or to negotiate an agreed upon play script. The requirements of dyadic make-believe play are different, but they may be no simpler than those of story construction.

A number of researchers have focused on the role of event knowledge or event schemas in children's play. For example, Wolf (1983) sees effects of event knowledge on both language and symbolic play. When symbolic play performance is placed in the larger framework of symbolic development, knowledge of what to do in play comes under the control of skills that govern semiotic function in general and skills particular to the domain of symbolic play (Gardner, 1983). In this approach, language and symbolic play are viewed as separate streams of symbolic development. However, language is a central medium for the symbolic play of preschool children, and its specific role in social play must be considered.

Garvey (1982) emphasized that the developmental history of role play is tied to interpersonal experience:

> Children learn to conduct such play, first with adult support or even explicit training or modeling, and then with age-mates, whose function grows during the third year of life from child partner to include role-play partner as well. (p. 83)

For Garvey and Berndt (1977), the knowledge basis of this social play is a schema:

> . . . the children share an abstract plan or representation of an event sequence. . . . The schema must be sufficiently abstract to subsume variant and specific guides to performance. These variants (of schemas), which we call action formats, direct pretend production. . . . Once the schema is formed, it is productive; i.e., it generates specific action formats that control the performances we observe. (p. 8)

In this way Garvey and Berndt have attempted to describe how children go from what they know to what they do in play. The researchers describe specific play schemas common to children's play, such as making a phone call, cooking/baking, dining, packing, and so on. However, they do not specifically address how children's utilization of schemas affects their discourse competence within play.

An analysis of play in terms of shared scripts is specifically directed toward explaining the role of knowledge in structuring peer play discourse. According to the scriptal view of children's dialogic capacities, "children's ability to engage in dialogue depends upon their ability to establish and maintain shared context based on mutual understanding of the situation and script" (Nelson & Gruendel, 1979). This view is based on the same assumptions as those behind the research on mother-child discourse described in Chapter 7, namely, that joint activity and joint talk require that both partners share an understanding of the event in progress. This requirement extends to the dyadic play of preschoolers in that successful cooperative play depends upon shared cognitive context, as we have defined it here, in the form of common ERs. In our view, talk in play cannot be separated from play itself; play analysis must include both verbal and nonverbal components. Analysis of conversations in play may yield greater knowledge about shared or conflicting ERs than the nonverbal component.

The scriptal view of play construction also suggests that play scripts themselves may enable children to carry through a play sequence smoothly. That is, children may develop expectations about how a particular play sequence should go, over and above their knowledge about the event on which the play is based. Thus, children may have "school play scripts" and "cooking play scripts" as well as school scripts and cooking scripts.

Understanding the use of event knowledge in imaginative play involves understanding both the individual child's organization of the sequence of events in play, and the social, interactive, goal-directed play of preschool peers. The first study reported in this chapter focuses on a comparison of the organization of children's reports of the same event in play and in real life. This study demonstrates that both real world knowledge and play scripts may be used to structure the sequence of events within pretend play. The second study explicates how scripts support both the conversations and the enactment of the shared play goal of preschool peers. This study describes developmental changes in children's use of event knowledge for social play across the preschool years.

SCRIPTS FOR PLAY AND REALISTIC EVENTS

Researchers on play have discerned a complex relationship between the content of play and reality. Garvey and Berndt (1977), in their observation that "the raw materials of make-believe are to a large extent those of the non-play world, recombined and modified within play orientation'' (p. 1), stress the ties of play to the real world. On the other hand, psychoanalytic formulations argue that "content of pretense . . . is not isomorphic with reality'' (Fein & Apfel, 1979, p. 87); pretense can change real event happenings and provide access to the conflicts and anxieties of the child.

Prior research has not been specifically directed toward determining whether children differentiate between the same event in play and in real life. In the previous section of this chapter it was shown that preschool children do not seem to differentiate between stories and scripts for real events. The same might be true of play. In a study by Evan and Rubin (1983), the methods of script research were used to investigate the developmental changes in children's reports of the sequence of events in their childhood games. In this study kindergarten, first-grade, fourth-grade, and eighth-grade children's reports of what happens when they play Simon Says, Musical Chairs, and Doggie, Doggie, Who's Got the Bone were compared. Evan and Rubin found that children of all ages volunteered game rules in an order that matched the game sequence. Younger children focused on the action elements of the games, whereas older children presented their report in a form that detailed how to play the game from beginning to end. Thus, the study confirms that in play events, as in the events of their everyday lives, children report the sequence of events in the order in which they experience the event. However, this is only a beginning step toward the comparison of children's knowledge of structure in play and in the real world.

The study reported here was designed to compare preschool and school aged children's reports of "what happens'' in some events that children both experience in real life and also use as themes for their socio-dramatic play. The three events chosen for this study were: (1) going to the store; (2) going on a trip; (3) going to the doctor. The 24 subjects in the study all attended the same private day school and were from mixed ethnic and socio-economic backgrounds. In the play condition, six preschool children (Mean Age = 5;1) and six school aged children (Mean Age = 8;5) were asked "what happens when you play'' each of the three events. In the reality condition, six preschool children (Mean Age = 5;4) and six school aged children (Mean Age = 9;1) were asked "what happens when you are going'' (1) to the store, (2) on a trip, (3) to the doctor. All of the event reports were recorded as they were given by each subject.

Each protocol was first coded for the number of propositions, that is, the utterances containing an argument and a predicate (Ochs, Schieffelin, & Platt, 1979). *Act propositions* (adapted from Hudson & Nelson, 1983) were defined as any action reported by the child in an event narrative, either realistically ("You buy things'') or fantasy based ("I pretend I have a kid''). *Relational statements* included both *act sequences* (i.e. "Well first me and my daddy walk in the store, and then I ask him how much food we are going to get'') and *conditionals*, which specify the conditions to be met for an act to occur (i.e., "If its a lot I get to ride in the shopping cart''). *Roles* indexed the number of people specifically mentioned in the event report, in the form of either pronouns (I, we), common nouns (father), proper nouns (Edith), or pretend roles ("John is the baby"). When pretend roles were assigned to a specific person, the person's name and the role were each counted separately. In all other cases, only the first mention of a role was included in this measure. *Slot fillers* were members of the same class of items (i.e., "tomatoes, spaghetti, potatoes" and "Get a check-up and a shot"). *Play props* was a measure applied exclusively to the play reports, and it indexed the mention of specific materials or locations for play (i.e., pennies for playing store and doctor set for playing doctor).

Event Comparison

Because of the small number of subjects in this study, these findings should be considered primarily as suggestive observations that may be useful in generating hypotheses for further research.

Amount of Information. Table 8.3 displays a comparison of the means of preschool and school-aged children for each measure coded in their event reports. Children of all ages apparently know less about playing doctor than about

TABLE 8.3
Comparison of the Means for Each Measure for the Play and Real Event Reports of Preschool and School Aged Children

	Events							
	Shopping		*Trip*		*Doctor*		*Total*	
	Play	*Real*	*Play*	*Real*	*Play*	*Real*	*Play*	*Real*
Propositions								
Younger	12.8	5.4	11.2	4.12	4.8	4.8	9.6	4.8
Older	8.3	8.5	8.8	10.00	7.2	6.6	8.1	8.4
Acts								
Younger	7.0	4.4	6.0	3.3	3.5	3.2	5.5	3.6
Older	7.5	5.6	6.0	6.2	5.7	5.0	6.4	5.6
Conditionals								
Younger	6.0	3.0	6.0	2.0	2.0	2.7	4.7	2.6
Older	6.3	4.8	4.8	6.3	4.3	4.3	5.1	5.1
Roles								
Younger	4.2	2.2	2.8	2.5	1.8	1.8	2.9	2.2
Older	1.8	1.6	1.7	2.3	1.8	2.5	1.8	2.1
Play Props								
Younger	1.3	0.0	0.8	0.0	0.7	0.0	0.9	0.0
Older	0.8	0.0	0.0	0.0	0.7	0.2	0.5	0.1
Slot Fillers								
Younger	4.7	0.8	1.5	0.7	0.8	0.8	2.3	0.8
Older	1.8	4.3	3.5	1.2	1.8	2.0	2.4	2.5

playing the other two events, as shown by the mean number of propositions generated for each event. There also appears to be more variability in the number of propositions across the play events than there is for the same events in realistic reports. Younger children's play reports average twice as many propositions (9.6) as do their realistic reports (4.8). Averaging across all play events, the preschool children also have twice as many conditional and slot fillers in the play reports as they do in the realistic event reports.

Why did the play reports contain more information than the realistic report of the same event? Garvey and Berndt (1977) suggested that representation of event sequences used for play "must be sufficiently abstract to subsume variant and specific guides to performance" (p. 8). That is, event sequences used for play do not rigidly determine children's plans for play. Rather, these play schemas are productive. For example, although many of Garvey and Berndt's preschool subjects utilized a Treat/Heal schema in peer play, these performances contained acts in which children healed dead pets, wounded snakes, and sick children. Additionally, children's play was often structured by the combination of multiple schemas.

The play reports of children in the present study also reflected the way schemas are used productively in play. The generative capacity of event knowledge used for play was manifested in the relatively greater production of conditionals, acts, and slot fillers in the play than in the realistic event reports. The content of play reports was more diverse than were the realistic reports of the same event. There is evidently an important distinction between young children's knowledge of events and their use of event knowledge in planning or reporting about play. Whereas script reports contain information on *usual* happenings, play reports contain information on *possible* happenings. The greater elaboration of play reports reflects the expansions that occur when preschoolers report on or perform in play.

On almost every measure, older children's play and realistic reports are more equivalent than younger children's reports. The reason for this is unclear, but we may speculate that older children may no longer play doctor, school, or shopping. This possibility was suggested by several children who stated that they did not play the events they were asked to report on. If this is so, it is possible that they utilized knowledge of the real life event structure in both their realistic and play event reports. This strategy would result in minimal differences in the amount of information in the two types of event reports.

A feature of preschool play reports, in contrast to realistic reports, is that they contain lists of related items. This suggests that play may provide an opportunity for the younger child to rehearse the membership of a class of objects. For example, play shopping event reports often contained lists of food items, play trips yielded lists of places, and doctor play reports sometimes had lists of medical procedures. This characteristic of play is also revealed in the actual play conversations of preschool dyads, as described later in this chapter.

Except for these differences, both play and reality scripts appear to have the same componential structure. Both are composed of sequentially ordered acts. Mention of roles is also central in both types of event reports.

For the younger child, play seems more closely tied to material objects than are real-event reports. This is shown by more frequent mention of both slot fillers and play props in the preschool children's play reports. On the other hand, school-aged children's play and reality measures are in close accord, possibly because, as noted earlier, older children may have generated realistic event reports in both the play and reality conditions.

Structure of Event Reports. The distribution of all play and reality event reports into categories of event structure described below is shown in Table 8.4. This table documents that the majority of both preschool and school-aged children's event reports were sequentially ordered. The structure of younger children's reports was more diverse in the play than in the reality condition. This suggests that event knowledge is not the only building block in the construction of play. Play reports are organized by diverse forms of knowledge, including scripts from everyday life and specific "scripts for play" that are sometimes embedded within the structure of their school day. The examples of each type of play report that follow reveal the differences in the composition of these play forms.

Act Sequence. This was the most common form of event report of the older children, in both play and reality conditions, and the most frequent reality report type of the preschool children. These reports match the sequence of the events as they occur in real life and have the classic structure of a script report (see Gruendel, 1980). Here, a five-year-old boy tells what happens when he plays going on a trip:

> Sometimes I pretend I'm in a car. And I get to the farm. I see horses, cows, and chickens.

TABLE 8.4
Frequency of Play and Reality Report Types of Preschool and School Aged Children Across All Events Combined

	Younger		*Older*	
Report Type	*Play*	*Reality*	*Play*	*Reality*
Act Sequenced	3	9	8	12
Act Play Sequenced	4	—	4	—
Act School Sequenced	3	—	—	—
Act Non-sequential	5	8	4	4
Miscellaneous	3	—	2	2
Total Reports	18	17	18	18

Another five year old boy offers the following ''scripted'' play report on going shopping:

> First I would go to the supermarket and buy stuff. And then I would buy something that I needed. Not food, but stuff that I needed to clean the house. Then I would go to the cash register and pay. Then I would walk out of the store.

This script for shopping, containing a beginning, a middle, and an ending, could provide this child with a solid content base for actually playing the game of going shopping with a friend. However, scripts are not the only type of knowledge children use to plan play.

Act Play Sequences. It has been suggested that children learn ''scripts for play'' in particular contexts that subsequently serve as guides to their play in that context (Seidman, 1983a). In this study, over one fifth of the play reports were characterized as act play sequences, in which children specified the particular objects, locations, and their transformed identities, which they utilized when playing particular dramatic play games.

The best example of these ''scripts for play'' is from a five-year-old girl reporting on doctor play:

> I use the doctor set. I doctor myself sometimes. And my friend doctors me. I lie on the bench. And then my friend doctors me. We used to have a blanket but we came to school one day, we couldn't find the blanket. So we have to use a dress. It looks like a blanket. We use the coat-dress like a blanket.

Note that this pretend game has a history, as seen in the statement ''we used to have a blanket.'' Note also the specific details in the same child's play script for shopping.

> I pretend I have a kid. So I tell them I'll be right back. And then I go in the other room. I'm going to go to the market to get some food. I really go to the bathroom and come right back. I keep going to the bathroom and come right back. And then Allison M., I play with her. So we both. . . One part we both pretend we have babies. So Nicki, she helps. She's Allison's kid. Casey is my kid. So we pretend Allison F. is the maid. And then. You know the carriage? There are a few kids. Allison F. uses the bed. Allison M. uses the crib. Nicki uses the floor. And then we all go to sleep. And then we pretend we get up it's morning. Then we go to the market again. Then we all go on a picnic in the playhouse. And then the table cloth in the playhouse. We put that on the floor and we spread it out. And we put dishes on the floor and pretend we are eating. And that is all.

With her friends, this little girl has developed a specific play identity for each player of the game. Playing shopping is, for her, embedded in her larger family role-play games. The play reports of other children are embedded within their scripts for the school day. Zach, for example, presented a very detailed script for playing trip, which he ended by saying:

> And then we put the stuff back. And we do different things, like having a little snack.

Act School Sequenced. Reports of play are sometimes tightly interwoven with the routine of the school day. Sometimes a request for a report on "what happens when you play" produced reports on what happens in a school day. This often occurred when the child did not have a well-articulated play report for a particular theme of play. The following four-year-old girl's report on playing shopping illustrates this type of report:

> I go upstairs. And I play with the children upstairs in the shop. Where it is at the coop. I don't go to stores. I just go to the coop. When I come to school I play house with Bessie. And then after I take meeting. And then after that we take a nap. First we eat lunch, and then we get up and draw. And then we go home. And Nora comes for school. So when the teachers are sick. And they have to stay home. And when Bianca sick, Nora stays with Mary.

For some children, then, it seems that the definition of play is more generally applied to what you do with friends at school. This finding suggests that play knowledge is organized both in a general form—as the activities you do with your friend in school—and in a specific form—as the activity you play with particular friends in particular locations.

Act Nonsequential. These reports were statements of a single act, followed by a list of related objects. This form of report was more common in the younger group's play and reality reports. A typical nonsequential play report for shopping is the following from a five-year-old boy:

> And sometimes we get apples, oranges, and chicken and beef and steak and bacon, milk, cheese, ham. One thing more is I get orange juice and apple juice.

Reports that were not clearly either play or reality based were coded *Miscellaneous.*

In summary, play and event reports generally share a common, sequential structure. However, the play reports of younger children rely on layers of knowledge derived from the events in real life, the pretend events as the children have learned to play them, and knowledge of playing in school. Scripts of real-life events, scripts for play and scripts for school, appear to be the pieces that structure the multiple layering of event sequences in the types of play investigated in this study.

EVENT KNOWLEDGE IN THE CREATION OF PRETEND PLAY

As the previous study and Evan and Rubin's (1983) research demonstrate, children know a great deal about "what happens" in their play. This knowledge provides them with a basis for knowing "what to do" in play. For example, it would be safe to assume that a child who can report the rules of baseball is a better player than one without any knowledge of the game; but, if both children know what happens in the game, then a better way to discover the better player is to watch them play. That is, understanding the cognitive basis for children's play requires examination of both their conceptions of play and their play performance.

The script and schema theories described earlier considered specifically how peer play dialogues related to the cognitive representational systems of young children. Garvey and Berndt (1977) proposed that the basis of verbal plans for play are schemas, which are defined as abstract plans or representations of an event sequence. In their model, these schemas guide play and are realized in the action formats of peer players. For example, cooking/baking, dining, travelling, provisioning/shopping, and building/repairing were common action formats for the young pretenders these authors observed.

Nelson and Gruendel (1979) also discussed how children's general knowledge systems influence their ability to converse with peers in play situations. They presented examples of both realistic and pretend dialogues of young peers audiotaped in their preschool. These conversations contained numerous exchanges of contingent, social speech and appeared to be organized around mutually shared scripts for events that the children were familiar with, such as mealtimes and the school day. Script theory suggests that, when a pair of children utilize a well-known event as the topic of their conversation, there is a high probability that both members of the dyad will be able to engage in an extended dialogue that is coherent in both form and content.

The dialogic hypothesis that was proposed by Nelson and Gruendel (1979) specifies the conditions necessary for peers to engage in extensive conversations: ". . . when both conversational structure and content knowledge are shared by young participants in a language situation, dialogue may be expected to occur" (Nelson p. 75). Given this proposal, the extent to which peers utilize script knowledge in play discourse and the function of scripts in the creation of shared fantasy emerge as important questions, and the research reported here was undertaken to investigate these issues.

Scripts for Play

The next study to be reported investigated the extent to which event-based fantasy is utilized by young peers. It was hypothesized that, if scripts are necessary for children to share fantasy, then peer conversations based on scripts should emerge in diverse play settings. To test this proposal, three pairs of children were audiotaped while each engaged in 15-minute sessions of sandbox, playdough, and toy telephone play. The longest dialogue was extracted from the speech corpus of each dyad. Analysis of the content of these conversations revealed two things. First, across the three different play settings, the majority of the longest play dialogues were scripted in the sense that they contained multiple, interrelated play acts that were sequentially organized. Second, each setting had a different, particular script that organized play in that context. Playdough play yielded conversations based on food preparation events, sandbox play was organized around birthday party scripts, and planning a visit structured telephone talk (Nelson & Seidman, 1984).

This study provided evidence that peers utilize events in sharing fantasy and that different events structure play in specific contexts. Similarly, Boynton and French (1983), in a study of the playtalk of a group of young children, found that a cooking fantasy emerged in the kitchen corner; the conversations in the block and jungle gym area were shorter, less elaborated, and did not focus on a single event. They concluded that the quality and quantity of peer speech "varied as a function of whether the *content* of the children's play is scripted, which in turn varies as a function of the physical *context* in which play occurs" (French et al., in press, p. 21). Given the contextual variability in the use of scripts in play, further understanding of how scripts structure the play interactions and talk of peers requires a systematic study of several dyads engaged in play in the same setting. Another study of sandbox players was designed toward this end.

Based on the prior work, it was proposed in this study that peer dialogues would emerge only when the young participants used shared script knowledge to structure their conversations (Nelson & Gruendel, 1979; Nelson & Seidman, 1984). To investigate this proposal, ten dyads between the ages of 36 and 63 months were audiotaped during a 12-minute session of sandbox play. The play materials were a sand-filled tank containing a plastic container with a top, a measuring cup, two shovels, and a large spoon. All of the talk of the participants was transcribed, and each utterance was coded both for its relevance to the partner's previous utterance and for its thematic content. Thematic measures captured the interactive goals that the dyad pursued through their talk. Thus, one or more exchanges of relevant talk with the same thematic content constituted a thematic conversation.

Thematic Content of Conversations. During sandbox play, children engaged in play dialogues around three different interactive goals: fantasy play, functional object play, and ownership of play materials. Fantasy play involved conversations that evoked or sustained an imaginative context, whereas object play was reality based. Children frequently shifted their interactive goals across their 12-minute play sessions. (Seidman, 1983b). Fantasy play conversations most often had an event-based structure: 79% of the utterances in fantasy play were classified as script based. Moreover, there were significantly more utterances in script-based conversations than in nonscripted play. Additionally, whenever a pretend play episode re-emerged in the stream of verbal interaction, it was almost always topically related to the events of play previously established in discourse. It became clear that events structured more than just one pretense conversation; scripts organized pretense across the entire verbal interaction. In contrast to pretend play, physical object play was structured by action sequences in which talk described or referenced play actions that accompanied the manipulation of familiar objects (see Nelson & Seidman, 1984).

In conclusion, there are both similarities and differences between the resources peers utilize when engaging in pretend and physical object play conversations. In general, maintenance of peer dialogues requires both social skill and conversational competence. Admittedly, children who have greater skill in peer interaction will have a broader repertoire of available techniques for engaging other children. Still, one of the major tasks faced by any young player is finding a relevant topic to talk about. In physical object play, children can utilize the "here and now" context of their actions to provide the support for dialogues about their own actions and properties of their play materials. However, the use of language in pretend play requires the ability to become free of the immediate context (Sachs, Goldman, & Chaille, 1984) and develop ideas in talk that go beyond the given identities of objects or people (El'konin, 1966). And as demonstrated here, shared event knowledge has a central role in enabling children to develop fantasy dialogues.

Developmental Changes in the Use of Event Knowledge for Fantasy Dialogues. We have presented evidence that scripts are important in enabling young peers to engage in elaborated and extensive pretend play dialogues. We have also found that event-based play has an important role in the maintenance and development of fantasy across an entire segment of peer interaction. However, there are developmental changes in the use of event knowledge for play talk. This is illustrated by an analysis of the fantasy conversations of each dyad during sandbox play. A pretend play conversation was defined as one or more exchanges of relevant talk in which the majority of the utterances evoked or sustained a fantasy.

Tables 8.5 and 8.6 list the content of every pretend play conversation that occurred in the 12-minute play sessions of each pair of sandbox players. Dyads are numbered in order of increasing age. For dyads 1 and 2, symbolic play was not the goal of their interaction; they focused instead on manipulation and talk about play materials. For the children approaching the end of their fourth year, pretense was an important goal of their interaction. Dyads 3 and 4 both displayed event-based pretend conversations, as did dyads 6, 7, 8, 9, and 10.

Creating conversation is based, in part, on the child's ability or willingness to

TABLE 8.5
Development of Content of Pretend Play Conversation of 3-Year-Old Dyads (1-4)

	Dyads			
Conversations	*1*	*2*	*3*	*4*
First	Got cake	It's cookies	Make playdough	Make cake
Second			Add H_2O to playdough	Sing Happy Birthday
Third			Mix playdough	Sing Happy Birthday
Fourth			Make playdough	Make coffee
Fifth			Make and cover playdough	Try to be Mommie
Sixth			Put playdough in bucket	Sing Happy Birthday
Seventh				
Eighth				
Ninth				
Tenth				
Eleventh				
Twelfth				

follow a turn-taking structure while talking with his or her co-player (Keenan & Schiefflin, 1976). Beyond this, there appear to be additional skills that facilitate the display of elaborate script sequences in conversations, as the following analysis reveals.

Transforming the Object. In this situation, before children could initiate an event-based play episode in the sandbox context, the transformed identity of the plastic container had to be mutually established. In the single pretend play conversation of dyads 1 and 2, this task was not accomplished. Here, 3-year-old N questions her friend, P:

N: What you doing.
P: Get the cake.
N: What? Get the cake?
P: Yeah.

In the statement, "Get the cake," P assumes that N knows the sand-filled bucket is a cake. N doesn't catch on, and these players never enter a play frame. Clearly, ability to play is a function both of thinking about re-naming objects and successfully communicating that transformation. In the next example from dyad 2, M has a hard time keeping track of her own transformation.

M: It's cookies. Wait!
T: Yeah it is.
M: Where is it?
T: Wait.

For the pretense to continue, the cookie identity of the bucket must be established again. However, the friends proceed to argue over ownership of the play materials, and event-based fantasy never develops. For pretense conversation to develop, it is necessary for object transformations of play material to be shared.

Event Structure from Real Life. Dyad 3 is successful in play, in part because they constantly reassert the make-believe identities of the materials in the sandbox. Once they successfully negotiate the transformation of the objects, they proceed to develop an event-based play scenario, which is woven across their twelve minutes of interaction as follows:

A: O.K. Playdough.
J: This is the flour.
A: The playdough.
J: This is the flour. I have to mix it.
A: Playdough.
J: So this will be playdough. And then you can get this and mix it. The playdough.

The event of the fantasy is making playdough, an occurrence they have frequently observed in their day care center. A is explicitly marking the transformed status of the container; J added the new information to recreate the script, and she continued to add additional elements.

J: You're putting the water to the playdough. Cause this playdough and that's the water.
A: Yeah.
J: You're putting some water.
A: Yeah.
J: You're putting some water.
A: Yeah.
J: Oh so it get so sparkerly. Oh! You are making alot of playdough. For later, right? Right A?
A: I'm the daddy.
J: Oh my!
A: It the water, water.

A knew exactly what J was talking about, even though she herself did not suggest any acts from the making playdough script. Note that in the last exchange, she takes up the suggestion about a transformation that was previously contributed by J. In subsequent conversations, the girls continued to make the playdough, as seen in Table 8.5. They ended by putting the "playdough" into the plastic container.

TABLE 8.6
Development of Content of Pretend Play Conversations of 4-Year-Old Dyads (6-10)

	Dyads				
Conversations	*6*	*7*	*8*	*9*	*10*
First	Establish egg and water	Build castle	Play bakery shop make cake	Make rice assign mother role	Make something
Second	Crack egg	Establish cake	Add sugar and mix	Make food place in fridge	Ask if know how to make cornmeal
Third	Private fantasy	Make jello	Add peanuts	Mother request water	Establish father feed him food father evaluates food
Fourth	Argue over making egg salad	Add pounds	Add more nuts give cake to truck	Ask mother what she wants	Suggest make pancakes
Fifth	Argue over making egg salad	Make cookies in bakery shop	Add chocolate	Ask mother what she wants	Make meatballs
Sixth			Add sugar	Add water and cook	Mix food Pancakes? Meatballs?
Seventh			Add chocolate and grape	Assign sister role	
Eighth				Ask about sister role	
Ninth				Make ice cream	
Tenth				Ask mother needs more ice cream	
Eleventh				Make coffee	
Twelfth				Cook make cake	

A and J's event-based dialogues reveal that agreement on the transformation of the objects is critical for successful play. They maintained this agreement by repeating the word playdough twenty times! Once there was a stable symbolic identity to play with, the children were able to add novel acts that were contained in their scripts for making playdough. Thus, their play had a high degree of cohesion across their entire interaction.

As Table 8.6 reveals, the pretend conversations of each dyad were not always structured by the same event. It is also possible to have multiple transformations of the same object, as shown by dyad 6. However, even in this case, real-life knowledge of the acts entailed in making food provided a structure for pretend play talk. Whereas younger children relied on the repetition of the pretend name of the object to sustain their conversation, older children utilized paradigmatic play acts to develop their play. Dyad 8 elaborated their cake fantasy by adding peanuts, chocolate, and grapes. The use of related objects to elaborate play performances was also a characteristic of the play reports of preschool children, in the first study reported here.

Playing Two Roles in an Event. In addition to knowledge of events, children in play display knowledge of the behavior and experiential capacities people have in common (Wolf, Rygh & Altshuler, 1983). When playing a role, people can express more than just the sequence of events; they can also express the needs, desires, and personalities of the characters. However, maintaining a character in play probably cannot occur until children are able to integrate reciprocal roles within an event sequence. This capacity was displayed by dyad 10, who assumed the roles of mother and father. The mother role was first enacted through the cooking activities of the girl player (see Table 8.6). After a period of cooperative cooking, the girl (A) assigned the boy (B) a complementary role:

A: Father?
B: What?
A: Ready. (She shows him her sand-filled container.)
B: I know. I need this. We need this.
A: I made it for you to taste. Be my guest. Is it good?
B: No. It needs a little bit more sugar.
A: O.K.
B: I'll do it.
A: O.K., that it?
B: Yeah.
A: Can we mix it? Now taste it.
B: It's good.
A: *Real* good?
B: Yeah.

Here, A and B judged each others actions from the perspective of their conception of mother's and father's roles in cooking. Enacting events in character may result in the repetition, addition or deletion of particular acts in the play scenario. For example, B, as the father-taster, decided to add more sugar, an act suggested by his pretend evaluation of the food. However, even when characters use roles, events still provide the settings that characters use to develop their roles. Garvey and Berndt (1977) have suggested that when both role and schemata govern play, the actions and events appear to be performed not for their own sake, but rather the events are dominated by the assumed identities of the characters. The interrelationships between event and role knowledge in the emerging competence of young peers in fantasy play is a topic that needs further investigation.

PLAY AND STORIES AS SYMBOLIC DEVELOPMENTS

Both the conversational and the play report studies provide new insights into the relationships among knowledge of what happens, of what to do, and of what to say in play. Although event knowledge structured both the make-believe play reports and social play conversations, the display of scripts was modified by the particular form used to orchestrate the play. In reporting the events of play, creating an event report requires that children select a sequence of acts to represent their play events. The social play conversations of children are more complex; they rely on the consistent transformation of play objects. Connections are established between pretend objects and events, and roles and events. Finally, multiple roles are integrated within an event structure. These constructions require the creation of coordinated sequences in both action and in language.

In contrast to the story-telling task, in the play situation children almost always have props available to support their make-believe, even though these props may need agreed-upon definitions, as in the sandbox study. Thus, although the two contexts may call on the same basic ERs and require some of the same skills in transforming reality into make-believe, they differ in the complexity of the activity itself and in the support offered by props and peers. Even though play requires cooperation, sharing knowledge and expectations about roles and event sequences, and coordinating action and dialogue, it appears to be the easier performance for young children. This apparent outcome may, however, be only a reflection of the fact that in our preschool culture children have a great deal of practice in fantasy play of different kinds, whereas their experience of story telling is primarily passive.

Before leaving this topic of the use of ERs in fantasy, we speculate on the possible relation between symbolic play, cognitive development and event knowledge. A number of authors (e.g., Saltz, Dixon & Johnson, 1977;

Smilansky, 1968) have claimed that practice or skill in symbolic play is associated with advances in cognitive development as assessed by standard tests. Symbolic play calls on a number of separate skills, including role-taking, negotiating with a partner, planning, and sequencing. All these skills require basic event knowledge. The observation that symbolic play is related in some way to general cognitive development may thus be a reflection of the relation between event knowledge and cognitive development, which is considered in Chapter 11. Cognitive advance might be related to ER development and thus to play skills either because well-structured ERs support symbolic play most effectively; or because the use of ERs in play enables their further development, analysis, and flexible use. Currently available research does not provide any basis for choosing between these alternative hypotheses; indeed, both may be true, reflecting an interactive relation between ER development and play. Whether skill in story telling reflects a similar relationship is not known, although there is a widely held belief that exposure to stories in early childhood facilitates cognitive development. These speculations suggest important relationships that deserve more systematic investigation.

9 Event Representations as the Basis for Categorical Knowledge

Joan Lucariello
Anthony Rifkin

Previous chapters in this book have documented the psychological importance of event knowledge in cognitive activities and in the understanding and production of language. The present chapter examines some knowledge organizations that may be derived or constructed from event representations. The major premise of this chapter is that event representations constitute knowledge of experience in the world and that cognitive processes operate on these (and presumably other representations) rather than on the perceived world. Such operations, in turn, may lead to the construction of new forms of knowledge. Thus, one course of early cognitive development is the evolution of different, more abstract forms of knowledge from a base of established representations. This kind of development can be thought of as a form of cognitive "creativity" involving the creation of new, higher order information not present in the original knowledge state.

In this chapter we describe two kinds of knowledge organization that can be derived or constructed from event representations. In the first section, we examine the relation between two contrasting types of knowledge organization, which have been described by Mandler (1979; 1983). One type, usually identified with semantic memory, is that of the taxonomic category, hierarchically arranged (Collins & Quillian, 1969; Tulving, 1972). This type of organization is based on class inclusion relationships among superordinate and subordinate classes. In this section we are concerned with *object* categories. The second type of organization is the schema, and in the focus of this chapter, the event schema, which has been described at length in previous chapters.

In the present proposal, these two types of knowledge structures are assumed to be complementary and derivationally related in the following sense. As the research presented in previous chapters indicates, event representations are a major form of conceptual representation for the young child. It is hypothesized here that the semantic system, or knowledge of taxonomic categories hierarchically arranged, develops through cognitive analysis, that is, through the abstraction of patterns of relationships present in the event representation base (see Nelson, 1985, for a fuller explication of this proposal).

In the second section of this chapter, we explore the kinds of organizations that event knowledge itself can enter into: both taxonomic and part-whole relations involving the embedding of events within one another. These different kinds of organization of event knowledge are described in terms of *event categories* derived from basic event representations.

OBJECT GROUPINGS

Children's knowledge of the taxonomic, hierarchical relationships among object categories has received considerable theoretical and empirical attention in the cognitive development literature. Two issues are centrally important here. One controversial issue is *when* children acquire this knowledge. There are those who propose that such knowledge is available to the child in the preschool years and even earlier (see Mandler, 1979, for review; also Smiley & Brown, 1979); but there is also evidence from a wide number of experimental paradigms indicating that such knowledge is either not available or not readily utilized until approximately 7 or 8 years of age, or even later. This evidence comes from tasks such as word associations (see Nelson, 1977 for review), semantic-priming (e.g., McCauley, Weil, & Sperber, 1976), list recall (see Ornstein & Corsale, 1979, for review), classification (e.g., Inhelder & Piaget, 1964; Olver & Hornsby, 1966; Rosch, Mervis, Gray, Johnson, & Boyes-Braem, 1976), and class inclusion (see Winer, 1980, for review).

A second, related issue is *how* children acquire knowledge of the taxonomic relationships among object categories. Within developmental psychology there have been four major proposals regarding this issue. One proposal, advanced by the Piagetian school (Inhelder & Piaget, 1964), is that the development of classification is an outcome of the development of logical operations in the concrete operational child. According to this view, preoperational or intuitive children cannot deal with class-inclusion relations and thus with hierarchical classification. Although they can add two subordinate classes ($A_1 + A_2$) to equal the superordinate class (B), they lack reversibility of the transformations, that is, the joint logical operations of addition and subtraction. In other words, they cannot reverse the additive operation (e.g., $B - A_2 = A_1$). This claim is supported by extensive research on class inclusion problems (Winer, 1980).

A second proposal as to how children acquire this knowledge has been advanced by Rosch and her colleagues (Rosch et al., 1976; Rosch, 1978) in connection with her theory of categorization. A major premise in this theory is that the perceived world is not an arbitrary, unstructured set of equiprobable, co-occurring attributes. Rather the material objects of the world are perceived as possessing a high degree of correlational structure. Rosch et al., (1976) found that the correlations among attributes vary at different hierarchical levels and are strongest and most apparent at what they termed the basic-level. Rosch et al. proposed a developmental order to the acquisition of subordinate-, basic-, and superordinate-level categories. Basic-level categories, and terms for them should generally be acquired before categories and terms at other levels of the hierarchy are acquired. The order of acquisition of category levels and terms has been the subject of considerable research activity in recent years, and this work has generally supported the primacy of the basic-level (see Anglin, 1977; Brown, 1958; Daehler, Lonardo, & Bukatko, 1979; Horton & Markman, 1980; Mervis & Crisafi, 1982; Rosch et al., 1976).

A third explanation of how children acquire understanding of the taxonomic relationships among object categories emphasizes *linguistic* factors, such as shorter names, greater frequency of name use, and the provision of information on category relations through the use of multiple labels and explicit instructions on inclusion relations. There has been considerable research describing adult, usually maternal, labeling practices (e.g., Blewit, 1983a; Wales, Colman, & Pattison, 1983), and studying the effect of such practices on the understanding and acquisition-order of categories in children (Blewitt, 1983b; Shipley, Kuhn, & Madden, 1983; White, 1982). This research supports the supposition that verbalization of and about category terms plays a role in the young child's acquisition of categorical knowledge.

Each of these three accounts points to different factors involved in the child's acquisition of knowledge about the taxonomic relations among object categories. Certainly, logical operations, the organized distribution of featural information provided by the perceived world, and language play a role in this knowledge-acquisition process. Yet, one factor not considered by these approaches is the child's understanding or conceptualization of the real world. As the empirical work presented throughout this book indicates, a primary way in which the child represents experience in the world or organizes knowledge about the world is through event schemas. An important question, then, is whether the *form* of this knowledge of the world is useful to the child in acquiring knowledge about the taxonomic organization of object categories.

To address this question, we look to a fourth approach to the study of children's knowledge of taxonomic relationships among object categories, that is, to a schema-based approach. The premise here is that object concepts are organized and learned within the framework of event representations and that only gradually are these concepts freed from the contexts in which they were learned and regrouped into hierarchical relationships on the basis of similarity, class membership, and logical differentiation (Mandler, 1979; Nelson, 1982a; 1983).

In this section we outline a schema-based account proposed by Nelson

(1982a; 1983), specifying *how* taxonomic knowledge is constructed from a basically schematically organized memory system. This account may help to resolve the issue of *when* knowledge of the hierarchical relationships among object categories is available to the child.

The Slot Filler Model

The research presented in the previous chapters indicated that young children understand the events they take part in within organized structures (e.g., lunch, bedtime) that include not only appropriate actions (e.g., eating, sleeping) but also appropriate objects that complement these actions. These objects share the same function and hence occur in the same position in a given event representation. They fill the slots that complement the actions, for example, the different items that can be eaten or drunk within a representation of lunch. Very often, these objects alternatively occupy the slots over different occurrences of the event. For example, on one occasion the child may eat chicken and peas for dinner, and on another occasion fish and potatoes may fill the same slots. Learning a simple category, such as dinner food, involves the abstraction of alternative fillers for the slots. Thus, these categories are based on alternatives, or on what are termed *paradigmatic*[1] relations.

Slot filler categories are formed on the basis of shared function. Shared function represents the principle of substitutability within a frame (the paradigmatic relation in linguistics), in this case the frame Act + _____. Since Hume, two bases of association have been recognized—similarity and contiguity in space-time—and these are reflected in the presumed bases for category formation and formation of thematic groups (e.g., cup and milk) respectively. Although the members of slot filler categories may be similar to one another (e.g., oranges and apples are both round) and may be seen contiguously in space-time (e.g., pants and shirts), the present claim is that neither of these conditions is necessary to the formation of the category and may not even be sufficient. Rather, shared function, or substitutability, is the essential relation in the formation of the child's early taxonomic categories.

Thus, it is hypothesized that slot fillers form the child's initial semantic category structures. The fully developed hierarchical taxonomic category draws on members from different event representations, and these usually represent different subcategories, for example, the subcategories of clothes for bed and outdoor clothes. (A note of caution here is in order because there are some subcategories that cross ER lines [e.g., meat as a subcategory of food]). In the

---

[1]The terms syntagmatic and paradigmatic are used here in their cognitive sense (Nelson, 1982a), and not in the strictly linguistic sense based on Saussure (Lyons, 1977). As here defined, syntagmatic relations are relations between elements of different types that occur in a sequential structure. Paradigmatic relations are relations between elements of the same type occurring in similar contexts in different structures.

formation of categories, objects that share the same function but that occur in different event representational structures (e.g., eat toast for breakfast; eat bologna for lunch) are joined into a single category, with the category term ("food") applied to both. This move is assumed to require a higher level of paradigmatic abstraction than the simple slot filler category and is, therefore, hypothesized to be a later, more advanced development.

This model also takes into account the role of linguistic factors in the acquisition of categorical knowledge. Language is thought to aid the cognitive disposition to join the subcategories from different event representations and may even be necessary to this move by applying the same term (e.g., "food") to all of them (see Nelson, 1985).

As the foregoing suggests, the slot filler model of categorical structure implies that different event representations may define different subcategories; ontogenetically, for categories derived from the child's real world experience, event representation based subcategories are combined into larger taxonomic categories as the child develops, learns, and is taught. The slot filler model, then, suggests a basis for categorical evolution. The contrast between taxonomic and slot filler presented here is a developmental one; it is assumed that the slot filler categories combine in time to form fully developed, hierarchically organized taxonomic structures.

The research reported here was undertaken to assess the psychological validity of slot filler categories. A list recall paradigm was utilized, following the established research tradition based on the assumption that children's recall and clustering of categorized word lists are indices of the implicit categorical organization of their knowledge base. (For a full report of this research see Lucariello and Nelson, 1985).

For the first experiment, two recall lists were constructed. By questioning preschoolers about objects associated with a single action in a given event, we elicited words in the categories of clothes, food, and animals. Within the clothes category, children were asked to report clothes they could wear in the morning, wear outside, and wear to bed. Within the animal category, they were asked for animals they could see at the zoo, the farm, or at home. Within the food category, they were asked for foods they could eat at breakfast, lunch and dessert. Next, the most frequently mentioned response for each subcategory question was used to compose a taxonomic list: pants, coat, pajamas, elephant, cow, dog, toast, cheese, ice cream. The slot filler list was composed of the three most frequent responses in each of the following subcategories: zoo animals, lunch foods, and morning clothes. The items were: elephant, tiger, lion; peanut butter, cheese, bologna; pants, shirt, socks.

Two groups of preschoolers were presented with the taxonomic list in either a free or constrained recall condition using taxonomic cues, such as "Tell me all the (clothes, food, animals) we just said." Two groups received the slot filler list in the same two conditions. In addition, the slot filler list only was used in a script-cue condition in which children were asked, "Tell me which of those things you could eat for lunch, see at the zoo, and wear in the morning." The first four conditions compare the effect of the composition of the categories from one or three different event representations; the last two compare the effect of taxonomic or script-cues on recall of the same list, the slot filler list.

The results are straightforward. Recall was significantly higher for the slot filler list than for the taxonomic list in both free and constrained recall conditions. Moreover, in free recall, clustering was significantly higher for the slot filler list. The highest level of recall was found for the slot filler list in the script-cue condition, indicating the salience of cues that reflects the basis on which categories are initially formed.

These findings indicate that slot filler categories, or event schema based subcategories, represent a closer match to the organization of semantic memory in the preschool child than do broad taxonomic categories. They illustrate the importance of event representations for the construction of object categories, and they support the position that taxonomic organization independent of experienced events is not very salient for the preschool child.

Components of Long-Term Memory

The results of our first slot filler experiment indicate that event representations are powerful in supporting the use of semantic categories for young children. However, two types of relationships are exhibited in event representations; syntagmatic or complementary relations, and paradigmatic or categorical relations. The organization of the event representation assumes that "lunch," for example, is a header or node under which are organized a sequence of acts, each of which may implicate objects that complement the act. These objects share the same function, and such object groupings form slot filler categories. It is important to reiterate that, in many cases, the objects that may complement an act are not present at the same time. For example, a child usually does not eat peanut butter or bologna at the same time but does know that they are slot fillers for things that can be eaten at lunch. The association among such items is based primarily on paradigmatic abstraction and is not based on contiguity in the same time-space; that is, it is not directly based on experience. Items that appear together in the same time-space are considered *complementary* or *thematic* relations (see Denney, 1974), and when they also bear some functional relation to one another they are considered *functional* or *syntagmatic* relations (see Denney & Ziobrowski, 1972). For example, peanut butter and bologna are considered slot fillers for the lunch event, but bologna and plate share a syntagmatic relation for the same event. However, even in cases where items from the same slot filler category do appear in the same time-space, for example, pants and socks, these items share more than a simple spatial-temporal link. Members of slot filler categories share a common function, and thereby substitute for one another within the same slot in an event representation. It is in these ways that they are essentially different from complementary or syntagmatic groupings.

It was important to examine whether shared function and position (slot) in an event representation provide a more powerful basis for object organization than do simple spatial-temporal associations among objects and whether spatial-temporal or syntagmatic associations may represent another basis for the organization of objects. The taxonomic and slot filler lists used in the first experiment were therefore presented to preschoolers in a free recall memory task, together with a new third list, a *complementary list.* The third list contained categorically different items that bear a functional relation to one another (but do not share the same function) and are present in the same spatial-temporal contexts as the slot fillers (but do not occupy the same slot). The list items were: elephant, peanuts, cage, sandwich, plate, cup, pants, closet, hanger.

Here again, the results were straightforward. Recall and clustering were significantly higher for the slot filler list than for either the taxonomic or the complementary list. There were no significant differences in recall and clustering between the taxonomic and the complementary lists.

The findings with respect to the slot filler and taxonomic lists replicate those of the first experiment and again indicate the salience of the slot filler categorical organization for the young child. These data support the position taken here that categorical semantic structures emerge from a conceptual base of knowledge initially organized schematically.

The findings regarding the slot filler and complementary lists are provocative. If event representations are a major form of conceptual representation for the young child, as they appear to be, then children can be expected to have knowledge of syntagmatic, that is, thematic or complementary, relations. How, then, can poorer memory performance on the complementary list compared to the slot filler list be explained? This is not an isolated finding; when complementary or syntagmatic lists have been utilized by other investigators, poor memory performance has also usually been observed (Bjorklund, 1980; Galbraith & Day, 1978). In fact, high levels of recall and organization are not displayed even on child-generated complementary groupings unless subjects are given an opportunity prior to recall to achieve stable sorting of the to-be-remembered items (Bjorklund, Ornstein, & Haig, 1977; Bjorklund & Zaken-Greenberg, 1981; Worden, 1976). Yet, an additional complication is that children do utilize knowledge of such complementary relations on tasks such as classification (e.g., Inhelder & Piaget, 1964; Olver & Hornsby, 1966; Vygotsky, 1962) and match-to-sample (e.g., Smiley & Brown, 1979).

This pattern of findings may be interpreted in terms of a theory of the differentiation between semantic and conceptual organization in long-term memory (Nelson, 1982a, 1983, 1985). This theory proposes that purely experientially based structures, such as those contained in the complementary list, do not enter into organization in semantic memory and, therefore, are not accessed in a verbal (i.e., semantic) task such as recall. Semantic memory consists of paradigmatic organizations, however, and the slot filler categories serve in the establishment of a semantic system by constituting the first and most salient paradigmatic structures. Taxonomic categories are more abstract and advanced semantic structures that draw on and organize the first event-representation-based subcategories. For this reason, they are less developed in the younger child. Accordingly, with increase in age, children's memory performance for lists of categorically related items improves. In nonverbal tasks or tasks not dependent on semantic memory as such, for example, object sorting and match-to-sample, the experientially based conceptual organizations (e.g., complementary relations) may be more salient for the younger child.

Summary

The research reported here supports the proposal that a conceptual system of event representations is subjected to cognitive analysis and that a more abstract system of knowledge organization, a semantic system, is derived or constructed from this analysis. Further research is underway to address some of the issues raised by these findings. For example, we are seeking to verify, through the use of other paradigms, the psychological reality of slot filler categories and to study the developmental fate of slot filler categories and their strength in relation to taxonomic categories with older children. We are also examining the differentiation of the conceptual and semantic systems in long-term memory and the relation of these to experimental tasks.

THE ORGANIZATION OF EVENT CATEGORIES

Taxonomic Organization

Taxonomic organizations of categories relate categories to one another in terms of class inclusion. The higher a category is within a taxonomy, the greater the inclusiveness of that category (i.e., the more categories it includes under it). The greater the inclusiveness of a category, the higher is its level of abstraction.

In the domain of objects, considerable knowledge about the taxonomic organization of natural language categories has been built up in recent years. As noted earlier, Rosch and her colleagues (Rosch et al., 1976; Rosch, 1978) have provided evidence that taxonomies of concrete objects are structured in such a way that one level of abstraction is "basic" in the organization of objects. Their evidence showed this level of categorization to be the highest level of abstraction at which category members: (a) possess a significant number of attributes in common; (b) share elaborated motor movement sequences used in interaction with them; and (c) have an identifiable averaged shape. These findings support the working assumption that, in the perceived world, there occur information-rich bundles of perceptual and functional attributes that form natural discontinuities and that basic cuts in categorization are made at these discontinuities.

If people apply similar principles of categorization to the domain of events, then we can expect to find commonly held taxonomic organizations of event categories, and a "basic" level should be identifiable within these taxonomies. Rosch (1978) reported preliminary evidence for the existence of basic-level event categories. She observed that people describe the previous days' activities most frequently in terms of event units that refer to particular, well-scripted activities—units such as "got dressed"—rather than larger units such as "prepared to go out" or smaller units such as "put on my shoes." Rosch inferred from this evidence that this size or type of unit may constitute basic-level events. However, unlike the relations of basic-level objects to higher and lower levels, these different types of event units bear part-whole relations to each other, not class inclusion (i.e., taxonomic) relations. For example, "put on my shoes" is a part of the "getting dressed" event. Thus, it remains unclear whether events can be classified in terms of taxonomic levels of abstraction and whether a "basic" level can be identified according to any of the operational criteria of Rosch et al. (1976).

On the other hand, Schank (1982) has proposed that event information can be accessed using different levels of abstraction, thus suggesting a possible basis for the taxonomic organization of event categories. To investigate this possibility, Rifkin (1984) conducted three experiments designed to ascertain if people organize events in terms of commonly held event taxonomies and if these taxonomies have a "basic" level. College students served as subjects so that the findings could be compared with the prior research on the taxonomic organization of objects.

In the first two experiments, commonly held event taxonomies with class inclusion relations were elicited. In the first experiment, subjects were given superordinate terms for categories of activities (entertainment, meals, transportation, housework, school activities, hygienic activities, shopping, sports, and crime) and were asked to list activities or events that are instances of these categories. In the second experiment, subjects were given the six most frequent responses for each of the superordinates in the first experiment and were asked to list the categories these activities belong to and the different types (or instances) of these activities they could think of.

Results from the first experiment revealed a consistently agreed upon set of middle-level categories elicited by the superordinate event terms. Results from the second experiment indicated that the superordinates were, in turn, most frequently listed as the categories to which the middle-level terms belong; and that a consistent set of subordinate terms were given as instances of the middle-level categories. Thus, commonly held event taxonomies based on class inclusion relations were identified in these experiments.

In the third experiment, Rosch et al.'s (1976) "basic-level" hypothesis was tested using the event category taxonomies constructed in the first two experiments. This hypothesis states that there exists a "basic" level that is the most inclusive level of categorization at which category members possess the greatest number of features in common. Obviously, the criteria of common shape and common motor movements applicable to objects would not be applicable to activities. Subjects were given the superordinate-, middle-, and subordinate-level category terms and were asked to list the features they felt were characteristic of these different activities. Results from this experiment revealed that the middle-level event categories constituted a basic level of categorization, similar to Rosch's basic level of object categories. That is, these categories elicited a significantly greater number of features than the superordinates, and no significant difference in the number of features was found between the middle- and subordinate-level categories. Moreover, few, if any, features were elicited for the superordinates. Thus, within the commonly held event category taxonomies, a basic level of abstraction was identified.

Other research has also provided evidence for adults' taxonomic organization of event categories and the inclusion and organization of a number of different types of features (actions, objects, roles, etc.) within the boundaries of these categories (see Cantor, Mischel, & Schwartz, 1982). Moreover, the taxonomic organization of event knowledge appears to have a specific function in the retrieval of event information. Reiser, Black, and Abelson (1983) found that basic-level event categories may provide an optimal constraint for the retrieval of autobiographical memories, given the amount of featural information organized at this level of abstraction. For example, the basic level category "the movies" may supply an optimal constraint for retrieval of memories of particular events, whereas the superordinate category "entertainment" would not.

In summary, then, although the content domains of event categories may be different from those of object categories—and the latter may be attributes of the former—the organizational principles of categorization appear to be the same.

Internal Structure and Event Category References

A closer consideration of the event category features elicited from subjects in the last experiment, in relation to the information on event categories elicited from adults in other investigations, reveals that different references to event categories may access different aspects of the internal structure of these categories.

In Rifkin's (1984) research, noun and noun phrase labels, rather than verb phrase labels, were used to elicit features for the event categories (e.g., "dinner" in contrast to "having dinner," or "the movies" in contrast to "going to the movies"). These labels were the terms given by the subjects in the first two experiments of this research. The features elicited by the noun and noun phrase labels for the basic and subordinate categories were found to be primarily concrete in nature. That is, rather than actions, roles, and personal (affective) states, primarily objects, physical attributes, and locations were listed as features of these categories (e.g., "ball," "cold," and "stadium" for football). Superordinates elicited few features, and these were primarily persons (e.g., "family" for meal), general actions rather than specific actions (e.g., "exercise" rather than "running" for sports), and personal states or attitudes (e.g., "fun" for sports).

The retrieval of concrete information for the middle-level and subordinate event categories is in contrast to the findings of Cantor, Mischel, and Schwartz (1982), who asked subjects for the characteristics of being in a situation or event (e.g., "being at a party"). Their subjects gave primarily action and person-oriented features for event categories. Similarly, in a pilot study, Rifkin (1984) used verb phrase labels for the event categories (e.g., "having dinner") and found that, in contrast to the noun phrase labels, these elicited more actions than objects. We speculate, then, that when a *participatory* reference is made to event categories through the use of verb phrase labels, person and action information related to event categories is accessed. *Nonparticipatory* references to events, such as the use of noun and noun phrase labels, access primarily concrete event information, that is, objects, physical attributes, and locations. Thus, it appears that different types of information relevant to events may be stored separately (or in distinguishable ways) and may be accessed through different types of references to these events.

It can be argued that the types of category information stored and the method of accessing this information are similar for both objects and events. The subjects in Rifkin's (1984) study gave concrete attributes for basic and subordinate level event categories and general actions for superordinate categories. Similarly, Rosch et al., (1976) found the same contrast for object categories at different levels. When they requested the characteristics of objects by using noun and noun phrase labels, that is, by invoking a nonparticipatory perspective for objects at the basic and subordinate level (e.g., hammer and claw hammer) they received primarily concrete features (e.g., "handle," "metalhead"). For superordinates, they received general action features as the few features listed (e.g., "make things" for tools). On the other hand, when Rosch et al. (1976) asked for what one does when interacting with these objects, thereby invoking a participatory perspective, subjects gave sequences of motor movements.

Note that the elicitation of scripts for events is accomplished through the use of a participatory perspective (e.g., "What happens when you go to a restaurant?"). This type of participatory request is similar to that used by Rosch et al. (1976) when invoking a participatory perspective, and the result is similar in both cases, that is, sequences of actions are reported. Thus, event representations appear to be organized from a participatory perspective. The abstraction of event categories may be accomplished through operations performed on the event representations, as proposed earlier. Once these event categories are established, both participatory and nonparticipatory perspectives can be used to access the different kinds of information comprising these categories.

Part-Whole Relations

The hierarchical organization of event knowledge is integral to the Memory Organization Packets (MOPs) proposed by Schank (1982). However, within Schank's model, event information can be referenced both independently at a given level of abstraction and as components of other activities. For example, the schema for the event "going on dates" can include the actions "make arrangements," "meet," "do activity," and "drop off date." Of these actions, "do activity," is a *placeholder slot* that can be filled with a number of different activities. Within this slot, the superordinate event category "entertainment" can generate the possible middle-level alternatives (e.g., the movies, the theatre), and then the subordinate level alternatives (e.g., horror movies, musical comedy). As this example demonstrates, event categories, once formed, can constitute part of event representations (e.g., "entertainment" as part of "going on dates"). The similarity to the slot filler object categories described in the first section of this chapter is obvious. Additionally, event categories may be accessed during everyday planning and decision making as proposed by Schank (1982). For example, when planning a date, the superordinate event category "entertainment" can function in the "do activity" slot to generate the basic-level alternatives (e.g., "the movies," "the theatre"). The information stored at the level of these basic category alternatives could be used to decide which of these events one might participate in.

In Rifkin's (1984) experiment, a distinct kind of part-whole relation involving the event categories themselves was found in the following forms. First, event categories from one taxonomy were listed as features of event categories from other taxonomies. For example, the basic-level categories "cooking" and "washing dishes," identified as types of the superordinate category "housework," were also named as attributes of the basic-level category "dinner" and of the subordinate level category "family dinner" under the superordinate category "meals." Thus, "whole" categories from one taxonomy (e.g., "cooking" and "washing dishes" from "housework") are "parts," that is, attributes of categories, of another taxonomy (e.g., "dinner" and "family dinner"). A similar situation was found within the *same* taxonomy. For example, "movies" and "parties" were among the most frequently listed instances of the category "entertainment" (in the first experiment), whereas subjects listed "movies" and "parties" as attributes of the superordinate category "entertainment" in the attribute-listing experiment. These findings illustrate that part-whole relations apply to event categories, not only in terms of their usage in placeholder slots within schemas, but also in terms of the taxonomic organization itself. Thus, the part-whole relations within event hierarchies appear to be more complex than those envisioned in the Rosch et al. (1976) scheme applicable to objects. They indicate the need for further investigation of the relations within and between these domains.

Developmental Considerations

A major developmental issue brought out in the study of event categories is that some aspects of event knowledge may be more or less available to the child at different points in development. From the research reported in earlier chapters, we know that the young child has available information on the sequential organization of actors, actions, and objects within an event. However, providing information on characteristics, features, or attributes of events, as required in the research of Rifkin (1984) and Cantor et al., (1982), appears to involve the decontexting or abstraction of event elements (e.g., persons, objects, actions, etc.) from the syntagmatic frames in which they were learned and in which they are initially embedded. If the availability of features indicative of category formation and necessary for taxonomic organization requires and results from further cognitive analysis of established event representations, then such information could not be expected to serve as the first round of event information for the young child. Assuming that feature knowledge associated with event categories results from the decontexting or abstracting of event components from the syntagmatic frames in which they were learned and are embedded, a major issue is whether there is an acquisition order related to the *kinds* of features that can be abstracted.

Features can be placed along a scale marking the concrete-abstract dimension. For example, Cantor et al. (1982) identified a category of event components termed *nonphysical,* which includes personality traits, feelings, attitudes, and socioeconomic status, as well as situation components, such as time of year and atmosphere. Physical characteristics for persons, such as sex, age, attractiveness, and neatness, and for situations, such as physical surroundings and objects in the room, were categorized as *physical*. The nonphysical categories appear to represent more abstract, and thus more complex information about events and situations than do physical categories.

In a consideration of the relation between features of event categories and event representations, it may be assumed that the initial representation of an event does not contain a high degree of abstract information. As the representation for any given event becomes more elaborated (see Chapter 4), more abstract information may become incorporated. Some evidence for this speculation is apparent in Fivush's (1984) study, as well as in Gruendel's (1980) data (see Chapters 3 and 4). If this supposition is true (and more direct investigation of this is required), then event categories may be formed on the basis of concrete/physical features, with more abstract features accruing to these categories as the schema develops and more complex information or features can be abstracted.

Although children's taxonomic organization of event categories has not yet been directly investigated, some evidence is available in children's script protocols. Kindergarteners have been found to use a type of hierarchical organization of events (Fivush, 1984; see Chapter 4). For example, when kindergarten children who had given scripts for their school day were further probed about these activities, rather than relating the sequence of actions within a given school day activity (e.g., reading), they gave lists of examples or instances of the activity (e.g., "find letters," "do riddles"). Although listing subordinate category examples is not evidence of fully developed class-inclusion relations, it is evidence of the use of categorical levels of abstraction in the organization of event knowledge.

Further, Fivush (1984) found that the hierarchical organization of event categories develops with repeated experiences with events, with more subordinate terms being listed as children gained experience with the event. Subordinate sets of activities were subsumed under more general category labels in later reports of the same events. That is, when children reported the activities of their school day, earlier reports of "play with blocks," "play with puppet," and "paint" were later subsumed under the general category "play."

This hierarchical structuring and use of event categories appears to begin after children form event representations. Such organization of event categories points to the possibility that the event schema plays a role in the organization of event categories similar to that of object categories. As evidenced earlier, subordinate event categories can occupy slots within an event representation in a way that is analogous to object categories. Moreover, just as slot filler object categories combine to form more general, more inclusive taxonomic categories, so do slot filler event categories, as when "play with blocks," "play with puppet," and "paint" are grouped and subsumed under the general category "play."

The relation between event features, event parts (that is, placeholder slots), and event categories, which was seen to be very complex in adult category organization, is a matter that requires additional developmental investigation. There is evidence (e.g., Markman, 1981, 1983) that children find part-whole relations easier to deal with than they do categorical (class inclusion) relations among object categories, and this should hold for events as well as objects. Thus, we might expect placeholder event categories to emerge as part of event schemas prior to the construction of hierarchical event category organization.

Summary

The research reported in this section indicates that event categories, derived from event representations, can enter into organizational systems involving more abstract knowledge of class inclusion and part-whole relations. Moreover, these systems have been found to interact with one another. Thus, through cognitive analysis of the initial representation of experience, event categories are formed and enter into interconnecting networks of knowledge. Additional research is needed to specify the kinds of cognitive processes involved in the origins and development of these networks and the role language (through naming and teaching practices) plays in their establishment.

GENERAL CONCLUSIONS

The research in this chapter has indicated that event representations may be thought of as "cognitive seeds." Once established, they yield higher order knowledge. However, we need to understand better the processes by which this is accomplished including the discovery of all the kinds of knowledge that can be derived from event representations. Moreover, for each form of knowledge, we need to specify the kinds of cognitive analyses or processes that are at work in its construction. The derivation of knowledge from event representations may involve both deliberate analysis (Galambos & Rips, 1982) and the operation of information-processing mechanisms, such as pattern analysis, that are not under deliberate control.

We also need to understand the role played by the culture and the language system in the constructive process. Moreover, we need to examine the development of these knowledge organizations as interactive systems, so that we can ascertain how the development of one system impacts on another. Only when all of this knowledge is available will the "seed-like" nature of event representations be fully understood.

10 The Application of Scripts in the Organization of Language Intervention Contexts

Catherine M. Constable

This chapter presents an application of scripts in the organization of language intervention contexts. Many of the ideas put forth here derive from clinical work carried out over the past 6 years. A major focus in that work has been to establish a functional interplay between script research and the development and analysis of language intervention practices. To understand the application of script theory in this context, it is necessary to be clear about the goals of a language intervention program as well as the nature of language disorders.

Language intervention, like any therapeutic practice, takes diverse forms. The diversity reflects differences in the nature of the language disorder to be treated, the linguistic or communicative competencies to be developed, the theoretical orientations of interventionists regarding the nature of language, and the clinical orientations that the interventionist brings to the task of facilitating communicative and linguistic skills in children who are having difficulty acquiring those skills. Thus, it is important to recognize that there is no one, universally accepted, comprehensively defined concept of language intervention per se. However, language intervention can be characterized generally as the practice of engaging language disordered children in experiences that promote communicative and linguistic abilities, which are progressive and are functional for interpersonal as well as intellectual activity (see Johnston, 1983; Rees, 1983).

Language intervention from this perspective involves designing and presenting events that are easily analyzable and highly functional for the language disordered child. Within these events, the various operations and relations that exist in and mediate between systems of linguistic form, semantic meaning, and pragmatic and problem solving functions need to be made extremely transparent. Further, language intervention entails making systematic and gradual modifications in the design and presentation of such events over time, in order to accommodate, as well as facilitate, continued development and reorganization in the child's communicative and linguistic systems.

Script research and theory is relevant to this perspective on language intervention for several reasons. First, script theory provides guidelines for the structure and content of the nonlinguistic features of intervention events. Second, scripted events presumably reduce cognitive workloads, thus increasing the resources that children can apply to the language learning task. Third, scripted events generally facilitate a display of children's more advanced communicative and linguistic performances (Chapters 6 and 7). A sensitivity to this idea is critical for interventionists as they attempt to aid children in deploying the upper bounds of their present linguistic system in different functional directions; and to facilitate an extension of the upper bounds of linguistic complexity via subtle modulations in the linguistic and nonlinguistic features of more familiar, routine events in which the child participates. Finally, script analysis makes possible an ongoing assessment of the structure and content of the social knowledge bases that language disordered children bring to the intervention context. Such an analysis is essential to the evolution of strategies for developing any linguistic skills that are to be used pragmatically.

In the program for young language disordered children that I directed we began to employ specifically scriptal frameworks about 5 years ago. Our first efforts in that direction clearly had positive effects on the socio-communicative and linguistic performances of a number of the children. We have since elaborated on this type of design, extending its application in a variety of clinical directions to address different linguistic and communicative problems. Thus, we have tested some implications of a scriptal view of event representation, albeit with a "diverse collection of children" referred to as "language disordered" (Aram & Nation, 1982, p. 1).

To provide the background for understanding our application of scripts to language intervention, I begin with a discussion of the nature and complexity of language disorder and follow with an overview of some recent trends in language intervention. I then present a detailed description of the specific clinical applications of script theory that we have developed and utilized over time. I conclude with a discussion of the importance of complementary efforts between basic research and applied programs in this area.

THE NATURE OF LANGUAGE DISORDERS

The term *language disorder* refers to a variety of behavioral manifestations of presumed disruption in the developments of semantic representation, syntactic and morphological operations, pragmatic presuppositions and intention, or any constellation of these. Heterogeneity epitomizes the description of the class of children who, despite adequate hearing and normal nonverbal or performance IQ, present a communicative or linguistic impairment.

The concomitant conditions and deficits associated with such impairments likewise vary. Symbolic or representational deficits, difficulty in discriminating rapid sequences of linguistic and nonlinguistic acoustic stimuli, attentional and memory deficits, generalized difficulty in temporal perception and production, mild neurological dysfunction, or combinations thereof, all have been implicated in language disorder in one sample or another of such children (Johnston & Ramstad, 1978; Kahmi, 1981; Morehead & Ingram, 1973; Tallal et al., 1976, 1981, 1983; Tallal & Piercy, 1973, 1974, 1975; Terrel & Schwartz, 1983; see also Johnston, 1982).

On the surface, many language impaired children appear to learn language content, form, and use in a normal sequence but at a slower rate with marked chronological delay (see Johnston, 1982 for an excellent review of the related research). Even when the course of language acquisition appears to reflect a normal, but slower, sequence, we need to be concerned about the impact of these early language delays on subsequent linguistic developments, general cognitive function, and participation in social and instructional interactions. The force of language as an intellectual tool, and its function in the construction of social and instructional contexts, make the nature and effect of "time displaced acquisitions" a subject of pervasive interest (see Bashir, Kuban, Kleinman & Scavuzzo, 1983). Furthermore, an impression that the linguistic system is developing normally, but slowly, can be drawn mistakenly if the diagnostic methods of analysis are not extremely comprehensive.

One case relevant to these issues involves a child who, at a chronological age of 3 years and 11 months was found to have a mean length of utterance (M.L.U.) in morphemes (Brown, 1973) of 4.07, which is within one standard deviation of the predicted mean for his chronological age (Miller & Chapman, 1981). This level of M.L.U. corresponds to a stage 5 assignment in Brown's theoretical system and is thus associated with the achievement of basic grammatical forms for coordinating simple sentences and propositional relations. Additional analysis, however, revealed that none of the 14 grammatical morphemes in Brown's (1973) system had been mastered, that is, were present in obligatory contexts 90% of the time; "ing," "plural s," "in," "on," and the irregular past forms "got" and "did" were the only grammatical morphemes that had emerged. Except for the irregular past tense, all the items in this particular cluster of grammatical morphemes are expected to be mastered around the same time, during stages 2 to 3, according to Brown. In this case, then, there appeared to be a developmental asynchrony between utterance length and grammatical morpheme development, a point to which return later.

A *Developmental Sentence Score* (derived from a syntactic analysis of spontaneous language, Lee, 1974) placed this child below the 10th percentile for his age group with respect to expressive syntax. Additional structural analyses, utilizing procedures found in Miller (1981), indicated that negation was coded typically by attaching the negative markers ''no'' or ''not'' outside the simple sentence (''no got too much,'' ''no put that there''). The use of ''can't'' and ''don't'' within the simple sentence were each noted only once (''moo cow can't come out,'' ''don't push that''). ''WH'' questions were performed by preposing the WH word before the simple sentence, e.g., ''where put that one?'' The semi-auxillaries ''wanna'' and ''gonna'' were apparent in two constituent utterances. These findings are consistent with a structural stage 2 or 3 assignment (Miller, 1981) and thus seem consistent with the level of grammatical morpheme development of this child's language.

Semantic analyses were more consistent with the child's M.L.U. level, however. For example, in many instances several semantic relations were coordinated within one utterance, such as ''no more big ones back here.'' In this utterance, the semantic relations coded include: nonexistence (''no more''), attribution (''big''), quantity ''s'' morpheme on ''ones''), and place (''back here''). Analysis of expressive vocabulary also indicated more age-appropriate performance. For example, the use of locative terms ''beside'' and ''in back'' appears to be more consistent with the child's chronological age (47 months) and M.L.U. age prediction (36.7–48.5 months) (see Johnston, 1981; Miller & Chapman, 1981), than with late stage 2 and early stage 3 structural assignment age predictions (± 1 standard deviation) of 24–35 months for WH questions, 24–41 months for negation, and 21–35 months for Verb Phrase Elaboration (Miller, 1981).

Finally, this child juxtaposed clauses and used the conjunction ''and'' to code coordinate (''you push, me push'') and causal relations (''close this and cow no get out''). Utterances of this type, though uninflected morphologically, accounted for some of the longest in the sample (see Bloom & Lahey, 1978, for definitions of semantic categories).

Results of the Test for the Auditory Comprehension of Language (Carrow, 1973) and the Peabody Picture Vocabulary Test (Dunn, 1965) indicated that grammatical comprehension and receptive vocabulary abilities (in picture pointing tasks) for this child were within one standard deviation of the mean for his age.

Based upon these analyses, this child appeared to be developing morphological and syntactic abilities in a normal sequence, but at a slower rate. The discrepancy between utterance length and the morphological and syntactic performances can be explained in a number of ways. According to Miller (1981), ''the developmental level of individual constructions can vary as much as one or on occasion, two stages on either side of M.L.U. stage assignment. . . .'' (p. 34). However, the grammatical morphemes (as opposed to syntactic constructions) were only emerging, and these included (except for two exemplars of irregular past tense) only stage 2 and stage 3 morphemes. A number of locative expressions in the sample were constructed with a locative + deictic construction (i.e., "up here," "down here," "back there"). On the other hand, some of the child's locative constructions ("up here," "back here," "down here") appeared formulaic and unanalyzed and thus may have produced an artifactually high M.L.U. score, not contributing to morphological or structural complexity.

Finally, it seems probable that semantic development accounted for the relatively long utterance length. This interpretation is based on the presence in the child's speech of juxtaposed utterances coding event relations, the intrasentential coordination of several different content categories with major verb relations, and C.A. appropriate locative and quantitative terms expressed.

Johnston (1982) has noted that the results of clinical case studies do point in the direction of atypical associations across the linguistic domains of the disordered child's system. As we have reported, some syntactic and morphological features of this child's linguistic system appeared to be developing normally although delayed in their emergence; whereas features such as the coordination of semantic categories, use of conjunction and clause juxtaposition, expressive and receptive vocabulary, grammatical comprehension, and mean length of utterance seemed comparatively more advanced.

Following a year of language intervention, this child's Developmental Sentence Score placed him above the 75th percentile for his age with respect to expressive syntax, and at this time all grammatical morphemes had been mastered. On the surface, then, it appeared that those aspects of the linguistic system that were initially delayed had subsequently been adequately developed. However, as noted earlier, it is important to be aware of the possible effects of early language delays on subsequent linguistic developments, particularly given recent research into the reorganizational processes involved in language development (see Bowerman, 1982).

Almost two years later this child, then 6 years 8 months, returned to our clinic. He was experiencing difficulties in school, particularly in developing early math and reading skills. The following are excerpts of his language at that time:

(#1)Child: "We play up on the hill."
Adult: "Where is the hill . . . near your house?"
Child: "It's, it's, we have a farm, but it's not ours it's Kline's, but he gots two barns he couldn't fit, he's got three barn but he had a get one down here so we got a hill, but that's his barn but he hasta come down here and feed 'em."

(#2) (referring to a picture of a boy holding a puzzle piece of a duck head in one hand while scanning a completed duck puzzle)

Adult: "Why can't the boy fit this piece into the puzzle?" (Blank, Rose & Berlin, 1979)

Child: "Cuz that, they already have a head in there, cuz it is that goes to another piece and it's a puzzle so it already has a head in so it a . . . don't have ya don't, ducks don't have black, black is like this so it means it goes to another puzzle."

The relationships between pragmatic functions, semantic expressions, and grammatical choices are quite complex, and there are several semantic and syntactic features that could be considered in the analysis of these discourse units (see Constable, 1983b). Indeed, example #1 speaks for itself as disordered language, both semantically and syntactically. Example #2 is of interest for pragmatic reasons as well. The first clause ("Cuz that, they already have a head in there . . . ") offers adequate explanation in response to the question, yet the child persisted in reformulations that were pragmatically redundant. Interestingly, these reformulations offer alternate semantic perspectives, which are logically correct. That is, the three different responses, ("cuz . . . they already have a head in there;" "that goes to another piece (puzzle);" "It's a puzzle so it already has a head"), represent different semantic expressions of a pragmatically and conceptually relevant notion.

This particular example illustrates that many language disordered children may appear to have problems sustaining discourse cohesion, extending topics, or making appropriate presuppositions as they are experiencing difficulty working out numerous interactions between the semantic roles and syntactic constructs of their developing linguistic system. (see Briton and Fujiki, 1982, for a discussion of pragmatic deficits in language disordered children.)

In sum, language disordered children present more complicated profiles than those that standardized assessments alone might indicate; a language disorder is a complex phenomenon. Furthermore, as our case demonstrates, language disorders change as the language system reorganizes; the complexity of the language disorder often reflects the complexity of the language system. Hence, our initial intervention was not ineffective. On the contrary, it appeared to facilitate syntactic and morphological development. Our program of intervention at that time, however, was shortsighted. As our child's language system continued to develop and reorganize, and as the complexity of the tasks for which he deployed his language likewise increased, his language disorder manifested itself once again, though in a different form.

This phenomenon is one that interventionists must address. The design of a scriptal approach to language intervention specifies gradual augmentation in the complexity of contextual and linguistic interactions over time. Several examples of how this incremental process can be carried out clinically are set forth in the application section of this chapter.

RECENT TRENDS IN LANGUAGE INTERVENTION

There was an information explosion in the language acquisition literature during the 1970s that quite naturally had a profound impact on approaches to language intervention. By the mid-1970s, the field of communication disorders began to temper its reliance on the use of operant procedures and the training of discrete psycholinguistic abilities (auditory sequential memory, sound blendings, etc.) as methods of facilitating language development in children with language disorders. The clinical activities that these orientations prescribed were straightforward and uncomplicated to administer; however, they had few significant effects on children's ability to use language to communicate (see Bloom & Lahey, 1978; Butterfield & Schiefelbusch, 1981; Rees, 1978).

Subsequently there was a proliferation of natural language learning approaches (Bloom & Lahey, 1978; McClean & Snyder-McClean, 1979). The unifying idea of these approaches was the belief that language intervention should occur in a variety of communicative contexts that highlight the pragmatic force of language as well as its formal features and semantic functions. Bloom and Lahey (1978) emphasized that meaning and intention originate in the child's experience, and thus language learning was for the most part dependent on the child's conceptual representation of that experience. They and others (see, for example, Bowerman, 1976) recommended that interventionists engage children in intervention activities that are similar to the children's everyday experiences, wherein the majority of materials utilized are dynamic, not static. The use of sand tables, cooking activities, playdough, art work, and waterplay was recommended (Bloom & Lahey, 1978; McClean & Snyder-McClean, 1979). One "pragmatically" based program (Miller, 1978) suggested that the interventionist's primary concern is to develop an interactive relationship with the child. Miller recommended that interventionists model communicative behavior of any type within a context of play that is chosen by the child.

All in all there was a growing concensus in the field that the goals and design of the language intervention programs must address the semantic content, structural forms, and pragmatic functions of children's language. Intervention, then, focused on the children's use of language and not the remediation of hypothesized underlying causes of the disorder.

It seemed that in one fell swoop the essence of the language intervention enterprise shifted from flipping pictures and pitching tokens to juggling semantic relations, grammatical morphemes, pragmatic presuppositions, expansions and models, copulas and modals, preschoolers and peanut butter! This shift in orientation seemed right minded, but the complexity it entailed presented a new set of challenges. Interventionists were forced to develop "a functional awareness of the various ways that routine event representations, paralinguistic cues, perceptual support and the language objectives of the child can interact with the multiple discourse functions of clinician/child utterances'' (Constable, 1983b, p. 118). The application of that awareness in creating and managing a communicative context is essential lest interventionists find themselves floundering ineffectually in the eye of a sociolinguistic hurricane.

THE DEVELOPMENT OF A SCRIPTED APPROACH TO LANGUAGE INTERVENTION

My initial interest in the application of scripts to language intervention was largely a result of my clinical experiences. From the beginning, we had designed our half-day, preschool language intervention program to be activity based. This orientation was in accord with the current views of the field as I have just discussed. Our first class of children, numbering seven, ranged in age from 3 to 5 years. These children all had a primary diagnosis of specific language impairment, though one child was later diagnosed as mildly retarded.

The language goals we set forth for the children were based on the analysis of spontaneous language samples that were collected over several days, in individual as well as in group interactions (see Bloom & Lahey, 1978 for analysis procedures). Some of the goals were as follows:

1. To develop coding of locative relations in 2–3 constituent utterances in order to comment or give a directive (e.g., ''take top off,'' ''pour water in'');
2. To develop coding of state relations in 3 constituent state relations in order to request or comment (e.g., ''I need a bowl'');
3. To develop 2 constituent action utterances coordinated with nonexistence (e.g., ''don't spill'), intention (e.g., ''gonna pour''), attribution (e.g., ''squeeze big one''), or recurrence (e.g., ''squeeze it again'') in order to comment or give a directive;
4. To develop juxtaposition of clauses in order to code temporal relations in order to respond to questions, or give directives (e.g., ''pour in, stir around'');
5. To develop use of copular forms to code state relations in order to request or comment (e.g., ''This is sticky,'' ''Are you hungry?'').

Thus, the goals that we wrote for the children initially (1978–1979) were based exclusively on Bloom and Lahey's (1978) assumptions that

> language is three dimensional and includes content/form/use interaction; the goals of language intervention should be based first on linguistic behavior and not on etiology or correlates of language disorder; the best hypotheses for determining goals of language intervention currently come from information about normal

> development; goals are best described in terms of the child's productions. . . . (p. 393)

The majority of our activities utilized real life materials that were dynamic, not static. Arts and crafts activities, cooking activities, toothbrushing, and waterplay were accompanied by a variety of verbal language facilitation strategies such as: models, expansions, communicative forms of elicited imitation, questions, questions with semantic and syntactic interactions embedded, directives, directives with semantic/syntactic interactions embedded, sentence completions and connectives. These strategies were used to encourage the children to talk to each other and with us. (See Constable, 1981, for a comprehensive review of verbal facilitation strategies.)

It became clear to us rather quickly that children used more language, employed more complex semantic-syntactic interactions, and oriented to the communicative acts of others more often during certain intervention activities than during others. This difference was evident in the daily analyses of children's spontaneous utterances that related to our language objectives. Furthermore, fairly complex analyses of semantic and syntactic relations across speaker turns (see Constable, 1981, 1983b) indicated that the effectiveness of verbal facilitation strategies was also event related. Not surprisingly, some of the basic characteristics that typified our more communicatively enriched activities were revealed to be those that reflected script inducing structures. First, these activities had a strong invariant temporal structure of component acts that had to be accomplished in order to meet some specified goal. Second, component acts obligated the use of certain objects. Third, the turn-taking conventions in our preschool often resulted in several repetitions of each component act before moving ahead to the next sequence. For example, one recipe for making playdough may require two cups of flour; when this activity was divided into equal turns for each of eight preschoolers, the result was eight turns at "scooping out and putting in" one-fourth of a cup of flour. As the reader can imagine, making the playdough (at least from our perspective) soon became the primary intervention activity, in contrast to playing with the playdough. Nonverbal, idiosyncratic exploratory and constructive play schemes typically constituted the play activity, although eventually we began to develop routines for playing with playdough as well.

Inasmuch as flexible, progressive, and relevant language use is a desirable outcome of language intervention, the activities we began to emphasize in our program were precisely those scripted activities that have just been characterized.

Thus, the early clinical experiences sensitized us to the importance of event structure. Subsequently we used the script framework of Nelson and Gruendel (1979) within which to conceptualize our program design more systematically.

It is important to emphasize the complexity of effecting clinical interactions that present language therapeutically without distorting language pragmatically. In order to effect "naturalistic" clinical interactions, the therapist must attend to and organize a multitude of linguistic and nonlinguistic contextual features, many of which often are not considered in less pragmatic therapies. In our early attempts at such organization, we often were overwhelmed by the complexity of the task facing children with impaired abilities in attending to and organizing the linguistically relevant features of their everyday experiences.

Normal language learners are able to extract patterns and develop representations from quite complex sociolinguistic experiences. Such abilities are especially critical in the early phases of language acquisition, providing children with data and knowledge bases from which:

1. to make fundamental form-meaning inductions;
2. to track the co-occurence of content words and grammatical morphemes;
3. to infer pragmatic force and perspective;
4. to abstract basic combinatorial rules;
5. to realize the constitutive function of talk in task accomplishment.

(See Dore, 1979; Maratsos, 1982; Peters, 1983.) These operations, of course, occur simultaneously with children's construction and use of linguistic and communicative means for creating social activity. Thus, language is not an outcome separate from its use.

What is genetically given, cognitively constructed, and/or socially transmitted regarding language acquisition remains debatable. However, experience using language in the social context is essential not only for pragmatic acquisition. Using the language in contexts of increasing complexity is an effective means of working through later semantic and syntactic reorganizations that are not necessarily motivated pragmatically.

Nelson and Gruendel (1981) have stressed the importance of understanding how the child selects from complexity and "how complexity is represented in a cognitive system" (p. 31). They proposed that young children initially encode the panorama before them in an analog form to which organizing and analyzing processes are applied, yielding a more generalized event representation, script, or set of subscripts (see Nelson, 1982a). The form these take (sequence of component acts linked together temporally and causally with specified actor and object slots) is quite consistent, suggesting that the more "scripted" an event is in context, the more efficiently it can be processed (see Nelson, Chapter 1 this volume). The content of scripts also influences the efficiency of event representation and processing. If external events are well matched in content to a child's script, the script may guide the child more or less automatically through those events

> . . . thus freeing (them) from constantly attending to the ongoing action. The cognitive space so gained can be used in consideration of the elements of situations that are problematic variations from routine, obstacles to the completion of a goal, negotiations between individuals engaged in an activity (and) problem solving activities of all kinds. (Nelson, 1981, p. 109; see also Chapter 7 this volume)

Shatz (1984) likewise cites the positive effects of more systemized knowledge. According to her, "the more organized one's knowledge, the less work required to retrieve the essential pieces of information and order them in appropriate ways for the task at hand" (p. 874).

To this point, then, scripting is an early process in the representation of experience (Nelson & Gruendel, 1981). The role of scripts as basic units of analysis within the cognitive system has been advanced by Nelson and Gruendel (1981) and Nelson (1982a). According to these accounts, ever more powerful pattern extractors scan across scripts. Presumably the outcomes of these operations include representations of relational concepts, object categories, discourse conventions, and a notion of substitutability in slot fillers across scripts (see previous chapters). Nelson (1982a) asserts that early word use and early semantic categories and relations are direct outcomes of this analysis.

Lucariello and Nelson (see Chapter 7) found that children between 24 and 29 months expressed a greater number of topics and referred to more "time displaced" events when the children were engaged in scripted event contexts. Similarly, Nelson and Gruendel (1979) indicate that preschoolers who share social scripts with their interlocutors are better able to engage in topic relevant dialogue (see also Chapter 8). Alternatively, when there is no shared script knowledge or when a script is not evoked (as in block play or artwork), the conversational support of the shared script will be lacking and egocentric speech may result.

The entailments of a script can be restrictive, preventing children from easily interpreting events that present a variety of familiar objects but in many different or novel roles (see Nelson, 1984, for a related discussion). Constable and Lahey (1984) hypothesized that event representations may be guiding a child in one direction while maternal efforts are being directed toward engaging the child in another sequence of activity. When children's interpretations of events are restricted in unrecognized ways, maternal utterances may be useless or even confusing to the child. Constable and Lahey concluded that the facilitative nature of many maternal speech acts cannot be determined without extensive event structure analysis and evidence of how the child is perceiving that event. Similarly, Shatz (1984) asserts that "differences in knowledge structures would have serious consequences in the ways children perform on communication tasks, virtually all of which make some demands for the retrieval of stored knowledge" (p. 98).

In light of these theoretical considerations, our early clinical experiences provide a rationale for our current clinical practice of presenting intervention events in a scripted format. From our point of view, the improved linguistic and communicative performances of our language disordered children in the more scripted activities were probably related to several factors: First, the structure of our activities acted as an organizational prosthetic; thus resources that ordinarily are required to organize information could be used by children to organize communicative acts and display their emerging linguistic skills (see Shatz, 1984; and Lucariello et al., Chapter 7, for similar points regarding normal language learners). Not all the language skills we observed had been *acquired* in these activities; rather these activities supported some of the earliest performances of newly developed competencies. The therapeutic value is in the opportunity for experience in language use that is essential to subsequent linguistic growth. Second, the turn-taking conventions in our preschool provided a redundant display of the subordinate structure of events. The extended presentation of verbally marked exemplars (i.e., eight turns at scooping, eight turns at stirring, etc.) within each slot of the script-like framework should enhance the construction of an event representation and the extraction of object knowledge and object relations to be linguistically represented. The predictability that the repetition of component acts confers on the event probably frees processing capacity for increased attendance to the acoustic features of talk. Third, the recurrent presentation of the more scripted events over time afforded the children the ability to share topics more easily (see Nelson & Gruendel, 1979). I suspect that the instantiation of shared knowledge bases drastically reduced the children's presuppositional workloads.

Professionals concerned with enhancing children's communicative competence establish, as part of their intervention procedure, means for monitoring how the structure and content of the knowledge bases that children bring to the intervention context change over time. Thus, we establish a repertoire of routine scripted events (in addition to other scripted though less recurrent events) that we construct with our preschoolers over and over again. As these events recur, we experience the effects that children's newly acquired linguistic and communication skills can have on the transformation of these events over time. For example, as the ability to code coordinate relations emerges, and as the child recognizes the obligatory actions for the completion of a particular event subscript, the child may initiate a suggestion to switch incidental person roles ("I poke David's. David poke mines!") A savvy interventionist may then elaborate on this particular speech act to develop a new slot in the event. Specifically, a potato switching routine constituted by an announcement ("Ryan pokes Joshua's and Joshua pokes Ryan's"), then action (boys switch potatoes), announcement then action, announcement then action, etc. . . . may be instigated to promote marking possessives.

Inasmuch as our clinical focus is on language and communication, the presentation of events must involve raising language as a figure from the interactional ground without obscuring its significance to the interaction. Thus, the accomplishment of component acts is often contingent on much prior negotiation (talk routines) to ensure that talk, from the child's point of view, constitutes much of what is to be done.

The observation, participation, turn-taking format that was described earlier in relation to making playdough, lends itself nicely to a talk/do, talk/do constitution of many activities we design for developing early communication and language abilities and insights. If a speech act, like any other act, can be processed as a slot in a script, then this format would certainly facilitate the representation of speech acts. This has implications for children's subsequent abstraction of the roles of communicative intents in constituting activity. For example, we have had children protest (e.g., "no, I hafta tell him") a violation in what they have come to perceive as a discourse convention for negotiating turn allocation. At other times, slots are constituted by spinning language out of a functional role in the accomplishment of action. A convention of playing with language content and form that is related to the immediate task at hand and then switching the mode of language use back to task accomplishment may be beneficial in a number of ways. As implied, this convention provides early experience in switching registers. In addition, we use play-with-language routines within a script, for different purposes, such as:

To catalyze segmentation by "introducing controlled variation" within learned chunks that as yet may not be fully analyzed at the morphological level (see Peters, 1983, p. 112).

Clinician: (while poking a potato) "I'm poking mine! . . . poke . . . poke . . . poke . . ."
Child 1: "poking mine! . . . poke . . . poke . . . poke . . ."
Child 2: "poking mine! . . . poke . . . poke . . . poke . . ."

2. To make salient grammatical morphemes that normally have little obvious pragmatic or semantic force:

Clinician: "Who's poking?"
Aide: "I am."
Clinician: "I am," (points to Child 1) "David is," (points to Child 2) "Ryan is," (points to Child 3) "Joshua's poking," (turns to Child 4) "Are you?"
Child 4: (starts poking again) Nods head
Clinician: "Yes you are; ask Laurie, Are you?"
Child 4: (turns to Laurie) "Are you?"
Laurie: (starts poking) "Yeah, I am."
Clinician: "I am," (points to Child 3) "Joshua is . . ."
David: "I am"
(Ryan looks up)
Clinician: (to Ryan) "Tell everybody (pointing to herself) "I am!"

Ryan: (looks to kids, points to self) "I am"
Clinician: "Yeah we all are!" "Everybody's poking!"

(See Constable, 1983a, for a discussion of communicative forms of elicited imitation.)

In these examples, redundant marking of the main verb (poke), mapping onto action in the previous component act (1), allowed the subsequent use of ellipsis in the next subscript (2). Thus, auxillaries ("are," "am," "is") could be represented meaningfully in an acoustically salient manner at the beginnings and ends of short phrases. We propose that conventionalizing play with language in a context of conceptual support and using language that is meaningfully tied to . the event free the child to begin reflecting on more abstract linguistic systems. We hope that this treatment of more abstract forms will stimulate later consideration of language as a "formal problem space" (see Karmiloff-Smith, 1979) and will increase other forms of language play that may be precursory to later metalinguistic developments.

Another intervention practice that derives from our observations of children's recurrent participation in routine events has to do with our systematic violations of the set of expectations that children have for those events. Intentional violations of various aspects of routine events (failure to initiate an obligatory action, withholding an obligatory object, transposing on action sequence) can be productive strategies for stimulating children's formulation of specific speech acts (i.e., protests: "no we can't use that!"; directives: "put the top on, *then* shake"), while at the same time providing salient opportunities for extending children's initiations regarding such violations in semantically or syntactically more complex ways. An example of this strategy is as follows:

Violation of a Routine Juice-Making Event. The clinician begins to shake a jar of juice, prior to placing the top on the jar.

1. Child 1: "No! Put the top on, then shake"
2. Clinician (using a sentence completion strategy): "If I don't put the top on . . ."
3. Child 1: "the juice come out"
4. Clinician (using a directive with semantic/syntactic structure embedded, to Child 2): "Tell everybody what we hafta do, or, what will happen if we don't . . ."
5. Child 2: "We hafta put the top on or the juice will come out"
6. Clinician: "That's right!" "Here, you put this top on, then the juice won't spill out when we shake it"

Here the clinician uses a violation of an event sequence to stimulate the children's initiation of a protest and also to focus on the conditional aspect of the initially expressed temporal relation. At first glance, the clinician's directive at turn 4 appears quite complex; and, in a different context, this sort of directive could be problematic for a preschooler. In this instance, we are using this superficially complex directive, as a *scaffold* to the development of linguistic expression of conditional relations as in utterance 5.

The order of the propositions "put the top on," "juice come out" is structured in the preceding discourse (turn 2 and turn 3) as a conditional elaboration of Child 1's initiation of a temporal relation (turn 1) to protest the violation of the event sequence. The clinician establishes this sequence of propositions by using a sentence completion strategy (turn 2). The basic structural format of the directive in turn 4 maintains this order, and the center embedded conditional conjunction "or" demarcates the clauses, as it is made acoustically salient by pause time. In addition to the syntactic frame, the directive provides the surface structure (*hafta* do; *will* happen) of the modal and temporal aspects of the verb elaborations that this particular conditional response entails. Schenkein (1980) and Levelt and Kelter (1982) present evidence that speakers utilize the surface forms of speech already produced in the discourse to generate their utterances. These researchers speculate that this may be an economical practice in linguistic formulation. Thus, event violation can provide a conceptual focus, whereas the structure of the discourse and the surface features of particular clinician utterances can scaffold semantic and syntactic aspects of linguistic formulation. Hence, in turn 5 we see evidence of processing off the text in the production of linguistically well-formed conditional notion.

A final point regarding routine events is that, as we repeatedly engage children in certain activities, we develop expectancies for their use of language in those contexts. We thus become more attuned to subtle though important linguistic changes that we otherwise might overlook. Awareness of this process assists in the precision of timing of various intervention goals and strategies.

CURRENT CLINICAL PROCEDURES IN THE APPLICATION OF SCRIPTS

A SCRIPTAL APPROACH TO THE FACILITATION OF EARLY SEMANTIC-SYNTACTIC RELATIONS IN PRESCHOOL DIALOGUE

In this section, I refer to two different schematic representations of a preschool activity. These representations frame a detailed discussion of specific examples of our approach, and they can be considered as scripts for activity plans based on the communication objectives developed for the children in our program. In using these plans, we attempt to communicate an event structure that fits the cognitive organization of the child and event content that is related to our language goals for the child. We underscore the fact that these plans guide our presentation of events, imposing an organizational structure that assists but does not restrict children's spontaneous expressions. As we have seen, there are a number of complex relationships among linguistic and nonlinguistic events that interventionists can create and exploit through this method. Consider now some specific demonstrations of how this might be accomplished in relation to Fig. 1.

Events are presented with the purpose of increasing the use of certain linguistic and communicative forms, functions, and operations, and for developing or stimulating the emergence of an awareness of others. Figure 1 is discussed as it relates to the following intervention objectives:

1. To increase the content coordinated with major verb relations in 2 and 3 constituent utterances, for example:
   a. To express *intention* (using the semi-auxillaries, wanna, gonna, hafta, spoesta) + locative action, to give a directive ("spoesta put in there")

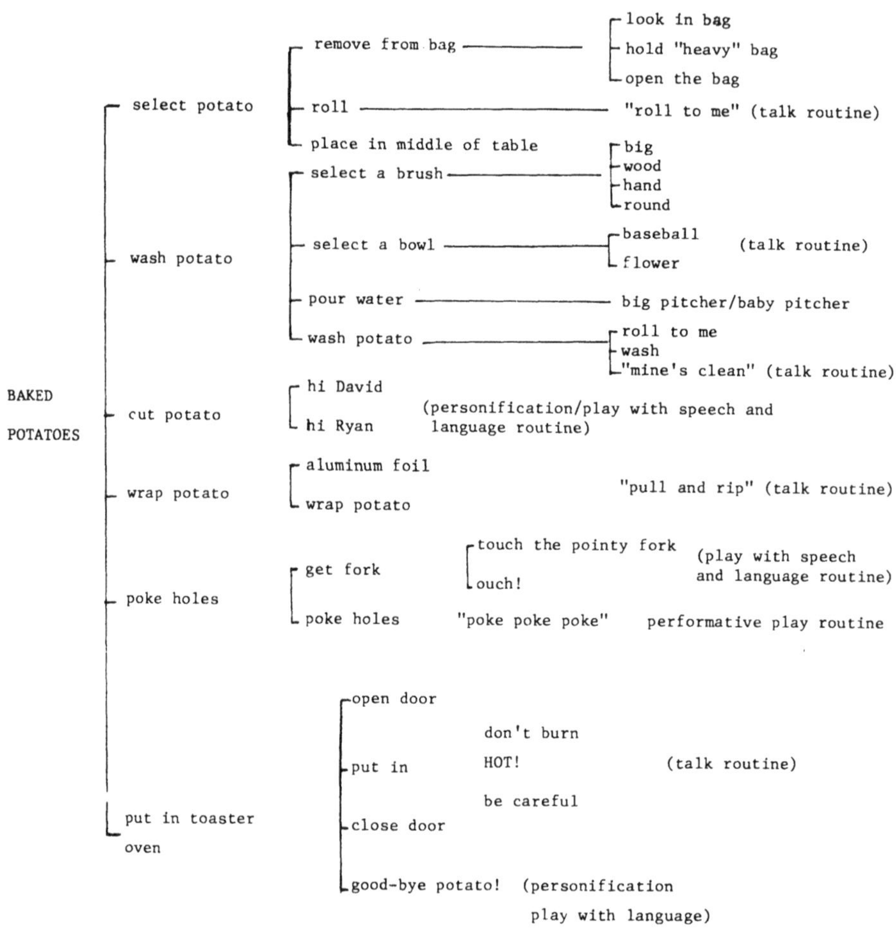

FIG. 10.1. A scriptal approach to the facilitation of early semantic-syntactic relations in preschool dialogue (Adapted from Nelson, 1982a)

+ notice, to request (''I wanna see'')
+ action, to answer or comment (''hafta wash it'')

b. To specify *place*
   + notice, to show or give a directive
   (''see potato in there,'' ''look in there'')
c. To express *attribution*
   + state (internal, possessive) to request, to announce (''I want wood brush,'' ''have a round brush'')
d. To code *possession*
   + locative, to give a directive (''pour some in my bowl'')
   + state (attributive), to show (''my potato (is) clean'')

2. To stimulate the emergence of non-present grammatical morphemes, or increase the use of productive grammatical morphemes in obligatory contexts.
3. To provide salient and functional exemplars of the various semantic roles and form classes that individual lexemes can take.
4. To increase the ability to generate linguistically and contextually contingent utterances in discourse.
5. To facilitate the use of the same semantic-syntactic units for different communicative and constitutive functions, within the same activity.
6. To increase play with morphological and syntactic mechanisms of the language.
7. To stimulate the awareness of language as an object (as a precursor to metalinguistic awareness).

These specific objectives were based upon our analysis of numerous language samples of each of our children during individual and group interactions. The developmental spread of the production objectives (1) and (2) reflects the heterogeneity of linguistic skills evident in our group of children. Objectives (3) and (6) are designed to enhance children's development of the awareness of various operations within the linguistic system. Together with the more pragmatically focused objectives, (4), and (5), these objectives are designed to promote flexibility in our language disordered children's communicative systems, as these systems are often characterized as inflexible and lacking creativity. Finally, objective (7) reflects a general concern for developing prerequisites for later secondary language skills that are typically troublesome for these children.

In Fig. 10.1, the schematic plan for the group activity of baking potatoes is outlined. The event is divided into major subscripts (e.g., selection, washing, cutting, etc.) with component acts and variations. The first example from Fig. 10.1 focuses on intervention objectives 1a, 1b, and 4. This particular segment relates to the very first act in the ''subscript'' of selecting a potato. The scriptal elaboration of this act, as in the following sequence from an actual implementation, demonstrates the ''talk/do'' turn-taking format discussed earlier.

1. (The clinician is holding a 10 lb. bag of potatoes) ''Hey! I see potatoes in here,'' (peering into mesh in the front of the bag) ''wanna see?'' (looking at Child 1) (several children respond affirmatively)

2. Child 1 nods head
3. Clinician: (gives bag to Child 1, who looks in bag) "See the potatoes?"
4. Child 1 nods head
5. Clinician: (to class) "David sees potatoes in that bag!" (to Child 2) "wanna see?"
6. Child 2: "yeah"
7. Clinician: (slides bag over to Child 2) "you hafta look in the window" (pointing to the mesh)
8. Child 2: "Hey! 'tato in there . . . (turns to Child 3) wanna see?"
9. Child 3: "yeah"
10. Clinician: (helping Child 2 slide bag) "Tell Ryan, he hasta look in the window."
11. Child 2: "hafta look in the window" (points to the mesh window)
12. Child 3: "Hey 'tatoes in that bag"
13. Clinician: (to Child 3) "Does Joshua wanna see in the bag?"
14. Child 3: (turns to Joshua) "Wanna see? . . . 'tatoes in this . . ."
15. Clinician: (as Child 3 tries to push bag to Joshua, Clinician looks to Child 6 across the table) "You're gonna look in the bag too! You're gonna see the potatoes"
16. Child 6: "I gonna see . . ."

In this example, every clinician utterance (with the exception of utterance (3) expresses the semantic content specified in the language objectives (1a,1b). Thus, an underlying function of each of these is to provide a model of semantic content and syntactic form. Furthermore, utterances that coordinate place with notice ("David sees potatoes in that bag," "I see potatoes in here") function primarily as announcements or comments while an experiencer is looking in the bag. On the other hand, utterances that coordinate intention with notice ("wanna see?," "you hafta look in the window") function primarily as requests or directives immediately prior to the actor or experiencer's action or notice.

Clinician turns 1 and 5 utilize this relationship between utterances content and function to create a discourse convention for task accomplishment. At turn 8, Child 2 uses the content-function (though reduced in form) models to constitute the task, just as the clinician did. Clinician turn 7 again models content and form specified in the intervention objectives. Later, in turn 10, the clinician uses a directive with those semantic-syntactic relations embedded in it in order to facilitate Child 2's coordination of notice and intention to direct Child 3 (see turn 11). We believe that the organizational structure and content redundancy present in the linguistic, discourse, and activity contexts is crucial to the development of such linguistically and contextually contingent utterances for sustaining discourse cohesion by language disordered children. Similarly, we assume that the knowledge of these conventionalized features of the discourse/activity context could be used to guide pragmatic inference. In turn 13, this assumption underlies the clinician's use of a question to elicit Child 3's turn (14), in which he uses targeted semantic content to make a request which is pragmatically valid.

The creation of the two "roll to me" events in Fig. 1 relates to intervention objectives 3, 5, and 6. In the second subscript of selecting a potato, the children engage in rolling a potato about the table. In this rather playful episode, children compete for acknowledgments of their requests ("roll me," "here," "roll it here"). The clinician during her turns provides models such as:

"I'm going to roll . . . to Ryan" (rolls potato)

"I'm going to roll . . . to David" (rolls potato)

Here the clinician intentionally segments the to + place/benefactive in the verb phrase, just prior to rolling the potato. Thus, the children's names represent beneficiaries as well as places.

Later, in a subscript of washing the potato, the children's expressions of the phrase to + Name similarly signal the clinician's action as follows:

Clinician:	"Ok, now you need your potatoes so you can wash them. (picks up a potato from the middle of the table) Here's David's so I hafta roll this one . . . to David (rolls). Here's Ryan's. I hafta roll this one . . . (points to Ryan and *witholds action*)
Children:	. . . "to Ryan!"
Clinician:	"This is Joshua's, I'm gonna roll this one . . ."
Children:	"to Josh . . ."

The models and functions of the clinician's acts in the first activity are designed to support the children's use of previously segmented phrases to complete the clinician's sentences in order to direct her action during the second activity. When the clinician witholds her action as a strategy, she presumes that the children have developed and will apply knowledge from the previous event to infer her intent. The causal relations coded by the clinician's talk in the second activity are designed to present the children's names in contrasting semantic roles (as possessor and benefactive/place). Also these sentences coordinate possessive state with locative action in the construction of the causal semantic relation that is soon to emerge and that can be construed obviously from the context.

In the next segment of Fig. 1, children accumulate the obligatory objects for washing potatoes. The presentation of each object (bowls, brushes, water) is accomplished in a scriptal fashion. The first two subscripts are designed to make salient the pragmatic force of attribution in specifying desired objects. An additional focus is to demonstrate how the language creates attributive roles and places these role markers in the prenoun position.

(The clinician approaches the table with a large bucket which is filled with brushes. The clinician remains standing.)

1. Clinician: "We need brushes to scrub our potatoes. I have big brushes." (places 2 large brushes on the table)
2. Clinician: ". . . this brush you can put your hand through, like this" (demonstrating) "Wanna put your hand through?"

(Children nod and take turns putting their hands through the hand brush while discussing the brush.)

3. Clinician: "OK, I have hand brushes." (places 2 hand brushes next to the big brushes)
4. Clinician: (taking another brush out of the bucket) "This one's round." (tracing finger around edge of brush)

(Children take turns touching the brush)

5. Clinician: "OK, big brushes, hand brushes, round brushes (placing round brush on the table) and a wood brush (places a wooden brush on the table) and another wood brush"
6. Clinician: (placing each type of brush back in the bucket) "big brushes, hand brushes, round brushes and wood brushes"
7. Clinician: (looking into the bucket she is holding) "I want a (selecting a brush) wood brush." (places the brush in front of herself)
8. Clinician: (looks to Child 2) "How about you?"
9. Child 2: "I want a hand one."
10. Clinician: "OK, David gets a hand brush. Here, you can put your hand through it." (Clinician looks to Child 3)
11. Child 3: "I want wood brush"
12. Clinician: (giving brush) "Here, now Ryan has a wood brush and I have a wood brush"
13. Clinician: "Ryan, ask Joshua if he wants a big brush (hands Ryan a big brush) or a hand brush" (hands Ryan the hand brush)
14. Ryan: (to Joshua) "big brush or hand brush?"
15. Joshua: "This one" (takes a hand brush)
16. David: "Hey, hand brush, hand brush . . ."
17. Clinician: "That's right David, you have a hand brush, and . . . (looks to Joshua)
18. Joshua: "I have hand brush"

The clinician uses turns 5 and 6 to provide recurrent markings of the attributes as well as to return the brushes to the bucket. The bucket is subsequently held out of the children's reach. Since the brushes are inaccessible to pointing, the pragmatic necessity to code attribution is created (unlike the circumstances that arise in turns 14 and 15).

Turns 7 and 8 together stimulate the coordination of the verb relation with the attribute in Child 2's turn 9. Turn 7 provides a semantic-syntactic model that is mapped onto selecting a brush. In turn 8, the clinician intentionally uses a nonspecific request form ("How about you?"). Had the clinician used a specific request form ("Which one do you want?"), it is likely that the child would have elided the verb want and simply responded "hand one." The clinician's goal here was to structure her discourse to provide a linguistic scaffold and pragmatic condition for the child's specification of a desired object by coordinating state with attribution in a three constituent utterance.

In turn 13, the clinician gives Ryan a turn to offer the brushes. Here, the clinician separates the final 2 noun phrases of her directive by handing Ryan a brush. Ryan subsequently uses the 2 final noun phrases (''big brush, hand brush''), maintaining discourse cohesion while responding to a directive with a pragmatically relevant request.

In turn 16, David makes an announcement analogous to the clinician's announcement in turn 12. Turn 17 has the multiple discourse functions of acknowledging David's remark and expanding his remark by using a sentence completion strategy. Consequently, Joshua makes a pragmatic inference and produces a linguistically contingent utterance that coordinates state and attribution.

The next major component act in Fig. 10.1 is cutting potato. (This is obligatory in our preschool to make the potatoes fit in the toaster oven.) A playful episode evolves from this component act (see Fig. 10.1). The potatoes are cut in half and subsequently made to ''talk'' to the children (similar to a pac-man design). Here are some of the utterances that constitute an activity:

Clinician: ''Hey he's talking to Ryan,'' ''I'll make him whisper in your ear,'' ''Mr. Potato is telling Josh a secret, psst, psst,'' ''Hi David, Hi Ryan (opening and closing each half of the potato.)'' ''Wanna hear him talk?'' ''Say cheese Mr. Potato.''

Children: ''Talk e me!,'' ''Hi 'tato!,'' ''talk, talk, talk,'' ''sh whisper,'' ''Tell him me,'' ''Cheese!''

Constable and van Kleeck (1984) suggest that words such as ''tell,'' ''ask,'' ''hear,'' ''talk,'' ''whisper,'' ''word,'' ''joke,'' ''sound'' be thought of in terms of a ''metalexicon.'' They suggest that these words, as well as expressions such as ''that's hard to say,'' ''what's that called,'' ''I didn't hear you,'' and ''say it again,'' focus children on speech and language. They assert that the ''frequency with which these words and expressions can be integrated into various activities may relate to the development of metalinguistic skill'' (p. 8).

A SCRIPTAL APPROACH TO THE FACILITATION OF EVENT RELATIONS AND COMPLEX STRUCTURES IN PRESCHOOL DIALOGUE

In the early phases of intervention, the turn-taking format for the accomplishment of each of numerous component acts within one event affords redundancy. This redundancy supports the development of event representations and abstractions of basic semantic and pragmatic relations. Hence, early on, the potato baking activity may constitute a major activity of the day.

The event knowledge that children develop during the early phases plays a major role in the transformation of events over time. In later phases of intervention routine events take on a different form. Many component acts are collapsed or accomplished by a division of labor among participants. This alteration coin-

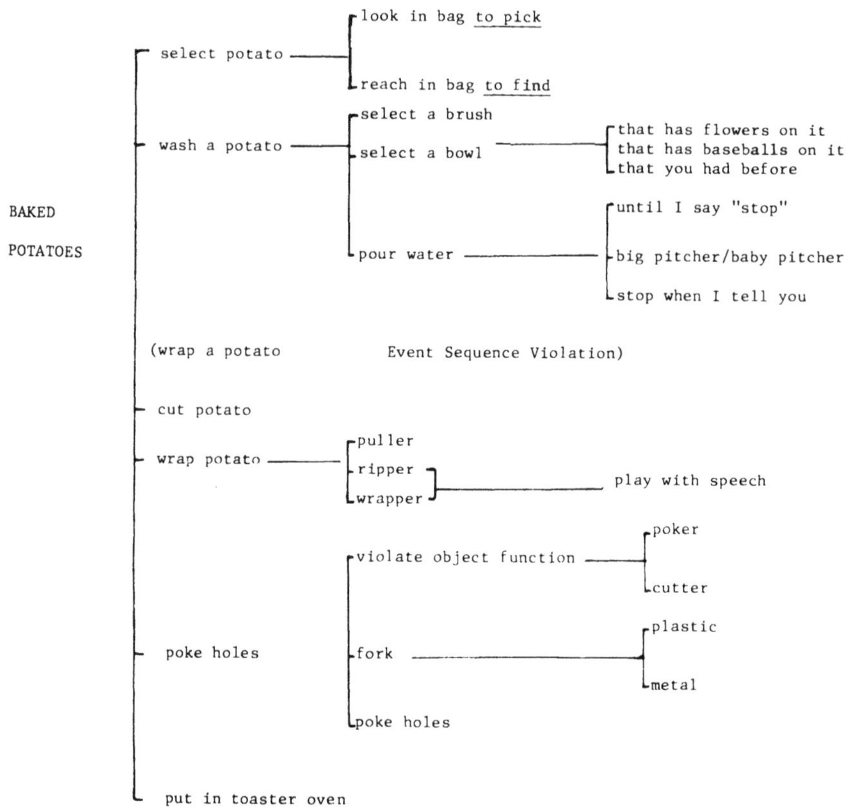

FIG. 10.2. Facilitation of Event Relations and Complex Syntax

cides with the evolution of new subscripts which the clinician guides (see Fig. 10.2). The clinician systematically alters the event in order to bring into focus more complex event relations and interactions commensurate with the childrens' unfolding linguistic and communicative developments.

In the introduction to the section on application, I discussed how clinicians can exploit event knowledge by intentionally violating childrens' presumed expectations for how events are to be accomplished. These violations often stimulate children to consider and express conditional and causal relations that hold within events, to hypothesize or predict. In addition, children's reactions to intentional alternations in event structure and content can reveal to us the accuracy of our inferences regarding their event representations.

The events presented in Fig. 10.2 make use of these event violations. Figure 10.2 is discussed as it relates to the following objectives:

1. To increase the use of simple infinitive clauses in complex sentences, in order to explain or specify essential actions or objects (i.e., use the fork to poke).
2. To increase coding of temporal relations using complex sentences conjoined by "and," "and then," "then," in order to retell or give directions (i.e., First you cut the potato, then you wrap and then you poke).
3. To increase coding of causal and antithetical relations using complex sentences conjoined by "so," "because," and "but" in order to explain relations between enabling states, actions, and results (i.e., This one can break, but this one won't, because this one is strong).
4. To develop coding of temporal/conditional relations using "if . . . then" structure, and temporal adverbs; while, before, until, when; to give a directive, complete a sentence or predict (i.e., If we cut it, it will fit).
5. To increase awareness of derivational mechanisms for changing form class.
6. To increase reference to events and actions in the future.

The following segment relates to objectives 2, 4, and 6. Here the children have just completed washing potatoes, and the clinician places aluminium foil on the table. A dialogue ensues around the event sequence violation that is specified in Fig. 2.

1. Child 1: "No, you hafta cut . . ."
2. Clinician: "That's right, you hafta cut the potatoes before . . ."
3. Child 1: "before you wrap em up"
4. Clinician: (to Child 2) "You tell us what we do first and what we do next."
5. Child 2: "First you cut the potato, then you wrap and then you poke."
6. Clinician: (to Child 3) "What will happen if we don't cut the potato?"
7. Child 3: "It can't fit"
8. Clinician: "That's right, if we cut it, then it will fit in the oven but if we don't cut it, then we can't fit the potato in."

The clinician's intentional violation of the event sequence stimulates a protest from Child 1 (and others). The clinician's utterance in turn 2 has several functions: it acknowledges the violation and expands the content using a sentence completion strategy that is subsequently elaborated by the child. Child 1 restates the temporal adverb by coordinating his utterance with the clinician, thus reiterating the temporal relation.

In turn 4, Child 2 receives a directive to retell. We begin making more instructional type demands such as this in order to prepare the children for the school contexts to come. Because these sorts of discourse conventions are new to the children, we introduce them in contexts that provide linguistic and conceptual scaffolds. The structure and content in clinician turn 4 sets up the temporal as well as the structural frame for Child 2's response. This formulation is guided by previous knowledge of Child 2's predisposition to "process off the text." Likewise, our awareness of his event knowledge ensures that the child has the conceptual resources to respond logically.

In turn 6, Child 3 is stimulated "to predict." Again, a more instructional task is first embedded in a predictable context. The clinician subsequently reiterates a conditional semantic perspective of the event (turn 8).

The following dialogue relates to objectives 1, 3, and 5 wherein the clinician begins handing out knives for the poking the potatoes segment (see Fig. 2).

1. Child 3: (amidst several protests) "No you need forks"
2. Clinician: "That's right, we use a fork to poke and . . . (extends a knife towards Child 4)
3. Child 4: ". . . use the knife to cut"
4. Clinician: "So the fork is the poker and the knife is the cutter!" (passes out plastic and metal forks) "Here's a poker for you and a poker for you and a poker for you . . ."
5. Child 4: (in response to receiving a plastic fork) "Hey I can't use this, I want the metal kind!"
6. Clinician: "Tell me why you can't use this (takes the plastic fork) but you can use this (hands a metal knife)"
7. Child 4: "This one can break, but this one won't . . ."
8. Clinician: "because . . ."
9. Child 4: "because this one is strong."
10. Clinician: "These plastic one's aren't very strong (breaks fork trying to poke a potato) so they break when we try to use them."

Here again, the clinician makes use of event knowledge, this time with respect to object roles that correspond to component acts, to bring a targeted semantic-syntactic focus into the discussion. Hence, the infinitive clause (to poke) can be modeled and used in a sentence completion to justify an initial protest (see turns 1–3). This discussion sets up the semantic focus for using the derivational mechanism for nominalizing their respective functions ("to poke," "to cut") to refer to the fork and the knife ("poker," "cutter"). Consequently the clinician refers to the fork as the "poker" several times in the context.

In turns 5–10, the topic is initiated by the presentation of a category member that is not substitutable in the activity because of its composition. A violation, which presupposes event knowledge, once again creates the semantic focus. This time the clinician is seeking to stimulate explanations for antithetical state relations and resultant actions. Once again, the clinician scaffolds the linguistic resources of the child by using a directive with the semantic-syntactic relations embedded (turn 6) and a sentence completion (turn 8). In turn 10, the clinician demonstrates the effects of the compositional attribute discussed, this time presenting the same causal relation, but using a different syntactic form (see Ammon, 1981 for a relevant discussion).

CONCLUSION

The human predisposition and ability to seek, recognize, extract, analyze, and reorganize patterns is basic to many linguistic developments (see Cicourel, 1974; Dore, 1983; Nelson, 1980; Peters, 1983; Shatz, 1984a, 1984b). Recent evidence (Conti-Ramsden & Friel-Patti, 1983; Johnson, 1984; Lasky & Klopp, 1982) from the analysis of parental talk suggests that the external linguistic data that is *available* for analysis by language disordered children is not significantly different from the linguistic data available for analysis by normal language learners. These findings imply that, at least initially, it is not an impoverished external source of linguistic data that lies behind the language disorder.[1] It seems probable that the resources for extracting from, organizing, and operating with an amalgam of perceptual, linguistic, social, and conceptual data (both internal and external) are in some way amiss in these children relative to the normal course of language acquisition. Although at the present time this is a speculative proposal, it provides a powerful tool for the analysis and remediation of language disorders.

The script analysis outlined in this volume and in previous papers (e.g., Nelson & Gruendel, 1979, 1981) have suggested how these basic resources in normal language learners fit into a system of cognitive operations upon social (external) experience, to yield internal products (scripts) that serve as the basic units for further processing. Just how scripted the events in context *need* to be, in order for normal children to develop their language system remains to be seen. However, the greater the extent to which an event in context is "scripted," the more easily it appears to be assimilated for the formation of a generalized event representation—a "basic building block" for further cognitive (and perhaps linguistic) analyses. (See Nelson & Gruendel, 1981, and previous chapters in this volume.)

In designing a language intervention program, I built upon these ideas, and the results of their application have been clinically successful. There is an intimate sense to the script-based intervention I have described, a sense of organizing their language experience with the children themselves. Based upon 6 years of experience with its development as well as descriptive data on the progress made by more than forty children, the efficacy of this approach has been well

[1]Although the long term effects of a child's language disorder on his or her linguistic environment are not clear, it is speculated that over time these effects may become more pronounced.

demonstrated (see also Constable, 1981). Language disordered children exhibit a desperate need for structure and redundancy of all kinds. A scriptal approach to intervention fulfills that need while simultaneously developing children's realization of language as the multifunctional tool that it really is.

I began this chapter by pointing out that heterogeneity characterizes the class of children referred to as language disordered. It is wrong to assume that any single intervention strategy would be sufficient to meet all the needs of every language disordered child. On the other hand, the kind of intervention context described here is flexible enough in its design and function to provide a structural foundation for the pragmatic presentation of a variety of linguistic and communicative experiences. Further, it provides dramatic evidence pointing to a psychological reality for scripts and their function in supporting cognitive, communicative, and linguistic processes. Intentional "scripting," followed by systematic variations in those scripted events, has proven clinically useful. This procedure may be a helpful investigative methodology for future researchers as they endeavor to establish further empirical evidence relative to the psychological reality of scripts.

ACKNOWLEDGMENT

I wish to acknowledge John Dore for stimulating my ongoing reconsiderations of what an intervention context can be.

11 Event Knowledge and Cognitive Development

Katherine Nelson

In the preceding chapters, a convincing case has been made that event knowledge plays a central role in the young child's language and thought. It has also been argued that such knowledge provides a basis for action and interaction and a framework for deriving abstract representational structures. In this chapter, the important findings are summarized first; then their implications for general theories of cognitive development are discussed in the context of different developmental paradigms. A representational theory of developmental change emerges from this discussion, and its most important proposals are brought out.

SUMMARY OF FINDINGS

A central finding of this research is that children as young as 3 years are sensitive to the temporal structure of events and are able to report act sequences of familiar events virtually without error. This contrasts with earlier reports (Fraisse, 1963; Piaget, 1969) that young children's memories are all jumbled up. Other research (see Brown, 1976; Mandler, 1983) had demonstrated that preschool children were able to sequence brief, causally connected stories and picture sequences. However, the present research has confirmed that this basic ordering ability is widely applied to everyday event sequences by children younger than previously supposed. Causal connections between acts appear to reinforce the temporal structure, whereas changes in spatial locations play a role in segmenting the overall event structure into discrete scenes and acts.

A second important finding is that young children form general representations of the events they experience rather than the specific idiosyncratic fragments often attributed to them. The language forms children use to report their scripts (general terms for subjects and, for "open slots," timeless present verb forms) and the open script structure, which can be filled in with more specific details when the description of a specific episode is called for (see Chapters 2, 3, 4, and 5) support this conclusion. The attribution of a general structure does not negate the possibility of a specific representation of an episode, which may or may not exist (see Chapter 5); however, the generalization of an experience appears to be a natural product of the child's mind. There is evidence that such generalization is formed on the basis of only one experience of an event, although factors such as what adults say about the event before, during, and after it is experienced may influence the degree to which this is the case.

Evident very early as well are other structural characteristics of event representations, including general role slots, the embedding of action sequences within higher order acts, and the identification of boundary events, goals, and associated central acts. The development of ERs involves increasing schematization, the identification of optional and required acts, conditional pathways, and the evolution of hierarchized structures, that is, structures with subgoals and their associated action sequences embedded within larger goal structures (see Chapters 3 and 4). These effects are similar both for increased experience over time and for increasing age. Developmental change is found also in the increasing flexibility of use of scripts in other structures and in a decreasing tendency to be "script-bound," that is, to stick close to the known script in memory, story generation, and action, real or play.

Event knowledge has been shown to have significant effects on memory, language acquisition, discourse processes, and categorization skills. The relation between memory for specific episodes and general representations of the same event appears to be complex and interactive. As more episodes of the same type are experienced, memories of them become more skeletal and general, similar to the GER, while the particular details associated with them become confused with one another (see Chapter 5). This suggests that, as the GER develops, the individual episodes associated with it become identifiable by way of specific details that vary from the norm, whereas the rest of the memory is retrievable through the general structure and its variable slot fillers, which may or may not have associations with that specific memory. Confusions among slot fillers then result. General structures apparently absorb specific memories; that is, specific memories become fused in general representations, becoming memorable in themselves only when they depart in some "weird" way from what can be expected in the general case.

One of the most provocative findings in this research is that, in describing their event knowledge, young children use relational constructions and linguistic terms that reveal an understanding of logical relationships in advance of that usually attributed to them. Hypothetical and conditional relations are appropriately noted by forms such as "if . . . then" or "when x then y." Causal relations are expressed by "because" and "so." Temporal relations are expressed by "then" but also by "before," "after," and "first," and repairs in the report of the temporal sequence are made using these terms. Adversative relations are coded by "but," and alternatives by "or." The acquisition of meaning for each of these terms has, on the basis of previous research assessing comprehension, generally been held to be a relatively late achievement, and deficiencies in logical understanding have been attributed to the young child on the basis of difficulties in understanding these terms. That young children produce these terms appropriately when needed in reporting on logical relationships in well understood events indicates that the problem is not in the child's logic or language but in some other factor. We have proposed, and have reported some experimental evidence to support the proposal, that the familiar ER itself supports the child's understanding and use of these relationships. If, as this research indicates, complex relational language is learned by being mapped onto the relationships evident in the child's event representations, it is clear that this process needs to be explored in more detail and its application to other language domains needs to be examined.

A less direct relation between the child's understanding of events and the learning and use of language is found in the examination of mother-child interactions in familiar and unfamiliar contexts. Here we find that familiar routines enable the child to learn the meanings of words and to engage in extended discourse with mothers; within these routines the child exhibits such relatively advanced skills as giving informative answers to questions and talking about nonpresent objects and events. We proposed that representations of routine events enable the child to attach meanings to already established representations, and that understanding the course of the unfolding activity enables the child to talk about it, within it, and because little attention needs to be paid to the activity itself, to talk about nonpresent events (also well understood). These effects lend additional weight to the proposals by Bruner, Snow and others that mother-child routines play an important facilitating role in children's language acquisition. Moreover, it was also shown that mother-child routines are important for the *establishment* of the child's event knowledge, which in turn affects both language and interaction within the routine.

Additional functions of ERs in children's thinking and discourse are found in story telling and play, where familiar scripts are evident as the basis for novel transformations in fantasy. With respect to stories, children seem to begin by simply reporting thinly disguised scripts as story episodes, and it is not until relatively late (8 years) that they manage to construct actual problem-resolution stories on the basis of their event knowledge. Similarly, in social play during the preschool years, the most successful play sequences (i.e., the longest and most coherent) are transparently based on shared social scripts.

The importance of ERs in young children's learning and thinking is evident as well in the demonstration reported in Chapter 10 that language-delayed children can be helped to achieve higher levels of functioning when they are supported by a program that provides the structure specified by the script model.

Perhaps the most provocative aspect of this research is the suggestion that ERs form the basis for more abstract cognitive structures, such as the formation of hierarchical categories. Research on both event hierarchies and object hierarchies based on slot fillers was reported in Chapter 9, and the logic behind this proposal was discussed there. Further attention is given to this and related matters in the following sections of this chapter.

COGNITIVE DEVELOPMENT FROM AN EVENT KNOWLEDGE BASE

The research reported here was designed to explore to the greatest extent possible the implications of the assumption that children work with representations of whole meaningful events in coming to understand social and object relations in the world around them. For this reason, the research has extended in many different directions rather than concentrating on one central problem, for example, the development of ER structure. This strategy has proven to be fruitful inasmuch as we have consistently found previously unsuspected effects of this type of knowledge structure, effects that have both methodological and theoretical implications. At the same time, this strategy has left many questions—even many basic questions—unanswered. For example, the question of how and when ERs begin to be formed has not received a definitive answer, although our observations have led us to the presumption that they are operative by 1 year of age (Nelson, 1982, 1983, in press; Nelson & Lucariello, in press; see also Mandler, 1983) and are important to cognitive and linguistic developments during the second year. Do ERs begin small, say, representative of a single "scene," and then become chained together, or do they begin as larger wholes that become differentiated? There is no definitive answer at the present time, although no differences in size or length of script (measured in real time extent rather than number of acts) between children of different ages from 3 to 8 have been observed. Other investigators have begun to explore these and related questions with respect to children's event representations (e.g., Bretherton, 1984; Fivush & Mandler, 1985; Gerard & O'Connell, 1985; Wolf, 1984; Worsley, 1984). Thus, more definitive answers to questions about how and when may be expected within the near future. Our present interest is to consider the implications of event knowledge for questions of cognitive development.

The Structure-Function Problem in Cognitive Development

Nelson and Gruendel (1981) claimed that event representations were "basic building blocks" of cognitive development, a claim that was restated in chapter

9. This notion is explored further in the remainder of this chapter. For this purpose it is necessary to place this research in the context of general developmental theory, which would be easier to do if there were general agreement on how developmental theory should be conceived. At the present time, however, there are competing views on this issue deriving from different theoretical traditions, and a brief consideration of those traditions that retain an influence on current developmental thinking is therefore in order.

In brief outline it would be correct to say that behavioristic or learning approaches to problems of cognitive development (insofar as the term itself was acceptable—see Kessen, 1962) dominated the field through the 1950s and into the early 60s (e.g., Kendler & Kendler, 1962). The hallmark of this approach is the assumption that change in the structure of behavior (or thought) is a function of learning contingencies in the environment. Thus, the child was viewed basically as a passive recipient of environmental stimuli, responses to which led to learning. Insofar as internal structure was recognized, it was as a mediator between external stimulus and external response and was a function of prior experience with stimulus-response contingencies. This tradition and its contemporary descendents (e.g., Whitehurst & Zimmerman, 1979) represent a kind of pure American functionalism (Boring, 1957), with cognitive structure viewed as largely irrelevant to the theory.

Piaget's resurgent influence began to be felt within the field in the mid-60s marked by Flavell's (1963) landmark book, soon thereafter making its way into the most unabashedly empirically oriented textbooks. Piaget was initially viewed as an organismic theorist similar to Heinz Werner (e.g., Langer, 1969) and in contrast to the mechanistic view of the learning theorists. In truth, however, Piaget's genetic epistemology was designed to solve the problem of the evolution of logical thought and the acquisition of scientific knowledge. Other concerns of the organism (e.g., emotional, aesthetic, social) lay outside his theoretical structure. Language, too, was considered of secondary importance to logical thought.

Piaget (1971) classified himself as a structuralist, emphasizing the importance of the organization of cognitive operations in a logical, mathematical structure. The notion of organization and structure was based in the biological analogy that Piaget invoked between intelligence and other biological functions, such as digestion. The same analogy produced the claim of the invariant functions of adaptation—assimilation and accommodation—that lay behind all cognitive change and that led inevitably to equilibration. It could be said that the functionally oriented field of American child psychology found it easier to accept the proposal of cognitive structure (which filled a vaccuum in the prevalent theory) than that of the invariant functions. Dissatisfaction with the latter stemmed from the apparent impossibility of sufficiently specifying in any given case which function would be operative and what the result of that operation would be. Thus, predicting change (or learning or the acquisition of new knowledge) in particular situations was not feasible. The result was that Piaget's functionalism became lost to view, whereas his structuralism became the hallmark of his system and the aspect that was tested in innumerable experiments in the 1960s and 1970s.

An important part of the structural claim was the proposed sequence of stages of cognitive development, from sensorimotor to preoperational to concrete operational and finally to the formal operations of adolescence and adulthood. Whether cognitive development should be conceived of in terms of stages or whether it is more fruitfully conceived of in terms of continuous development remains controversial (Brainerd, 1978 and responses; Flavell, 1971, 1982). It might be noted that the major stages demarcated by Piaget coincide with major periods recognized by many other theoretical approaches, including maturational theories (e.g., Gesell & Ilg, 1946) and psychodynamic theories (e.g., Erickson, 1950; Freud, 1952). That is, it is widely recognized that there are major shifts in functioning during childhood; the real question is whether they can be accounted for in terms of the structural shifts in the organization of intelligence posited by Piaget.

During the same period in which Piaget's theory began to have a major influence on child psychology, a different theoretical approach was being developed, drawing on the information processing models of cognitive psychology, which both utilized computer analogies in building models and also used computer simulations to test them (e.g., Neisser, 1967; Norman, 1970; Norman & Rumelhart, 1975). In this approach, cognition is modelled as a series of stages in the processing of data encountered by the subject. The subject is viewed as using strategies and rules to process data and solve problems or store information in memory. This approach is basically a functional one and in many of its assumptions resembles its learning theory predecessors. For example, the organism is essentially a passive recipient of information (although an active processor); the processing mechanism is "hard-wired" and does not develop (although some recent developmental models propose maturational change in the structure of the "hardware"). On the other hand, information processing models resemble Piaget's theory in being equally oriented toward logical thought and problem solving by the individual and unconcerned with social, emotional, or esthetic aspects of development. The distinguishing characteristic of information processing models in contrast to earlier learning models is their concentration on the internal data processing mechanisms rather than on external response mechanisms. Within this tradition, development is viewed as the acquisition of more adequate rules or skills for dealing with problems presented by the environment, and a basic unresolved problem for these models is how developmental change takes place (see Sternberg, 1984).

A related paradigm within cognitive science, deriving initially from Chomsky's (1965, 1975) views of language acquisition, is what has been called the *new nativism*. This view has been most strongly articulated by Fodor (1972, 1975, 1980), who argues that all concepts and all logical structures are innate. Less extreme variations propose that all essential cognitive operations and structures are present or potentially present in the human neonate and that any observable structural changes (whether in "hardware" or "software") are a product of maturation. Within this tradition much research is directed toward demonstrating that, when appropriately tested, younger children display many of the same capacities and competencies that older children do, although their knowledge base is less developed (e.g., Chi, 1978; Gelman, 1978; Keil, 1979).

Interestingly, this position has been occupied by both those who see social input as essentially irrelevant to development (e.g., Goldin-Meadow, 1981) and those who see teaching as a likely source of skill learning, even though the capacity for the skill is "built-in" (e.g., Gelman, 1978). Proponents of this position may be either structuralists or functionalists, depending on whether primary emphasis is put on innate structure or on processes of acquisition and development.[1]

A different influence on developmental theory began to be felt in the 1960s and grew in importance during the 70s and 80s, that of the ideas of Lev Vygotsky, the Soviet theorist who wrote in the 20s and 30s. Vygotsky's influence in this country began with the publication of the translation of his book, *Thought and language,* in 1962, and increased as such scholars as Cole, Scribner, Meachem, and Wertsch articulated his theoretical concepts and translated his works and those of his Soviet co-workers and followers (e.g., Cole, John-Steiner, Scribner, & Souberman, 1978; Luria, 1976; Wertsch, 1984). Vygotsky cannot easily be characterized in terms of either a structural or functional position. His approach to cognitive development, unlike that of Piaget or the information processing approaches, was explicitly based on social influence and on language and culture. In that sense, it was closer to the assumptions of the learning theorists, but its conception of the historical cultural context was far richer than that of American psychology, and the assumed influence of cultural context on thought was more far reaching. Vygotsky also proposed a progression of developmental stages of thought that has much in common with Piaget's, although they differed on the source of developmental change.

Many researchers have now adopted a point of view that may be termed "social transactionism," which depends to a greater or lesser degree on Vygotsky's approach and in particular adopts his notion of the Zone of Proximal

---

[1]This characterization leads to the observation that the learning position and the nativist position, once seen as diametrically opposed, have found an interesting accommodation in recent years. Nativists such as Chomsky have always asserted that behaviorists implicitly assumed a great deal of innate structure in order to make their models work, whereas it has been obvious to learning theorists that innate structure alone could not lead to the acquisition of such culture-specific knowledge domains as language. What has been needed, and what seems to have come about in many cases, is that some of the theorists originally deriving their assumptions from modified learning theory have accepted the idea of innate structure, while some of the nativists have acknowledged the necessity of learning, thus leading to the position occupied by the new nativists, whose answer to the question "What develops?" often seems to be "nothing."

Development (ZPD). The ZPD proposes that at any given time the child's cognitive state covers a range that extends from his or her own relatively limited ability within a domain to a much greater potential that can be tapped and made accessible through adult help and instruction. In this model there is an interaction between the child's cognitive status and the social world.

As implied in the foregoing discussion, each current explicit or implicit proposal regarding cognitive development places primary emphasis on either cognitive structure or function. There is little agreement, however, on how to characterize cognitive structure and none at all on the mechanisms of cognitive change. Further, the relative contributions of the social world and the individual child to cognitive development differ widely from model to model. Learning models and the ZPD put major emphasis on the contribution of others to cognitive advance, whereas the Piagetian conception and the information processing models tend to view the child in a social vacuum, bound to his or her own cognitive processes. If a general model of development is to result from these traditions, it will need to propose cognitive structure that relates to functions and functional change consistent with what we know about children's growing competence, and it will need to reconcile the contributions of the social world with internal changes in the child's cognitive system. Although we do not claim to have the answers to these problems at the present time, we believe that considering cognition as resting on a representational system that begins with whole events holds promise of progress in this direction.

In Chapter 1, I outlined some of our basic assumptions about the structure of the cognitive system that seem necessary to the functioning of a representational system. In particular, I suggested that such a system consisted of levels and layers of representations together with processes operating on them to produce new cognitive structures (representations). Thus, change in the system would be a function of invariant processes, but these processes are more specific than the assimilation and accommodation processes of Piaget's. They include such factors as pattern analysis; categorization; relational, part-whole, and attribute analysis (differentiation); and synthesis (integration).

What is important about this proposal is that what is represented and how that representation is structured are crucial to both current functioning and future development. This follows from the assumption that higher level (more abstract) structures are derived from the initial representation of reality. Thus, knowledge acquisition is assumed to be the basic developmental force, but this force is more a matter of internal change through cognitive analysis than simply a greater accumulation of "learning." This conception is not radically new, although it departs from the models sketched above even as it reflects their influence. Moreover, it has much in common with a number of current models of language development (e.g., Bowerman, 1982; Karmilov-Smith, 1979; Maratsos, 1982; Nelson, 1985).

Given the assumption that both the content and the structure of what is represented of experience is vital to current functioning and further development, the structure of representations becomes an important matter for investigation. The research reported here has documented that the child's representations of events display a coherent part-whole structure organized in terms of causal-temporal sequences. The structure is general, containing open slots for specific fillers, and it embeds smaller sequences within larger ones. These structural characteristics have important implications for the kinds of more abstract structures that can be derived from them. For example, as outlined in Chapter 9, the open slot structure provides a basis for forming categories of slot fillers. The sequential structure enables the analysis of cause-effect relations. Embedding provides a way of entering optionality and conditionality into the structure. All of these have been found to be aspects of the development of children's event representations, as shown in Chapters 3 and 4.

The representational system functions through the activation of relevant cognitive representations in situations in order to make possible the interpretation of the activity in that situation. Event representations are instantiated in familiar situations to guide action and interaction, both verbal and nonverbal. They make it possible for the child (or the adult) to predict what will happen next and to organize their own actions and verbalizations accordingly. ERs also may affect what is perceived within a situation through the expectations brought up. They influence what is remembered of an event and how it is remembered. Effects of this kind were documented in Chapters 5 and 7.

Higher level cognitive functions may be supported by the basic event representations. For example, the ability to make and carry out plans may begin with simply instantiating a script and proposing slot fillers, and become more complex as different scripts are combined to solve different planning functions. In Chapter 6 evidence was presented to suggest that the cognitive function of reversibility was first manifested on the symbolic level within the familiar script, and also that the meaning of certain terms referring to logical relationships was restricted at first to well-understood scripts. Chapter 8 showed that the generation of fantasy productions was first based on well-known scripts. We also have beginning evidence to suggest that children's ability to make inferences about missing information arises within the context of filling in information from well-known scripts before it is extended to logical implications (Slackman & Hudson, 1984).

All these findings suggest that the script supports cognitive functions before they are manifested in unfamiliar or unstructured situations. A key question is how these functions "break loose" to become transcontextual. We return to this question later.

Before we leave the question of function as conceived here, it should be noted that different types of representations may be activated and may compete within a given situation. This suggestion can be only tentatively advanced at this point, but it seems to offer considerable explanatory power when the behavior of young children is in question. On the one hand, different scripts may compete with one another, for example, play scripts and eating scripts. Or, in some experimental tasks functional schemas (e.g., scripts) may compete with categorical structures in solving problems. It seems probable that earlier established structures win out in such competitions. Thus, if one can in some way shut out the inappropriate structure, one may induce the child to rely on the more abstract structure considered more appropriate to the task. Older children may simply be more adept at managing competing representations. Of particular interest in this regard is the possibility that perceptual representations may compete with higher level cognitive representations and vice versa.[2]

In the following sections, some of the central problems in developmental theory that this view of cognitive development can illuminate are considered.

The Integration of Social and Physical Knowledge

As noted in the previous section, a basic problem for developmental theory is the relative contribution of the social world to advances in cognition in comparison with individual construction of knowledge. Most of the current theoretical positions outlined earlier, with the exception of Vygotsky's, consider the individual in a vacuum, subject to stimuli but not engaged in social interaction. The failure of cognitive theories to take social interaction into account has been felt most strongly in studies of language development, discourse processes, play, and other interactive situations where both cognition and communication are centrally involved and where what knowledge the child gains from the situation and how it is gained are central questions. A model of cognitive development that fails to consider the mechanisms by which the child incorporates knowledge gained from and within social interactive situations is inadequate to most of the problems that such a model needs to address. It is not coincidental that much of this book has focused on problems in language and discourse where these issues arise.

In most theories of cognitive development, knowledge of the physical world and knowledge of the social world are bifurcated, and integration of the two is seen as a problem. At best, as implied in the earlier discussion, social partners are viewed as aiding in acquisition of knowledge about the physical world. Taking event knowledge as basic in the child's knowledge representation system avoids this problem (Nelson, 1981; French, in press). Social interactions are as much a part of such events as the physical objects that are embedded within them. In fact, objects take on meaning only within events (see Nelson, 1985).

---

[2]Some effects of this type have been seen, for example, in the experiment by Fivush briefly reported in Chapter 4, in which children were incapable of screening out inappropriate pictorial representations of an event, even though, when reporting such events without pictorial support, they did not include inappropriate elements. (See also Bruner, 1966.)

The scripts that children produce reveal that both types of knowledge are integrated into a single structure. Social roles are as evident as physical props, and both physical and social causality enter into the structure of children's event reports. Our assumption—and it is still only an assumption—is that this integration is as true for the 1-year-old as for the 3-year-old and that the bifurcation seen by the theorist is a product of sophisticated analysis, not a product of the child mind (see also Glick, 1978). This is by no means to say that the child is not able to distinguish animate and inanimate or confuses people with things. Rather, the child's knowledge of the world is not divided up into two compartments, as their theoretical separation implies.

The young child's ability to sequence events is by now well established, yet only a short time ago lack of sequencing ability was standardly thought to be one of the preschooler's deficiencies. As long as children were asked to sequence arbitrary arrays of objects and actions, their abilities were bound to be underestimated. The kinds of events that make sense to young children, and that are therefore represented in script-like form involving causal-temporal sequences, are those that have understandable social goals, even if the goal is only to be together, as in the book reading routines that young children enjoy. It is not only that children understand sequences organized in terms of understandable goals, it is also that the socially organized events they take part in are sequentially organized, and to understand those events is necessarily to understand their sequences. The finding that sequential knowledge is basic to children's event knowledge, that is, that children are almost flawless in their sequencing of familiar events, is strong evidence that social and physical knowledge are not separate systems in the child's knowledge representations. Objects enter into the sequences that children represent as a consequence of people's actions, not as arbitrary independent acts. In other words, the temporal-causal sequencing revealed in these studies is a natural concomitant of the event representation base and the integration of social and physical knowledge systems. The proposal that such sequencing ability is an innate property of the human cognitive system appears unavoidable.

Many indications of children's understanding of logical relationships have been found in their script reports (see Chapters 3 and 6), including causal relations of different kinds, and hypothetical and conditional propositions. We do not suggest, however, that the acquisition of ERs is dependent on or necessarily reflective of logical thinking. Instead, we suggest that the proposal of ERs as a basic form of representation incorporates the possibility of many types of relationships, some of which will be recognized in due time as resting on logical necessity and others as conventional or as the outcome of alogical human concerns—moral, emotional, communal. It is not necessary for a child (or an adult) to distinguish among the reasons that an event is organized in the way that it is or to understand why it includes particular components in order for it to be represented accurately.

That ERs may include alogical as well as logical relationships may explain some of the responses young children give in tasks ostensibly calling for logical reasoning. Although we have not emphasized it in this report, young children seem to rely on reasoning that reflects their own understanding of human relationships, even when a task apparently calls for abstraction from real world events and consideration of strictly logical relations (Donaldson, 1978). Moreover, as Scribner (1977) has emphasized, young children are not alone in this tendency. Adults in less educated cultures also rely on real world human relationships rather than abstract logic when questions about human activity are asked. For example, in response to an experimenter-posed syllogism such as: "All Kpelle men are rice farmers. Mr. Smith is not a rice farmer. Is he a Kpelle man?" an unschooled adult in this culture may reply: "I don't know the man in person. I have not laid eyes on the man himself . . . Since I do not know him in person I cannot answer that question" (Scribner, 1977, p. 490). Understanding human relationships in their moral, emotional, and communal terms is certainly as complex an achievement as learning to use abstract logical reasoning skills. Abstracting such relationships from event representations should be viewed as an achievement and not dismissed as being of a lower order or of less importance than abstract deductive reasoning.

The integration of social and physical knowledge has implications for the process of acquisition of that knowledge as well. The process we hypothesize is one of *participatory interaction,* that is, one in which children participate in the activity as it is taking place and build up representations of their own actions and those of others (including the speech acts) within the activity (see Chapter 7). The child, guided by the adult, at first participates without full knowledge of the structure of the event; the participatory acts then become part of the child's representation. Although we believe that scripts can be built up through observation alone, this seems to call for imaginative participation, that is, taking an imaginative role in the action. Although the process of participatory interaction needs to be investigated further, our observations of mother-child interaction support the proposal that it facilitates the acquisition of sequential and causal structure so evident in the child's scripts.

Context Effects

One of the standard explanations for young children's deficiencies in performance on cognitive tasks is that they are context bound, that is, that they may display competence in some restricted context, but cannot generalize it across contexts. Such a description, however, explains little. One needs a theory of context that suggests why children are so restricted. Why is one context supportive and another not?

We suggested in the first chapter that instantiating a GER in a given situation serves the child as "cognitive context" and that it is this context, not the external objective context, that does or does not serve to support performance in a given situation. This follows from the proposition that cognitive operations operate on cognitive representations and not on the real world. If the child has a GER that "fits" the current situation appropriately (that is, maps the relations that are relevant to the task at hand), that representation will support any performance that the child understands to be relevant to it. If the child does not have a relevant GER to instantiate, for example in an experimental situation, an inappropriate GER may be called on or performance may deteriorate as the child tries to "make sense" by analyzing the perceptual representation for its salient characteristics, of which the social component may appear to be the most important.

The effect of cognitive context was seen here in the studies on language and play in Chapters 7 and 8, where both language skills and play sequences were more advanced when the children could rely on their knowledge of well-understood events. Improved learning and performance by language-delayed children when they were given the appropriate scripts, that is, provided with the appropriate cognitive context, was demonstrated in Chapter 10. Other studies have reported effects that may be interpreted in this way. For example, White and Glick (1980) demonstrated that, when ghetto children could draw on a context of a "slick trickster" in a conservation task, they performed significantly better than under standard conditions. One can suggest that these children from ghetto neighborhoods had well-established "street scripts" that included slick operators and thus were able to bring the appropriate analytic skills to bear on the transformations.

Another thesis that follows from the cognitive context concept and from the considerations advanced earlier is that children come to understand logical relations within specific event representations, which are then subject to abstraction and integration processes, resulting eventually in generalization across and beyond specific GERs. This proposition received its most persuasive support from the data reported in Chapter 6, where it was shown that children use relational language to describe their event knowledge at an age when they do not display knowledge of these relations in less specifically contextualized situations. It was also shown that even 3-year-olds display the ability to reverse temporal and causal relations within well-understood GERs, that is, to move back and forth within them. Such reversibility, the hallmark of concrete operations in Piagetian theory, is not displayed in less familiar and structured sequences until children are much older (see also Fivush & Mandler, 1985). It should be emphasized that neither familiarity of the event nor temporal-causal event structure is by itself sufficient to support such ability; rather, the temporal-causal structure needs to be established in the child's GER, and this requires familiarity with it.

It seems probable that reversibility, unlike sequencing itself, is a cognitive manipulative skill that is not in the strict sense innate but rather depends on the establishment of a certain degree of stable componentially partitioned structure that can be operated upon and transformed in a number of ways. The first GERs that children establish are likely to be too cohesive and undifferentiated to allow for this sort of manipulation.

A pervasive problem in the study of both cognitive and linguistic development has been the relation between comprehension and production. In the studies reported here, this relation has been observed several times. For example, in the discussion of the production of relational terms it was noted that children seemed to be able to produce these terms appropriately long before they could display accurate comprehension of them in experimental tasks. In contrast, it was noted that children seemed to understand the story structure long before they could generate stories adhering to that structure themselves.

The discrepancy between production and comprehension of relational terms may be interpretable in light of the cognitive context proposal as follows. The relational structure of the GER facilitates the child's understanding of the logical relations within it, and thus the terms that express these relations can be learned and used accurately in scripted contexts. If no GER is available for supporting the interpretation, the young child must construct a representation of the relation relying on the very language that is used to express it. Constructing a logical relation between events on the basis of language alone is evidently a difficult—perhaps impossible—task for the young child, one that calls on more cognitive capacity or skill than can be brought to bear, and the child fails.

This analysis indicates why children are almost always correct in their production of relational terms (and other language constructions). It is not because listeners interpret their intention to fit the meaning of the terms and thus fail to catch inappropriate uses. Rather, children usually know what they are talking about; that is, they produce language in situations that they have accurately represented to themselves. In contrast, the comprehension task places two different kinds of demands upon them. In one case, they may be asked to access a known relationship and interpret it in terms of the language used to describe it. In the other case, they are asked to construct a novel relationship using their knowledge of the language. In the first comprehension situation they will succeed, whereas in the second they will not, as the research reported in Chapter 6 documented.

The case of story production and comprehension is somewhat different. Story production involves using generative rules to create a novel construction on the basis of content available from event knowledge structures. Thus, a number of complex structures and skills must be combined and integrated in this process. Interpreting stories, and using the implicit structure of the story to identify important parts, is evidently a far less demanding task. It seems that the notion of cognitive context plays less of a role in explaining the differences in these two tasks than do the actual skills involved in the two situations, although, as suggested in Chapter 8, GERs may facilitate the child's ability to perform either task.

Other comprehension-production discrepancies found in both linguistic and cognitive domains may be explicable in terms of the differential support provided by the child's cognitive context to the operation of a particular skill. Such effects remain to be analyzed and tested.

The Basis for Categorical Structures

The discussion in Chapter 9 brought out the importance of substitutability as a basis for the formation of concepts and categories. Substitutability among category members is essentially the paradigmatic relation found in the analysis of linguistic structures. It contrasts with contiguity of members known as the syntagmatic relation between unlike elements in a structure (see Nelson, 1982a, 1983, in press). Members that are substituted for each other in a script structure (or in linguistic structures such as sentences) need not have a basis in similarity; rather they fit into functional slots in an event structure. Of course, one can propose that they are functionally similar, as, for example, ice cream and roast beef are similar because they are both foods and can both be eaten. However, this stretches the notion of similarity beyond usefulness and produces a circularity in the explanation of the formation of categories. Rather, contiguity, similarity and substitutability should all be viewed as independent grouping principles.

Unlike similarity and contiguity, substitutability is of interest because it often cannot operate on temporally contiguous perceptual relations. Rather, recognizing that elements can substitute for one another in similar situations depends on the analysis of cognitive representations of those situations and the abstraction of members that fit into the common event structure, which is itself abstracted. That the substitutability principle is evident in the language and thought of the very young child is further evidence for representations as the basis of cognitive growth.

In research on categorization principles utilized by young children, the contrast has generally been drawn between those based on contiguity, that is, a thematic or functional basis, and those based on similarity of color or form. The relation between a pipe and smoke, or a cup and saucer exemplify the first principle; whereas a red square and a red circle exemplify the second. Logical classification has often been tested in terms of whether children group objects according to an exhaustive analysis of similarity, whereas grouping according to contiguity is viewed as "infra-logical." Classification tasks seldom allow for grouping according to substitutability principles. For example, even if a group of objects were to include different clothing items, a child who grouped on the basis of substitution within a script would form small nonexhaustive groups, putting together those items that can be put on in the morning but not worn outside, for example. Effects of this kind have, in fact, been reported by Saltz and his colleagues (Saltz, Dixon, & Johnson, 1977). As the discussion in Chapter 10 suggests, and as our initial research on children's categories indicates, such categories appear to have a basis in functional substitutability. Moreover, the analysis of the abstraction possibilities of this principle indicates that such a basis can carry the individual a long way toward the formation of hierarchical taxonomic structures (Nelson, 1982a, 1983, 1985).

Contiguity, similarity, and substitutability can all be recognized at more and less abstract levels. That is, there is no reason for supposing that one principle is more basic than another. Young children do recognize perceptual similarity and classify objects on that basis (Sugarman, 1982). And their propensity to group on the basis of contiguity in the real world has been well demonstrated by Inhelder and Piaget (1964), Vygotsky (1962), and others since. Moreover, Markman (1983) has demonstrated the importance in young children's thinking of collections, which have a part-whole rather than an inclusion structure; these can be viewed as a type of category based on the contiguity relation. Thus it is clear that young children, as well as older children and adults, rely on all three types of relations for forming conceptual structures.

The claim is sometimes advanced that children rely for their object groupings exclusively on the relations apparent in perceptual arrays. Recognizing the importance of the substitutability principle for young children diminishes the force of this claim. Indeed, the bulk of the evidence supports the supposition that the child's cognitive representation often overrides the relations apparent in the perceptual array.

This discussion also suggests that schemas of the ER type are complementary to categories formed on different bases and, in some important cases, provide the basis for categorical formation. However, we hypothesize that logical inclusion relations of the hierarchical taxonomic type depend on the joint availability of "basic level" categories and a linguistic structure that encodes these higher order relations. This proposal goes beyond the evidence or even the speculations possible from the present data; it is discussed at greater length in Nelson (1985).

FURTHER DEVELOPMENTAL IMPLICATIONS

In addition to these problems, which the event representation proposal may aid in solving, there are some implications of the proposal that relate to the characteristics of development itself. First, the very notion of a mental representation implies the achievement of stability in the face of a continuously changing reality. The representation of events involves organizing elements and relations that change over time and that involve different tokens on different occasions. The achievement of a stable structure of this kind provides the child with an instrument for interpreting and acting on a reality that would otherwise be unpredictable and in some sense unknowable. A child who faces a world that is constantly changing, that does not provide the kind of repeatable event structure that makes a stable event representation possible, cannot achieve this kind of stability. We call this the *chaos factor* and speculate that it may have broad repercussions for the impairment of cognitive functioning when stable representations are not established and thus do not become available for cognitive processing.

Because stability is important to making sense of the experienced world, young children tend to rely heavily on their established representations and in this sense become "script bound." We have seen this effect in many different situations, from memory for stories (Chapter 3) to language comprehension (Chapter 6). The ability to manipulate or transform scripts, to use them flexibly in situations and tasks is a later achievement, one that apparently follows the establishment of a repertoire of stable representations. We found that this was characteristic of developments taking place at about 5 to 7 years. At this point, the evidence we have on these matters is suggestive and not direct, but the research reported here points in this direction.

Another implication of the present proposal to be emphasized is that content is as important to the cognitive system as is structure. The event representation is general and structured, but it is also specific to particular times, places, and people. Inasmuch as it serves as the basis for further structural abstraction (of categories, roles, event hierarchies, for example), these are abstracted across particulars. That is, abstractions never emerge without content. The upshot of this is that the child can be observed to be both specific and abstract. While the specifics of a situation may direct thought and action in that situation, at the same time the child may relate specifics on the basis of highly abstract relations. For example, children readily see that adults who fill a certain role may all be given the same name, i.e., "the teacher." Development, then, does not consist of a move from concrete and specific to abstract and general. Rather, these labels are misplaced; the child's thought is general and specific, concrete and abstract all at the same time.

A number of other developmental implications and implications for further research have been raised during the course of the discussion in the various chapters of this book. At this point, we rest our case for the importance of event representations in the cognitive structure and functioning of the young child. It is already clear that considerable interest in the topic exists and that further research in this area is underway. If we have overstated the case, these investigations will no doubt redress the balance. We think it more likely that evidence will continue to accumulate indicating that children think in terms of and within events and that this fact has significance for many areas of their cognitive performance and development.

REFERENCES

Abbott, V. A., & Black, J. B. (1980). *The representation of scripts in memory.* (Technical Report No. 5). New Haven, CT: Yale University, Center for Cognitive Science.

Abelson, R. P. (1981). Psychological status of the script concept. *American Psychologist, 36* (7), 715–729.

Ames, L. B. (1966). Children's stories. *Genetic Psychology Monographs, 73,* 337–396.

Ammon, M. (1981). Understanding of causality in preschool children: From action to explanation. *Topics in language disorders—cognition and language in the preschool years, 2* (1), 33–50.

Anderson, J. R. (1978). Arguments concerning representations for mental imagery. *Psychological Review, 85,* 249–277.

Anglin, J. (1977). *Word, object and conceptual development.* New York: Norton.

Appleby, A. N. (1978). *The child's concept of story.* Chicago: University of Chicago Press.

Aram, D. M., & Nation, J. E. (1982). *Child language disorders.* St. Louis: C. V. Mosby.

Ashmead, D. H., & Perlmutter, M. (1980). Infant memory in everyday life. In M. Perlmutter (Ed.), *Children's memory: New directions for child development* (No. 10, p. 1–16). San Francisco: Jossey-Bass.

Barclay, C., Wellman, H., & Abrams, N. S. (1982, August). *Recognition and dating of everyday, autobiographical memories.* Paper presented at the meeting of the American Psychological Association, Washington, DC.

Barrett, M. D. (1983, September). Scripts, prototypes and the early acquisition of word meaning. In L. French (Chair), *The cognitive context of language use.* Symposium conducted at the meeting of the British Psychological Society Developmental Section Annual Conference, Oxford.

Barsalou, L., & Sewell, D. (1984). *Contrasting the representation of scripts and categories.* Manuscript.

Bartlett, F. C. (1932). *Remembering: A study in experimental and social psychology.* Cambridge, England: Cambridge University Press.

Bashir, A. S., Kuban, K., Kleinman, S. N., & Scavuzzo, A. (1983). Issues in language disorders: Considerations of cause, maintenance and change. In J. Miller, D. Yoder, & R. Schiefelbusch (Eds.), *Contemporary issues in language intervention.* ASHA Reports 12, Rockville, MD.

Bates, E. (1979). *The emergence of symbols.* New York: Academic Press.

Beilin, H. (1975). *Studies in the cognitive basis of language development.* New York: Academic Press.

Beilin, H. (1977). Inducing conservation through training. In G. Steriner (Ed.), *Psychology of the 20th century: Vol. 7 Piaget and beyond* (pp. 260–289). Zurich: Kinder.

Bittetti-Capatides, J., Fiess, K., & Bloom, L. (1980, October). *The contexts of causality.* Paper presented at the meeting of the Fifth Annual Boston University Conference on Child Language, Boston.

Bjorklund, D. F. (1980). Children's identification of category relations in lists presented for recall. *Journal of Genetic Psychology, 136,* 45–53.

Bjorklund, D. F., Ornstein, P. A., & Haig, J. R. (1977). Development of organization and recall: Training in the use of organizaional techniques. *Developmental Psychology, 13,* 175–183.

Bjorklund, D. F., & Zaken-Greenberg, F. (1981). The effects of differences in classification style on preschool children's memory. *Child Development, 52,* 888–894.

Blank, M., Rose, S., & Berlin, L. (1979). *The preschool language assessment instrument.* New York: Grune and Stratton.

Blewitt, P. (1983a). Dog versus collie: Vocabulary in speech to young children. *Developmental Psychology, 19,* 602–609.

Blewitt, P. (1983b, April). *What determines order of acquisition of object categories?* Paper presented at the meeting of the Society for Research in Child Development, Detroit.

Bloom, L. (1970). *Language development: Form and function in emerging grammars*. Cambridge, MA: MIT Press.

Bloom, L. (1973). *One word at a time: The use of single word utterances before syntax*. The Hague: Mouton.

Bloom, L., & Lahey, M. (1978). *Language development and language disorders*. New York: Wiley.

Bloom, L., Lahey, M., Hood, L., Lifter, K., & Fiess, K. (1980). Complex sentences: Acquisition of syntactic connectives and the semantic relations they encode. *Journal of Child Language, 7*, 235–261.

Bordan, G., & Harris, K. (1980). *Speech science primer*. Baltimore: Williams and Wilkens.

Boring, E. G. (1957). *A history of experimental psychology*. New York: Appleton-Century-Crofts.

Botvin, G. J., & Sutton-Smith, B. (1977). The development of complexity in children's fantasy narratives. *Developmental Psychology, 13*, 377–388.

Bower, G. H., Black, J. B., & Turner, T. J. (1979). Scripts in memory for text. *Cognitive Psychology, 11*, 177–220.

Bowerman, M. (1976). Semantic factors in the acquisition of rules for word use and sentence construction. In D. M. Morehead & A. E. Morehead (Eds.), *Normal and deficient child language* (pp. 99–170) Baltimore: University Park Press.

Bowerman, M. (1982). Reorganizational processes in lexical and syntactic development. In E. Wanner & L. Gleitman (Eds.), *Language acquisition: The state of the art* (pp. 319–346). New York: Cambridge University Press.

Boynton, M., & French, L. A. (1983, October). *Holding it together: Preverbal children's play in a scripted setting*. Paper presented at the meeting of the Eight Annual Boston University Conference on Language Development, Boston.

Brainerd, C. J. (1978). The stage question in cognitive-developmental theory. *The Behavioral and Brain Sciences, 1* (2), 173–213.

Bransford, J. D., & McCarrell, N. S. (1974). A sketch of a cognitive approach to comprehension: Some thoughts about understanding what it means to comprehend. In W. B. Weiner & D. S. Palermo (Eds.), *Cognition and the symbolic processes*, (pp. 189–230). Hillsdale, NJ: Lawrence Erlbaum Associates.

Brenner, J., & Mueller, E. (1982). Shared meaning in boy toddlers' peer relations. *Child Development, 53*, 380–391.

Bretherton, I. (Ed.) (1984). *Symbolic play: The development of social understanding*. New York: Academic Press.

Briton, B., & Fujiki, M. (1982). A comparison of request-response sequences in the discourse of normal and language-disordered children. *Journal of Speech and Hearing Disorders, 47*, 57–62.

Brown, A. L. (1976). The construction of temporal succession by preoperational children. In A. D. Pick (Ed.), *Minnesota symposium on child psychology* (Vol. 10, pp. 28–83). Minneapolis: University of Minnesota Press.

Brown, R. (1958). How shall a thing be called? *Psychological Review, 65*, 14–21.

Brown, R. (1973). *A first language: The early stages*. Cambridge, MA: Harvard University Press.

Brown, R., & Bellugi, U. (1964). Three processes in the child's acquisition of syntax. *Harvard Educational Review, 34*, 133–151.

Brown, R., & Kulick, J. (1977). Flashbulb memories. *Cognition, 5*, 73–99.

Bruner, J. S. (1966). On cognitive growth: I. In J. S. Bruner, R. R. Olver, & P. M. Greenfield (Eds.), *Studies in cognitive growth* (pp. 1–29), New York: Wiley.

Bruner, J. S. (1978a, March). *The acquisition of language: The Berlyne Memorial Lecture*. Toronto: University of Toronto.

Bruner, J. S. (1978b). The role of dialogue in language acquisition. In A. Sinclair, R. J. Jarvella & W. J. M. Levelt (Eds.), *The child's conception of language*. Berlin: Springer-Verlag.

Bruner, J. S. (1983). *Child's talk: Learning to use language*. New York: W. W. Norton & Co.

Bruner, J. S., Olver, R. R., & Greenfield, P. M. (Eds.) (1966). *Studies in cognitive growth*. New York: Wiley.

Butterfield, E. C., & Schiefelbusch, R. L. (1981). Some theoretical conditions in the design of language intervention programs. In R. L. Schiefelbusch & D. D. Bricker (Eds.), *Early language: Acquisition and intervention*. Baltimore: University-Park Press.

Campbell, R. N. (1979). Cognitive development and child language. In P. Fletcher & M. Garman (Eds.), *Language acquisition* (pp. 419–436). Cambridge, England: Cambridge University Press.

Cantor, N., Mischel, W., & Schwartz, J. C. (1982). A prototype analysis of psychological situations. *Cognitive Psychology, 14,* 45–77.

Carni, E. (1982). *The ups and downs of "before" and "after": Contextual controls of understanding*. Unpublished doctoral dissertation, City University of New York.

Carni, E., & French, L. A. (1984). The acquisition of *before* and *after* reconsidered: What develops? *Journal of Experimental Child Psychology, 37,* 394–403.

Carrow, E. (1973). *Test of auditory comprehension of language* (5th ed.). Boston: Teaching Resources Corporation.

Chi, M. T. H. (1978). Knowledge structures and memory development. In R. S. Siegler (Ed.), *Children's thinking: What develops?* (pp. 73–95). Hillsdale, NJ: Lawrence Erlbaum Associates.

Chomsky, N. (1965). *Aspects of the theory of syntax*. Cambridge, MA: The M.I.T. Press.

Chomsky, N. (1975). *Reflections on language*. New York: Pantheon.

Cicourel, A. (1974). *Cognitive sociology*. New York: Free Press.

Clark, E. V. (1971). On the acquisition of the meaning of *before* and *after*. *Journal of Verbal Learning and Verbal Behavior, 10,* 266–275.

Clark, E. V. (1973). How children describe time and order. In C. A. Ferguson & D. I. Slobin (Eds.), *Studies of child language* (pp. 585–606). New York: Holt, Rinehart & Winston.

Clark, E. V. (1983). Meanings and concepts. In P. H. Mussen (Ed.), *Carmichael's manual of child psychology, Volume 3: Cognitive development* (edited by J. H. Flavell & E. M. Markman) (pp. 787–840). New York: Wiley.

Clark, H. H., & Clark, E. V. (1977). *Psychology and language: An introduction to psycholinguistics*. New York: Harcourt Brace Janovich.

Colegrove, F. W. (1899). Individual memories. *American Journal of Psychology, 10,* 228–255.

Collins, A. M., & Quillian, M. R. (1969). Retrieval time from semantic memory. *Journal of Verbal Learning and Verbal Behavior, 8,* 240–247.

Constable, C. M. (1981, July). *Creating communicative context: Analyzing linguistic and nonlinguistic event interaction*. Paper presented at the meeting of the American Speech, Language and Hearing Association, Philadelphia.

Constable, C. M. (1983a, November). *Analyzing cohesive relations in normal and disordered language: Clinical applications*. Paper presented at the meeting of the American Speech, Language and Hearing Association, Cincinnati.

Constable, C. M. (1983b). Creating communicative context. In H. Winitz (Ed.), *Treating language disorders*.Baltimore: University Park Press.

Constable, C. M., & Lahey, M. (1984). Analyzing interactional episodes: Does the method make a difference? *Proceedings of the Fifth Annual Symposium on Research in Child Language Disorders*. University of Wisconsin, Madison.

Constable, C. M., & VanKleeck, A. (1984). *From social to instructional uses of language: Bridging the gap*. Unpublished manuscript, Department of Speech and Hearing Sciences, City University of New York.

Conti-Ramsden, G., & Friel-Patti, S. (1983). Mothers' discourse adjustments to language impaired and non-language impaired children. *Journal of Speech and Hearing Disorders, 48* (4), 360–367.

Corrigan, R. (1978). Language development as related to stage 6 object permanence development. *Journal of Child Language, 5,* 173–189.

Cromer, R. F. (1968). *The development of temporal reference during the acquisition of language.* Unpublished doctoral dissertation, Harvard University.

Crovitz, H. F., & Quina-Holland, K. (1976). Proportion of episodic memories from early childhood by years of age. *Bulletin of the Psychonomic Society, 7,* 61–62.

Crovitz, H. F., & Schiffman, H. (1974). Frequency of episodic memories as a function of their age. *Bulletin of the Psychonomic Society, 4,* 517.

Daehler, M. W., Lonardo, R., & Bukatko, D. (1979). Matching and equivalence judgments in very young children. *Child Development, 50,* 170–179.

D'Andrade, R. G. (1981). The cultural part of cognition. *Cognitive Science, 5,* 179–195.

DeLoache, J. S. (1980). Naturalistic studies of memory for object location in very young children. In M. Perlmutter (Ed.) *Children's Memory: New Directions for Child Development* (10) pp. 17–32. San Francisco: Jossey Bass.

Denney, N. (1974). Evidence for developmental changes in categorization criteria for children and adults. *Human Development, 17,* 41–53.

Denney, N. W., & Ziobrowski, M. (1972). Developmental changes in clustering criteria. *Journal of Experimental Child Psychology, 3,* 275–282.

Donaldson, M. (1978). *Children's minds.* New York: W. W. Norton.

Dore, J. (1979). Conversation in preschool language development. In P. Fletcher, & M. Garman (Eds.), *Language acquisition* pp. 337–361). Cambridge, England: Cambridge University Press.

Dore, J. (1983). Feeling, form and intention in early language acquisition. In R. Golinkoff (Ed.), *The transition from communication to language* (pp. 167–190). Hillsdale, NJ: Lawrence Erlbaum Associates.

Dudycha, G. J., & Dudycha, M. M. (1932). Some factors and characteristics of childhood memories. *Child Development, 4,* 265–278.

Dunn, L. (1965). *Expanded manual: Peabody Picture Vocabulary Test.* Circle Pines, MN: American Guidance Service.

Edwards, D. (1973). Sensory-motor intelligence and semantic relations in early child grammar. *Cognition, 2,* 395–434.

Eisenberg, A. R. (1982). *Specificity and organization in two-year-olds' descriptions of past experiences.* Paper presented at the meeting of the Boston University Conference on Child Language, Boston.

El'Konin, D. (1966). Symbolics and its function in the play of children. *Soviet Education, 8,* 35–41.

Emerson, H. F. (1979). Children's comprehension of "because" in reversible and non-reversible sentences. *Journal of Child Language, 6,* 279–300.

Emerson, H. F. (1980). Children's judgments of correct and reversed sentences with "if." *Journal of Child Language, 7,* 137–155.

Engel, S., Kyratzis, A., & Lucariello, J. (1984, April). *Early past and future talk in a social interactive context.* Paper presented at the meeting of the International Conference on Infant Studies, New York.

Erickson, E. H. (1950). *Childhood and society.* New York: Norton.

Evans, M. A., & Rubin, K. H. (1983). Developmental differences in explanations of childhood games. *Child Development, 54,* 1559–1567.

Fein, G., & Apfel, N. (1979). Some preliminary observations on knowing and pretending. In N. Smith & M. Franklin (Eds.), *Symbolic functioning in childhood* (pp. 87–100). Hillside, NJ: Lawrence Erlbaum Associates.

Feldman, A., & Acredolo, L. (1979). The effect of active vs. passive exploration in memory for spatial location in children. *Child Development, 50,* 698–704.

Ferreiro, E., & Sinclair, H. (1971). Temporal relations in language. *International Journal of Psychology, 6,* 39–47.

Fivush, R. (1981, August). *Young children's knowledge about familiar events.* Paper presented at the meeting of the American Psychological Association, Los Angeles.

Fivush, R. (1984). Learning about school: The development of kindergarteners' school scripts. *Child Development,* 55, 1697–1709.

Fivush, R., Hudson, J., & Nelson, K. (1984). Children's long-term memory for a novel event: An exploratory study. *Merrill-Palmer Quarterly, 30* (3), 303–316.

Fivush, R., & Mandler, J. M. (1985). *Developmental changes in the understanding of temporal sequence.* Paper presented at the biennial meeting of the Society for Research in Child Development, Toronto.

Fivush, R., & Nelson, K. (1982). *When pictures fail: The disruption of children's ability to sequence events.* Unpublished manuscript, City University of New York.

Flavell, J. H. (1963). *The developmental psychology of Jean Piaget.* Princeton: D. Van Nostrand Co. Inc.

Flavell, J. H. (1971). Stage-related properties of cognitive development. *Cognitive Psychology, 2,* 421–453.

Flavell, J. H. (1982). Structures, stages, and sequences in cognitive development. In W. A. Collins (Ed.), *The Minnesota symposia on child psychology* (Vol. 15, pp. 1–28). Hillsdale, NJ: Lawrence Erlbaum Associates.

Fodor, J. A. (1972). Some reflections on L. S. Vygotsky's *Thought and language. Cognition, 1,* 83–95.

Fodor, J. A. (1975). *The language of thought.* New York: Crowell.

Fodor, J. A. (1980). On the impossibility of acquiring "more powerful" structures. In Piatelli-Palmarini, (Ed.), *Language and learning: The debate between Jean Piaget and Noam Chomsky* (pp. 142–162). Cambridge, MA: Harvard University Press.

Ford, W. G. (1976). *The language of disjunction.* Unpublished doctoral dissertation, University of Toronto.

Fraisse, P. (1963). *The psychology of time.* New York: Harper and Row.

Freidson, E. (1953). Adult discount: An aspect of children's changing tastes. *Child Development, 24,* 39–49.

French, L. A. (1985a). Acquiring and using words to express logical relationships. In S. A. Kuczaj, & M. D. Barrett (Eds.), *Development of word meaning.* New York: Springer-Verlag.

French, L. A. (1985b). Real world knowledge as the basis for social and cognitive development. In J. B. Pryor & J. D. Day (Eds.), Developmental perspectives on social cognition. New York: Springer-Verlag.

French, L. A., & Brown, A. L. (1977). Comprehension of *before* and *after* in logical and arbitrary sequences. *Journal of Child Language, 4,* 247–256.

French, L. A., Lucariello, J., Seidman, S., & Nelson, K. (in press). The influence of discourse content and context on preschoolers' use of language. In L. Galado & A. Pellegrini (Eds.), *Narrative language and play.* Norwood, NJ: Ablex.

French, L. A., & Nelson, K. (1981). Temporal knowledge expressed in preschoolers' descriptions of familiar activities. *Papers and Reports on Child Language Development, 20,* 61–69.

French, L. A., & Nelson, K. (1982). Taking away the supportive context: Preschoolers' talk about the "then-and-there." *The Quarterly Newsletter of the Laboratory of Comparative Human Cognition, 4,* 1–6.

French, L. A., & Nelson, K. (1985). *Children's acquisition of relational terms. Some ifs, ors, and buts.* New York: Springer-Verlag.

Freud, S. (1952). *A general introduction to psychoanalysis.* New York: Washington Square Press.

Freud, S. (1953). Three essays on the theory of sexuality. In J. Strachey (Ed. and Trans.), *The standard edition of the complete psychological works of Sigmund Freud* (Vol. 7). London: Hogarth Press. (Original work published 1905.)

Freud, S. (1963). Introductory lectures on psycholoanalysis. In J. Strachey (Ed., and Trans.), *The standard edition of the complete psychological works of Sigmund Freud* (Vols. 15–16), London: Hogarth Press. (Original work published 1916–1917.)

Galambos, J. A., & Rips, L. J. (1982). Memory for routines. *Journal of Verbal Learning and Verbal Behavior, 21,* 260–281.

Galbraith, R. C., & Day, R. D. (1978). Developmental changes in clustering criteria? A closer look at Denney and Ziobrowski. *Child Development, 49,* 889–891.

Gardner, H. (1983, April). The nature of symbolic skills. In H. Gardner (Chair), *The development of early symbolic skills.* Symposium conducted at the meeting of the Society for Research in Child Development, Detroit.

Garvey, C. (1982). Communication and the development of social role play. In D. Forbes & M. Greenberg (Eds.), *New directions for child development: Children's planning strategies* (No. 18). San Francisco: Jossey-Bass.

Garvey, C., & Berndt, T. R. (1977). The organization of pretend play. *Catalogue of selected documents in psychology, 7,* No. 1589.

Geertz, C. (1973). *The interpretation of cultures.* New York: Basic.

Gelman, R. (1978). Cognitive development. *Annual Review of Psychology, 29,* 297–332.

Gelman, R., & Gallistel, C. R. (1978). *The child's understanding of number.* Cambridge, MA: Harvard University Press.

Gesell, A., & Ilg, F. (1946). *The child from five to ten.* New York: Harper and Row.

Glick, J. (1978). Cognition and social cognition: An introduction. In J. Glick and K. A. Clarke-Stewart (Eds.) *The development of social understanding.* New York: Gardner Press.

Gopnik, A. (1982). Words and plans: Early language and the development of intelligent action. *Journal of Child Language, 9,* 303–318.

Graesser, A. C., Gordon, S. E., & Sawyer, J. D. (1979). Recognition memory for typical and atypical actions in scripted activities: Tests of a script pointer and tag hypothesis. *Journal of Verbal Learning and Verbal Behavior, 18,* 319–332.

Graesser, A. C., Woll, S. B., Kowalski, D. J., & Smith, D. A. (1980). Memory for typical and atypical actions in scripted activities. *Journal of Experimental Psychology: Human Learning and Memory, 6* (5), 503–515.

Gruendel, J. M. (1980). *Scripts and stories: A study of children's event narratives.* Unpublished doctoral dissertation, Yale University.

Hall, G. S. (1899). Note on early memories. *Pedagogical seminary, 6,* 485–512.

Halliday, M. A. K. (1975). *Learning how to mean: Explorations in the development of language.* London: Edward Arnold.

Hanawalt, N. G., & Gebhart, L. J. (1965). Childhood memories of single and recurrent incidents. *Journal of Genetic Psychology, 107,* 85–89.

Harms, J. M. (1972). *Children's responses to fantasy in relation to their stages of intellectual development.* Unpublished doctoral dissertation, Ohio State University.

Henri, V., & Henri, C. (1898). Earliest recollections. *Popular Science Monthly, 53,* 108–115.

Hood, L., & Bloom, L. (1979). What, when, and how about why: A longitudinal study of early expressions of causality. *Monographs of the Society for Research in Child Development, 44* (6, Serial No. 181).

Horton, M. S., & Markman, E. M. (1980). Developmental differences in the acquisition of basic and superordinate categories. *Child Development, 51,* 708–719.

Hudson, J. (1984). *Recollection and reconstruction in children's autobiographical memory.* Unpublished doctoral dissertation, City University of New York.

Hudson, J., & Fivush, R. (1983). Categorical and schematic organization and the development of retrieval strategies. *Journal of Experimental Child Psychology, 36,* 32–42.

Hudson, J., & Nelson, K. (1983). Effects of script structure on children's story recall. *Developmental Psychology, 19* (4), 625–635.

Hudson, J., & Nelson, K. (1984). *Repeated encounters of a similar kind: Effects of repetition in children's autobiographic memory*. Manuscript submitted for publication.

Hurlock, E. B., & Schwartz, R. (1932). Biographic records of memory in preschool children. *Child Development, 3*, 230–239.

Inhelder, B., & Piaget, J. (1964). *The early growth of logic in the child.* New York: Norton.

Johnson, B. D. (1984). Mother and adult linguistic interaction with children who have a specific language disorder: Response or strategy? *Proceedings of the Fifth Annual Symposium on Research in Child Language Disorders*. University of Wisconsin, Madison.

Johnston, J. R. (1981). On location: Thinking and talking about space. *Topics in language disorders—cognition and language in preschool years, 2* (1), 17–32.

Johnston, J. R. (1982). The language disordered child. In N. J. Lass, L. V. McReynolds, J. L. Northern, & D. E. Yoder (Eds.), *Speech, language, and hearing: Vol. 2. Pathologies of speech and language* (pp. 780–801). Philadelphia: W. B. Saunders Company.

Johnston, J. R. (1983). Discussion: Part I: What is language intervention? The role of theory. In J. Miller, D. Yoder, & R. Schiefelbusch (Eds.), *Contemporary issues in language intervention* ASHA Reports 12, 52–60. Rockville, MD.

Johnston, J. R., & Ramstad, V. (1978). Cognitive development in pre-adolescent language impaired children. In M. Burns & J. Andrews (Eds.), *Selected papers in language and phonology* Evanston, IL: Institute for Continuing Professional Education.

Kail, M. (1980). Étude génétiques des présupposés de certains morphemes grammaticaux. Un exemple: MAIS. [Developmental studies of the presuppositions of grammatical morphemes. An example: But.] *Approaches du langage, 16*, 53–62.

Kamhi, A. (1981). Nonlinguistic, symbolic and conceptual abilities of language impaired and normally developing children. *Journal of Speech and Hearing Research, 24*, 446–453.

Karmiloff-Smith, A. (1979a). *A functional approach to child language*. Cambridge, England: Cambridge University Press.

Karmiloff-Smith, A. (1979b). Language as a formal problem-space for children. In W. Deutsch (Ed.), *The child's construction of language*. Cambridge, England: Cambridge University Press.

Kavanaugh, R. D. (1979). Observations on the role of logically constrained sentences in the comprehension of "before" and "after." *Journal of Child Language, 6*, 353–357.

Keenan, E. O., & Schieffelin, B. (1976). Topic as a discourse notion: A study of topic in the conversations of children and adults. In C. Li (Ed.), *Subject and topic*. New York: Academic Press.

Keil, F. (1979). *Semantic and conceptual development: An ontological perspective*. Cambridge, MA: Harvard University Press.

Kendler, H. H., & Kendler, T. S. (1962). Vertical and horizontal processes in problem-solving. *Psychological Review, 69*, 1–16.

Kessen, W. (1962). "Stage" and "structure" in the study of children. *Monographs of the Society for Research in Child Development, 27* (2).

Kintsch, W. (1974). *The representation of meaning in memory*. Hillsdale, NJ: Erlbaum.

Kosslyn, S. M. (1980). *Image and mind*. Cambridge, MA: Harvard University Press.

Kreye, M. (1984). Conceptual organization in the play of preschool children: Effects of meaning, context, and mother-child action. In I. Bretherton (Ed.), *Symbolic play: The developing of social understanding* (pp. 299–336). New York: Academic Press.

Kuczaj, S. A. (1981). Factors influencing children's hypothetical reference. *Journal of Child Language, 8*, 131–137.

Kuczaj, S. A., & Daly, M. J. (1979). The development of hypothetical reference in the speech of young children. *Journal of Child Language, 6*, 563–579.

Kyratzis, A., Lucariello, J., & Nelson, K. (1984, October). *The social origins of event knowledge: Its roots in narrative language*. Paper presented at the meeting of the Ninth Annual Boston University Conference on Child Language, Boston.

Langer, J. (1969). *Theories of development.* New York: Holt, Rinehart and Winston, Inc.
Lasky, E. Z., & Klopp, K. (1982). Parent-child interactions in normal and language disordered children. *Journal of Speech and Hearing Disorders, 47* (1), 7–18.
Lee, L. (1974). *Developmental sentence analysis.* Evanston, IL: Northwestern University Press.
Levelt, W., & Kelter, S. (1982). Surface form and memory in question answering. *Cognitive Psychology, 14,* 78–106.
Linton, M. (1975). Memory for real-world events. In D. A. Norman & D. E. Rumelhart (Eds.), *Explorations in cognition* (pp. 376–404). San Francisco: W. H. Freeman & Co.
Linton, M. (1979, August). *Cueing events in adults' and children's autobiographic memory.* Paper presented at the meeting of The American Psychological Association, New York.
Linton, M. (1982). Transformations of memory in everyday life. In U. Neisser (Ed.), *Memory observed* (pp. 77–91). San Francisco: W. H. Freeman & Co.
Loftus, E. G. (1975). Leading questions and the eye-witness report. *Cognitive Psychology, 7,* 560–572.
Lucariello, J. (1983, April). Context and conversations. In K. Nelson (Chair), *Relations between event representations and language use.* Symposium conducted at the meeting of the Society for Research in Child Development, Detroit.
Lucariello, J., & Nelson, K. (1982, March). *Situational variation in mother-child interaction.* Paper presented at the meeting of the Third International Conference on Infant Studies, Austin, TX.
Lucariello, J., & Nelson, K. (1985). Slot-filler categories as memory organizers for young children. *Developmental Psychology, 21,* 272–282.
Luria, A. R. (1976). *Cognitive development: Its cultural and social foundations.* Cambridge, MA: Harvard University Press.
Lyons, J. (1977). *Semantics* (Vol. 1). New York: Cambridge University Press.
Macnamara, J. (1972). Cognitive basis of language learning in infants. *Psychological Review, 79,* 1–13.
Mandler, J. M. (1978). A code in the node: The use of a story schema in retrieval. *Discourse Processes, 1,* 14–35.
Mandler, J. M. (1979). Categorical and schematic organization in memory. In C. R. Puff (Ed.), *Memory organization and structure* (pp. 259–299). New York: Academic Press.
Mandler, J. M. (1983). Representation. In J. H. Flavell & E. M. Markman (Eds.), *Cognitive development.* Vol 3 of P. Mussen (Ed.), *Handbook of child psychology* (4th ed., pp. 420–494). New York: Wiley.
Mandler, J. M., & DeForest, M. (1979). Is there more than one way to recall a story? *Child Development, 50,* 586–589.
Mandler, J. M., & Johnson, N. S. (1977). Rememberance of things parsed: Story structure and recall. *Cognitive Psychology, 9,* 111–151.
Mandler, J. M., & Murphy, C. (1979). Subjective active judgments of script structure. *Journal of Experimental Psychology: Learning, memory, and cognition, 9* (3), 534–543.
Maratsos, M. (1982). The child's construction of grammatical categories. In E. Wanner & L. Gleitman (Eds.), *Language acquisition: The state of the art* (pp. 240–266). New York: Cambridge University Press.
Maratsos, M. (1983). Some current issues in the study of the acquisition of grammar. In J. H. Flavell & E. M. Markman (Eds.), *Cognitive development.* Vol 3 of P. Mussen (Ed.), *Handbook of child psychology* (4th ed., pp. 707–786).
Markman, E. M. (1981). Two different principles of conceptual organization. In M. Lamb & A. Brown (Eds.), *Advances in developmental psychology* (Vol 1, pp. 199–236). Hillsdale, NJ: Lawrence Erlbaum.
Markman, E. M. (1983). Two different kinds of hierarchical organization. In E. K. Scholnick

(Ed.), *New trends in conceptual representation: Challenges to Piaget's theory?* (pp. 165–184). Hillsdale, NJ: Lawrence Erlbaum.

Markman, E. M., Horton, M. S., & McLanahan, A. G. (1980). Classes and collections: Principles of organization in the learning of hierarchical relations. *Cognition, 8,* 227–241.

Markman, E. M., & Siebert, J. (1976). Classes and collections: Internal organization and resulting holistic properties. *Cognitive Psychology, 8,* 561–577.

Marshall, J. C. (1980). On the biology of language acquisition. In D. Caplan (Ed.), *Biological studies of mental processes* (pp. 106–148). Cambridge, MA: The MIT Press.

McCartney, K. A., & Nelson, K. (1981). Children's use of scripts in story recall. *Discourse Processes, 4,* 59–70.

McCauley, C., Weil, C. M., & Sperber, R. D. (1976). The development of memory structure as reflected by semantic-priming effects. *Journal of Experimental Child Psychology, 22,* 511–518.

McClure, E., Mason, J., & Lucas, P. (1979). An exploratory study of story structure and age effects on children's ability to sequence stories. *Discourse Processes, 2,* 213–249.

McCune-Nicolich, L. (1981). The cognitive bases of relational words in the single word period. *Journal of Child Language, 8,* 15–34.

McLean, J., & Snyder-McLean, L. (1979). *A transactional approach to early language training.* Columbus: Charles E. Merrill.

McNeill, D. (1970). *The acquisition of language.* New York: Harper and Row.

McNeill, D. (1979). *The conceptual basis of language.* Hillsdale, NJ: Lawrence Erlbaum Associates.

Mead, G. H. (1934). *Mind, self, and society.* Chicago: University of Chicago Press.

Menig-Peterson, C. L., & McCabe, A. (1978). Children's orientation of a listener to the context of their narratives. *Developmental Psychology, 14,* 582–592.

Mervis, C. B., & Crisafi, M. A. (1982). Order of acquisition of subordinate-, basic-, and superordinate-level categories. *Child Development, 53,* 258–266.

Miller, J. (1981). *Assessing language production in children.* Baltimore: University Park Press.

Miller, J. F., & Chapman, R. S. (1981). The relation between age and mean length of utterance in morphemes. *Journal of Speech and Hearing Research, 24* (2), 154–161.

Miller, L. (1978). Pragmatics and early childhood language disorders: Communicative interactions in a half hour sample. *Journal of Speech and Hearing Disorders, 43,* 419–436.

Morehead, D., & Ingram, D. (1973). The development of base syntax in normal and linguistically deviant children. *Journal of Speech and Hearing Research, 16,* 330–352.

Neimark, E. D. (1970). Development of comprehension of logical connectives: Understanding of "or." *Psychonomic Science, 21,* 217–219.

Neimark, E. D., & Slotnick, N. S. (1970). Development of the understanding of logical connectives. *Journal of Educational Psychology, 61,* 451–460.

Neisser, U. (1967). *Cognitive psychology.* New York: Meredith Publishing Co.

Neisser, U. (1967). Cultural and cognitive discontinuity. In T. E. Gladwin & W. Sturtevant (Eds.), *Anthropology and human behavior* (pp. 54–71). Washington, D.C.: Anthropological Society of Washington, D. C.

Neisser, U. (1981). John Dean's memory: A case study. *Cognition, 9,* 1–22.

Neisser, U. (1982). Snapshot or benchmarks? In U. Neisser (Ed.), *Memory observed: Remembering in natural contexts* (pp. 43–48). San Francisco: W. H. Freeman & Co.

Nelson, K. Structure and strategy in learning to talk. *Monographs of the society for research in child development,* 38 (1–2, Serial No. 149).

Nelson, K. (1974). Concept, word, and sentence: Interrelationships in acquisition and development. *Psychological Review, 81,* 267–285.

Nelson, K. (1977). The syntagmatic-paradigmatic shift revisited: A review of research and theory. *Psychological Bulletin, 84,* 93–116.

Nelson, K. (1978). How young children represent knowledge of their world in and out of language. In R. S. Siegler (Ed.), *Children's thinking: What develops?* (pp. 255–273). Hillsdale, NJ: Lawrence Erlbaum Associates.

Nelson, K. (1979a, August). *Children's long-term memory for routine events.* Paper presented at the meeting of the American Psychological Association, New York.

Nelson, K. (1979b). *Time and space in children's event descriptions.* Paper presented at the meeting of the New York Child Language Conference, New York.

Nelson, K. (1980, August). Characteristics of children's scripts for familiar events. In J. Martin (Chair), *The development of knowledge structures.* Symposium conducted at the meeting of the American Psychological Association, Montreal.

Nelson, K. (1981). Social cognition in a script framework. In J. H. Flavell & L. Ross (Eds.), *Social cognitive development: Frontier and possible futures* (pp. 97–118). New York: Cambridge University Press.

Nelson, K. (1982a). The syntagmatics and paradigmatics of conceptual representation. In S. Kuczaj (Ed.), *Language development: Language, thought and culture* (pp. 335–364). Hillsdale, NJ: Lawrence Erlbaum.

Nelson, K. (1982b, May). *The transition from infant to child memory.* Paper presented at the meeting of the Erindale Conference on Infant Memory, Toronto.

Nelson, K. (1983). The derivation of concepts and categories from event representations. In E. Scholnick (Ed.), *New trends in conceptual representation: Challenges to Piaget's theory* (pp. 129–150). Hillsdale, NJ: Lawrence Erlbaum Associates.

Nelson, K. (1984). The transition from infant to child memory. In M. Moscovitz (Ed.), *Infant memory,* Vol. 10 of *Advances in the study of communication and affect.* New York: Plenum Publishing Corporation.

Nelson, K. (1985). *Making sense: Development of meaning in early childhood.* New York: Academic Press.

Nelson, K., Engel, S., & Kyratzis, A. (in press). The evolution of meaning in context. *Journal of Pragmatics.*

Nelson, K., Fivush, R., Hudson, J., & Lucariello, J. (1983). Scripts and the development of memory. In M. T. H. Chi (Ed.), *Contributions to human development:* Vol. 9. *Trends in memory development research* (pp. 52–70). New York: Karger.

Nelson, K., & Gruendel, J. M. (1979). At morning it's lunchtime: A scriptal view of children's dialogues. *Discourse Processes, 2,* 73–94.

Nelson, K., & Gruendel, J. (1981). Generalized event representations: Basic building blocks of cognitive development. In M. E. Lamb & A. L. Brown (Eds.), *Advances in developmental psychology* (Vol. 1, pp. 131–158). Hillsdale, NJ: Erlbaum.

Nelson, K., & Hudson, J. (in press). Scripts and memory development: Functional relationships in development. In F. E. Weinert & M. Perlmutter (Eds.), *Memory development: Universal changes and individual differences.*

Nelson, K., & Lucariello, J. (1985). The development of meaning in first words. In M. Barrett (Ed.), *Children's single-word speech.* Sussex, England: Wiley.

Nelson, K., Rescorla, L., Gruendel, J., & Benedict, H. (1978). Early lexicons: What do they mean? *Child Development, 49,* 960–968.

Nelson, K., & Ross, G. (1980). The generalities and specifics of long-term memory in infants and young children. In M. Perlmutter (Ed.), *Children's memory: New directions for child development* (No. 10, pp. 87–101). San Francisco: Jossey-Bass.

Nelson, K., & Seidman, S. (1984). Playing with scripts. In I. Bretherton (Ed.), *Symbolic play: The development of social understanding* (pp. 45–71). New York: Academic Press.

Nelson, K. E., & Nelson, K. (1978). Cognitive pendulums and their linguistic realizations. In K. E. Nelson (Ed.), *Children's language:* Vol. 1, (pp. 223–285). New York: Gardner Press.

Nineo, A., & Bruner, J. S. (1978). The achievements and antecedents of labelling. *Journal of Child Language, 5,* 1–16.

Norman, D. A. (1970). *Models of human memory.* New York: Academic Press.

Norman, D. A., & Rumelhart, D. E., and the LNR Research Group. (1975). *Explorations in cognition.* San Francisco: Freeman.

Nottenburg, G., & Shoben, E. J. (1980). Scripts as linear orders. *Journal of Experimental Social Psychology, 16,* 329–347.

Ochs, E., Schieffelin, B., & Platt, M. (1979). Propositions across utterances and speakers. In E. Ochs & B. Schieffelin (Eds.), *Developmental pragmatics* (pp. 251–268). New York: Academic Press.

O'Connell, B., & Gerard, A. (in press). Scripts and scraps: The development of sequential understanding. *Child Development.*

Olver, R. R., & Hornsby, J. R. (1966). On equivalence. In J. S. Bruner, R. R. Olver, & P. M. Greenfield (Eds.), *Studies in cognitive growth* (pp. 68–85). New York: Wiley.

Ornstein, P. A., & Corsale, K. (1979). Organizational factors in children's memory. In C. R. Puff (Ed.), *Memory organization and structure* (pp. 219–257). New York: Academic Press.

Palmer, S. E. (1978). Fundamental aspects of cognitive representation. In E. Rosch & B. B. Lloyd (Eds.), *Cognition and categorization* (pp. 259–303). Hillsdale, NJ: Erlbaum.

Paris, S. G. (1973). Comprehension of language connectives and propositional logical relationships. *Journal of Experimental Child Psychology, 16,* 278–291.

Paris, S. G., & Lindauer, B. K. (1976). The role of inference in children's comprehension and memory for stories. *Cognitive Psychology, 8,* 217–227.

Peters, A. (1983). *The units of language acquisition.* New York: Cambridge University Press.

Pezdek, K., & Stevens, E. (1984). Children's memory for auditory and visual information on television. *Developmental Psychology, 20,* 212–218.

Phillips, J. (1973). Syntax and vocabulary of mothers' speech to young children: Age and sex comparisons. *Child Development, 44,* 182–187.

Piaget, J. (1955). *The language and thought of the child.* New York: World Publishing.

Piaget, J. (1962). *Play, dreams and imitation in childhood.* New York: W. W. Norton & Co.

Piaget, J. (1969). *The child's conception of time.* London: Routledge & Kegan Paul.

Piaget, J. (1971). *Structuralism.* London: Routledge & Kegan Paul.

Piaget, J. (1978). *Success and understanding.* London: Routledge & Kegan Paul.

Piaget, J., & Inhelder, B. (1971). *Mental imagery in the child.* London: Routledge and Kegan Paul.

Pillemer, D. B. (in press). Flashbulb memories of the assassination attempt of President Reagan. *Cognition.*

Pitcher, E. G., & Prelinger, E. (1963). *Children tell stories: An analysis of fantasy.* New York: International Universities Press.

Posner, M. I., & Snyder, C. R. R. (1974). Attention and cognitive control. In R. L. Salso (Ed.), *Information processing and cognition: The Loyola Symposium.* Potomac, MD: Erlbaum.

Potwin, E. B. (1901). Study of early memories. *Psychological Review, 8,* 597–601.

Pradl, G. M. (1979). Learning how to begin and end a story. *Language Arts, 56,* 21–25.

Purcell, K. (1953). Memory and psychological security. *Journal of Abnormal and Social Psychology, 47,* 433–440.

Ratner, H. H. (1980). The role of social context in memory development. In M. Perlmutter (Ed.), *Children's memory: New directions for child development* (No. 10, pp. 49–67). San Francisco: Jossey-Bass.

Ratner, N., & Bruner, J. S. (1978). Games, social exchange, and the acquisition of language. *Journal of Child Language, 5,* 391–402.

Reber, A. S., & Allen, R. (1978). Analogic and abstraction strategies in synthetic grammar learning: A functionalist interpretation. *Cognition, 6,* 189–221.

Reber, A. S., Kassin, S. H., Lewis, S., & Cantor, G. W. (1979). *On the relationship between implicit and explicit modes in learning of complex rule structures.* Unpublished manuscript, Brooklyn College.

Reber, A. S., & Lewis, S. (1977). Toward a theory of implicit learning: The analysis of the forms of a body of tacit knowledge. *Cognition, 5,* 331–361.

Rees, N. (1978). Pragmatics of language. In R. Schiefelbusch (Ed.), *Bases of language intervention,* (pp. 191–268). Baltimore: University Park Press.

Rees, N. (1983). Language intervention with children. In J. Miller, D. Yoder, & R. Schiefelbusch (Eds.), *Contemporary issues in language intervention.* ASHA Reports No. 12, 309–316. Rockville, MD.

Reiser, B. J. (1983). *Contexts and indices in autobiographical memory* (Tech. Rep. No. 24). New Haven, CT: Yale University, Center for Cognitive Science.

Reiser, B. J., Black, J. B., Abelson, R. P. (1983). *Knowledge structures in the organization and retrieval of autobiographical memories* (Tech. Rep. No. 22). New Haven, CT: Yale University, Center for Cognitive Science.

Rice, M. (1983). Contemporary accounts of the cognition/language relationship: Implications for speech-language clinicians. *Journal of Speech and Hearing Disorders, 48* (4), 347–359.

Rifkin, A. (1984). *Event categories, event taxonomies, and basic level events: An initial investigation.* Manuscript.

Robinson, J. (1976). Sampling autobiographical memory. *Cognitive Psychology, 8,* 578–595.

Rosch, E. (1978). Principles of categorization. In E. Rosch & B. Lloyd (Eds.), *Cognition and categorization* (pp. 27–48). Hillsdale, NJ: Erlbaum.

Rosch, E., Mervis, C. B., Gray, W. D., Johnson, D. M., & Boyes-Braem, P. (1976). Basic objects in natural categories. *Cognitive Psychology, 8,* 382–439.

Rozin, P. (1976). The evaluation of intelligence and access to the cognitive unconscious. *Progress in Psychology and Physiological Psychology, 6,* 245–280.

Rubin, D. C. (1982). On the retention function for autobiographical memory. *Journal of Verbal Learning and Verbal Behavior, 21,* 21–38.

Sachs, J. (1983). Talking about the there and then: The emergence of displaced reference in parent-child discourse. In K. E. Nelson (Ed.), *Children's language* (Vol. 4, pp. 1–28). New York: Gardner Press.

Sachs, J., Goldman, J., & Chaille, C. (1984). Planning in pretend play: Using language to coordinate narrative development. In A. D. Pellegrini & T. D. Yawkey (Eds.), *The development of oral and written language in social contexts* (pp. 110–128). Norwood, NJ: Ablex.

Saltz, E. (1971). *The cognitive basis of human learning.* Homewood, IL: Dorsey Press.

Saltz, E., Dixon, D., & Johnson, J. (1977). Training disadvantaged preschoolers on various fantasy activities: Effects on cognitive functioning and impulse control. *Child Development, 48,* 367–380.

Schactel, E. G. (1947). On memory and childhood amnesia. *Psychiatry, 1,* 1–26.

Schank, R. C. (1982). *Dynamic memory: A theory of reminding and learning in computers and people.* New York: Cambridge University Press.

Schank, R. C., & Abelson, R. P. (1975). Scripts, plans, and knowledge. *Proceedings of the Fourth International Joint Conference on Artificial Intelligence.* Tbilisi.

Schank, R. C., & Abelson, R. P. (1977). *Scripts, plans, goals and understanding.* Hillsdale, NJ: Lawrence Erlbaum Associates.

Schenkein, J. (1980). A taxonomy for repeating action sequences in natural conversation. In B. Butterworth (Ed.), *Language production: Vol. 1. Speech and talk.* New York: Academic Press.

Scribner, S. (1977). Modes of thinking and ways of speaking: Culture and logic reconsidered. In P. N. Johnson-Laird & P. C. Wason (Eds.), *Thinking: Readings in cognitive science* (pp. 483–500). Cambridge, England: Cambridge University Press.

Seidman, S. (1983a, April). Eventful play: Preschoolers' scripts for pretense. In K. Nelson (Chair), *Relations between event representations and language use*. Symposium conducted at the meeting of the Society for Research in Child Development, Detroit.

Seidman, S. (1983b, October). *Shifting sands: The conversational content of young peers at play*. Paper presented at the meeting of the Eighth Annual Boston University Conference on Language Development, Boston.

Shatz, M. (1977). The relationship between cognitive processes and the development of communication skills. In C. B. Keasey (Ed.), *Nebraska symposium on motivation* (Vol. 25, pp. 1–42). Lincoln: University of Nebraska Press.

Shatz, M. (1979). Learning the rules of the game: Four views of the relation between grammar acquisition and social interaction. In W. Deutsch (Ed.), *The child's construction of language* (pp. 17–38). Cambridge, England: Cambridge University Press.

Shatz, M. (1983). Communication. In J. H. Flavell & E. M. Markman (Eds.), *Cognitive development* (pp. 841–889). Vol. 3 of P. Mussen (Ed.), *Handbook of child psychology* (4th ed.). New York: Wiley.

Shatz, M. (1984, July). *Bootstrap operations in child language*. Keynote address at the meeting of the Third International Congress for the Study of Child Language, Austin, TX.

Shipley, E. F., Kuhn, I. F., & Madden, E. C. (1983). Mothers' use of superordinate category terms. *Journal of Child Language 10*, 571–588.

Siegler, R. S. (Ed.) (1978). *Children's thinking: What develops?* Hillsdale, NJ: Lawrence Erlbaum Associates.

Slackman, E. (1985). The effect of event structure on learning a novel event. Doctoral dissertation, City University of New York.

Slackman, E., & Hudson, J. (1984, October). *Filling in the gaps: Inferential processes in children's comprehension of oral discourse*. Paper presented at the meeting of the Ninth Annual Boston University Conference on Language Development, Boston.

Slackman, E., & Nelson, K. (1984). Acquisition of an unfamiliar script in story form by young children. *Child Development, 55*, 329–340.

Smilansky, S. (1968). *The effects of sociodramatic play on disadvantaged preschool children*. New York: Wiley.

Smiley, S. S., & Brown, A. L. (1979). Conceptual preference for thematic or taxonomic relations: A non-monotonic trend from preschool to old age. *Journal of Experimental Child Psychology, 28*, 249–257.

Smith, M. E. (1952). Childhood memories compared with those of adult life. *Journal of Genetic Psychology, 80*, 151–182.

Snow, C. E. (1979). Conversations with children. In P. Fletcher & M. Garman (Eds.), *Language acquisition* (pp. 363–375). Cambridge, England: Cambridge University Press.

Snow, C. E., Dubber, C., & DeBlauw, A. (1982). Routines in mother-child interaction. In L. Feagans & D. C. Farran (Eds.), *The language of children reared in poverty: Implications for evaluation and intervention* (pp. 53–72). New York: Academic Press.

Snow, C. E., & Goldfield, B. A. (1983). Turn the page please: Situation-specific language acquisition. *Journal of Child Language, 10*, 551–569.

Stein, N. L., & Glenn, C. G. (1979). An analysis of story comprehension in elementary school children. In R. O.Freedle (Ed.), *New directions in discourse processing* (Vol. 2, 53–120). Hillsdale, NJ: Erlbaum.

Stein, N. L., & Trabasso, T. (1982). What's in a story? In R. Glaser (Ed.), *Advances in instructional psychology* (Vol. 2, pp. 213–267). Hillsdale, NJ: Lawrence Erlbaum Associates.

Sternberg, R. J. (1984). Mechanisms of cognitive development. New York: W. H. Freeman & Co.

Sugarman, S. (1983). *Children's early thought: Developments in classification*. New York: Cambridge University Press.

Tallal, P., & Piercy, M. (1973). Developmental aphasia: Impaired rate of non-verbal auditory processing as a function of sensory modality. *Neuropsychologia, 11*, 389–398.

Tallal, P., & Piercy, M. (1974). Developmental aphasia: Rate of auditory processing and selective impairment of consonant perception. *Neuropsychologia, 12*, 83–93.

Tallal, P., & Piercy, M. (1975). Developmental aphasia: The perception of brief vowels and extended stop consonants. *Neuropsychologia, 13*, 69–74.

Tallal, P., Stark, R., & Curtiss, B. (1976). Relation between speech perception and speech production impairment in children with developmental dysphasia. *Brain and Language, 3*, 308–317.

Tallal, P., Stark, R., Kallman, C., & Mellits, D. (1981). A reexamination of some nonverbal perceptual abilities of language impaired and normal children as a function of age and sensory modality. *Journal of Speech and Hearing Research, 24*, 351–357.

Tallal, P., Stark, R., & Mellits, E. D. (1983). *Identification of language impaired children on the basis of rapid perception and production skills*. Manuscript.

Taylor, S. E., & Winkler, J. D. (1980, August). *The development of schemas*. Paper presented at the meeting of the American Psychological Association, Montreal, Canada.

Terrel, B., & Schwartz, R. (1983). Object transformation: The linguistic aspect of symbolic play? *Proceedings of the Fifth Annual Symposium on Research in Child Language Disorders*. University of Wisconsin, Madison.

Todd, C. M., & Perlmutter, M. (1980). Reality recalled by preschool children. In M. Perlmutter (Ed.), *Children's memory: New directions for child development* (No. 10, pp. 69–86). San Francisco: Jossey Bass.

Tulving, E. (1972). Episodic and semantic memory. In E. Tulving & W. Donaldson (Eds.). *Organization of memory* (pp. 382–403). New York: Academic Press.

Umiker-Seboek, D. J. (1979). Preschool children's intraconversational narratives. *Journal of Child Language, 6*, 91–109.

Vygotsky, L. S. (1962). *Thought and language*. Cambridge, MA: The M.I.T. Press.

Vygotsky, L. S. (1978). *Mind in society*. Cambridge, MA: The M.I.T. Press.

Waldfogel, S. (1948). The frequency and affective character of childhood memories. *Psychological Monographs, 62*, 1–39.

Wales, R., Colman, M., & Pattison, P. (1983). How a thing is called—A study of mother's and children's naming. *Journal of Experimental Child Psychology, 36*, 1–17.

Walker, C., & Yekovich, F. (1984). Script-based inferences: Effects of text and knowledge variables on recognition memory. *Journal of Verbal Learning and Verbal Behavior, 23*, 357–370.

Wertsch, J. V. (1978). Adult-child interaction and the roots of metacognition. *The Quarterly Newsletter of the Institute for Comparative Human Development, 2*, 15–18.

Wertsch, J. V. (1979). From social interaction to higher psychological processes: A clarification and application of Vygotsky's theory. *Human Development, 22*, 1–22.

Wertsch, J. V. (Ed.) (1984). *Culture, communication, and cognition: Vygotskian perspectives*. New York: Cambridge University Press.

Wertsch, J. V., McNamee, G. D., McLane, J. B., & Budwig, N. A. (1980). The adult-child dyad as a problem-solving system. *Child Development, 51*, 1215–1221.

White, D. E., & Glick, J. (1978). *Competence and the context of performance*. Paper presented at the meeting of the Jean Piaget Society, Philadelphia.

White, S. H., & Pillemer, D. B. (1979). Childhood amnesia and the development of a socially accessible memory system. In J. F. Kihlstrom & F. J. Evans (Eds.), *Functional disorders of memory* (pp. 29–74). Hillsdale, NJ: Erlbaum.

White, T. G. (1982). Naming practices, typicality, and underextension in child language. *Journal of Experimental Child Psychology, 33*, 324–346.

Whitehurst, G. J., & Zimmerman, B. J. (1979). *The functions of language and cognition*. New York: Academic Press.

Winer, G. A. (1980). Class-inclusion reasoning in children: A review of the empirical literature. *Child Development, 51*, 309–328.

Winograd, E., & Killinger, W. A. (1983). Relating age at encoding in early childhood to adult recall: Development of flashbulb memories. *Journal of Experimental Psychology: General, 112*, 413–422.

Wolf, D. (1983, April). Event-structures: The first wave of symbolic understanding. In H. Gardner (Chair), *The development of early symbolic skills*. Symposium conducted at the meeting of the Society for Research in Child Development, Detroit.

Wolf, D., Rygh, J., & Altshuler, J. (1984). Agency and experience: Actions and states in play narratives. In I. Bretherton (Ed.), *Symbolic play: A social cognitive perspective*. Orlando, Florida: Academic Press.

Wood, D. J. (1980). Teaching the young child: Some relationships between social interaction, language, and thought. In D. R. Olson (Ed.), *The social foundations of language and thought* (pp. 280–296). New York: Norton.

Worden, P. E. (1976). The effects of classification structure on organized free recall in children. *Journal of Experimental Child Psychology, 22*, 519–529.

Yarmey, A. D., & Bull, M. P., III. (1978). Where were you when President Kennedy was assassinated? *Bulletin of the Psychonomic Society, 11*, 133–135.

Author Index

Subject Index

A

B

C

D

T

V

For Product Safety Concerns and Information please contact our EU representative GPSR@taylorandfrancis.com
Taylor & Francis Verlag GmbH, Kaufingerstraße 24, 80331 München, Germany

www.ingramcontent.com/pod-product-compliance
Ingram Content Group UK Ltd.
Pitfield, Milton Keynes, MK11 3LW, UK
UKHW022219190926
475702UK00003B/452
9781041276982